D0205463

LOVE YOUR LOOKS

How to Stop Criticizing and Start Appreciating Your Appearance

CAROLYNN HILLMAN, C.S.W.

A FIRESIDE BOOK
PUBLISHED BY SIMON & SCHUSTER
NEW YORK LONDON TORONTO SYDNEY TOKYO SINGAPORE

FIRESIDE
Rockefeller Center
1230 Avenue of the Americas
New York, NY 10020

DESIGNED BY BARBARA M. MARKS

Manufactured in the United States of America

10 9 8 7 6 5 4 3 2 1

Library of Congress Cataloging-in-Publication Data
Hillman, Carolynn.
Love your looks : how to stop criticizing and start appreciating your appearance
/ Carolynn Hillman.
p.   cm.
Includes bibliographical references.
1. Beauty, Personal.   I. Title.
HQ1219.H55   1996
155.3´33—dc20   95-40721
                                    CIP

ISBN 0-684-81138-3

For my wonderful husband, Steve,

who nurtures and sustains me

and truly special daughters, Nurelle and Robyn

PHENOMENAL WOMAN

Pretty women wonder where my secret lies.

I'm not cute or built to suit a fashion model's size

But when I start to tell them,

They think I'm telling lies.

I say,

It's in the reach of my arms,

The span of my hips,

The stride of my step,

The curl of my lips.

I'm a woman

Phenomenally.

Phenomenal woman,

That's me.

— MAYA ANGELOU

Contents

Acknowledgments

The writing of this book has been a labor of love: my love for my subject and the love of those around me who have supported me through the inevitable trials and tribulations of research and writing. Most of all, I want to thank my husband, Steve Harrigan, who held down the fort through the year and a half I spent nearly all my "nonworking" hours glued to my computer in the dining room—"so near and yet so far." In addition to functioning as chief cook, chauffeur, and general manager, he doubled as research assistant, tracking down books and articles as needed. Even more importantly, his belief in me, and in the importance of this book, has sustained me throughout. I also want to thank my teenage daughters, Nurelle and Robyn, who tried to keep their requests to a minimum (well, at least not to a maximum), and who were always there to cheer me on. Nurelle, in addition, spent many hours roaming libraries to find and copy articles from academic journals, and Robyn was always there to give me a hug when I needed one. Thanks, kids!

I also want to thank my editor, Cindy Gitter, who has been a delight to work with, and my friends and fellow therapists who took time from their very busy schedules to review all or part of my manuscript and were helpful and generous in their suggestions: Alan Lefkowitz, Beverly Lefkowitz, Rita Sherr, and especially Isabel DeMaster for her invaluable comments, recommendations, and sharing of herself.

Most of all I want to thank the women in my practice and workshops who exposed their anguish and pain to me, together with their creativity, aliveness, hope, courage, and determination. Many of their voices and stories appear throughout, though to respect their confidentiality they appear as composites. I hope their experiences will inspire you, as they have me, to dare to learn to love the way that you look.

Introduction

My determination to find ways for women to appreciate their natural looks grew out of my experiences in my self-esteem workshops and psychotherapy practice, as well as from my own struggles in learning to like the way I look. I found that whenever I gave a workshop or talked with women about self-esteem, no matter what the women's backgrounds, races, or sexual orientations, the subject of looks kept coming up, and with it the anguish of not liking their bodies, faces, and themselves. How, women wanted to know, could they like themselves when they were so fat, or so bony, or had large thighs, or big hips, or small breasts, or protruding stomachs, or pendulous breasts, or thick legs, or large rears, or terrible complexions, or unattractive faces?

Many of these women were well aware that their bad feelings about their appearance and themselves were a reflection of society's lookism, which demands that women meet a narrowly defined beauty ideal. Still, they found it was one thing to intellectually recognize the near impossibility of this standard, but it was quite another to be able to like their looks and themselves when their faces and bodies failed to resemble those on magazine covers. The more I spoke with women about looks and self-esteem, the more I realized that for women to be able to really value themselves, they needed to be able to learn how to like the way that they look.

At the same time, I was also going through my own personal struggles. Having been a fat kid who was made fun of, and a constant yo-yo dieter as an adult, since at least puberty I had hung my entire sense of attractiveness on what the scale said. If it was way down, I was pretty, sexy, and desirable. When the numbers went up, as they invariably did, I felt fat and ugly. In my forties, while working on my first book, *Recovery of Your Self-Esteem: A Guide for Women,* I became convinced of the hazards and futility of dieting, and I finally decided to abandon dieting forever and to learn to like the way I looked at whatever weight I might settle into. This was not easy. I had spent my whole adulthood terrified of being fat. One pound more on the scale had been cause for dismay, unhappiness, and self-blame. Now, as my weight rose, I had to learn a whole new way of being with my body and myself. Determined to maintain my self-esteem, I developed methods and techniques that have enabled me and the women I work with to appreciate our appearances and ourselves, whatever our size or physical attributes. I am glad to share them with you.

This book is for every woman of any age, race, and background, straight or gay, who has ever looked in the mirror and gotten a sick feeling in her stomach or wanted to look away; for every woman who didn't want to go somewhere, do something, or apply for something because she didn't feel she looked good enough at the time, or ever; for every woman who believes she can't find happiness the way she presently looks; for every woman who has ever looked at a beautiful woman and thought, She looks so good I just hate her; for every woman who is afraid to take up the place in the world that her body demands; and for every woman who wants to really like her looks and herself. While this book is not explicitly addressed to the special challenges that face the disabled (I haven't had enough experience working with disabled women to speak with authority), I hope that if you are disabled you will find it to be of some help, nonetheless.

Many of the techniques presented are in the form of hands-on exercises because it's hard to make changes just by reading about something. Change is most easily achieved through doing and experiencing. The exercises are designed to involve your heart, mind, and senses so that all of you can learn to like the way you look. You may want to read the book through before starting any of the exercises. That's fine, but to get the maximum benefit, I encourage you to do as many of the exercises as feel appropriate to you.

Some of the exercises entail relaxation and visualization. Relaxation followed by visualization is a powerful tool for change. It is not only a rehearsal for new ways of feeling and acting, it actually helps induce a transformation in your experience of yourself.

Both relaxation and visualization require that you close your eyes and go into yourself. For that reason, it is best to have someone else read the instructions to you, or to tape the directions to these exercises, reading slowly and pausing to give yourself ample time to experience at each comma, and wherever else feels appropriate to you. Or, if you prefer, you can order a complete set of audiotapes with the instructions for all the visualization exercises (see the back ad at the end of the book).

All the visualization exercises are introduced by the same simple, deep-breathing relaxation exercise because with repetition relaxation becomes easier and easier. After the first time, to avoid being repetitive, the relaxation instructions are presented only in abbreviated form, but I strongly recommend that you tape the full instructions (see the Appendix, page 267) and listen to them in full before each of the visualizations. (If you are familiar with relaxation and wish to use some other technique, that's fine, too.) After relaxing it's important to keep your eyes closed and go into yourself, and really experience the visualizations, rather than merely read them. When you read them, you are learning on the mental level. When you actually visualize, you are learning in your feelings and in your core how to value the way that you look. As you go through the exercises, you will learn how to see yourself as attractive and desirable.

Perhaps you don't believe it's possible for you to ever really feel attractive, looking the way you do now. If so, I don't blame you for being skeptical. Not so long ago I would have been just as skeptical. But I hope you'll give yourself the chance to discover that you really can learn to love your looks.

CHAPTER 1

THE BEAUTY IMPERATIVE

*f I only looked like that . . . How many times have you had that thought, longing to look like a beauty? If you're like most women, the answer is, More times than I can remember. This wish contains the anguish most of us feel about wanting to be beautiful and believing we don't measure up.

Most of us dislike something about how we look, and many of us hate part or all of our faces and bodies, wishing fervently that we could lose weight; grow shorter or taller; have thinner thighs, hips, or stomachs; larger or smaller breasts; more shapely legs; firmer, more rounded or smaller butts; better complexions; improved faces; or other alterations. Even if you think you look good, it may be at the cost of so much time, money, and effort—makeup, creams, hair treatments, clothes, diets, workouts—that you may feel like an impostor, believing that it is this "artificial" product that is attractive, not the real you.

However you feel about the way you look, you may wish you could place less emphasis on your appearance and instead be proud of yourself for your personal qualities and accomplishments; yet, try as you might, you may find, like most women, that you can't help wanting to be great-looking.

Allie: *I work in a lab, doing research. I really enjoy it, and I'm proud of the quality of my work. What bothers me, though, is the way that I look. I wish it didn't bother me so much, but it does. I hate my small breasts and wide hips and thighs. And my face is so ordinary. I just wish I were beautiful.*

Lucinda: *I feel like such a fraud. I'm a therapist, and my clients look up to me and think I have it all together. I'm always encouraging them to take risks and go to social events. Yet I haven't ventured into the social scene since my breakup a year ago. I keep trying to get myself to make an effort, but I can't help thinking: Who's going to want me the way that I look with these extra twelve pounds on?*

Gwen: *I'm a nurse's aide, and I really enjoy cheering patients up. I'm known for my sense of humor, and it gives me a good feeling to know that the patients look forward to seeing me. Most of the time I don't think that much about my looks. I'm too busy working and taking care of my family. But sometimes when I have a big occasion coming up, I'll want to look really special, and that's when I get this bad feeling in my chest and stomach. Shopping just makes it worse because I keep looking at myself in the mirror and hating what I see. I'm overweight and have this big nose, which throws my whole face out of whack. Usually by the time of the event I've been depressed for days.*

Sally: *I'm a college student. I work hard and get good grades, and I do have a great relationship, but I think it's because I have a nice personality. My friends and lover keep telling me that I'm very pretty and thin and look*

good, but I know they're only trying to make me feel
better. I mean, I know I'm not ugly, but I have these sad-
dlebags on my thighs, and my stomach sticks out, and
my butt is flabby, and my ankles are too thick. I mean,
how can this be pretty?

Do these women's concerns sound familiar to you? If you met them, you would never recognize them by their descriptions of themselves because they are all attractive; however, like most women, they are so focused on the ways in which they fall short of the beauty ideal that they fail to recognize their true appeal. Instead, they're convinced that their looks are deficient and that they're failing at the most important game in town: being beautiful. Well, who can blame them?

Most of us can't help being very concerned with how we look because we are continually told that there is nothing more important for a woman than being beautiful, and that if we are to have any hope of being happy, successful, and respected, or of establishing and maintaining a relationship, we'd better look good. This is the Beauty Imperative, which says that a woman has to be attractive to be considered admirable and of value. Her personal qualities and accomplishments may be fine and good, the Beauty Imperative tells us, but if she is not attractive and well dressed, she can readily become an object of ridicule. A recent example of the Beauty Imperative at work can be found in Janet Reno, the first woman attorney general of the United States. I have heard many people make fun of the way she looks, calling her overweight, horsey, or dowdy, as though her looks are the measure of her worth, not her groundbreaking achievement or how she does her job.

The Beauty Imperative undermines women's self-esteem because it measures a woman's importance by something that to a very large degree she has no control over—her features and body type—and what's more, it is something that she will inevitably lose. Every woman knows that in trying to look beautiful, as defined by society, she is playing a losing game. Sooner or later age will get her.

As a woman, I know I don't have to tell you about the anguish that wanting to be beautiful and feeling you don't measure up can cause. It's like carrying within you a constant source of irritation and dissatisfaction with yourself. Sometimes it may be relatively quiescent, so that you may hardly notice it. Other times it breaks out in full force, undermining your positive regard for yourself, so that you feel ugly, undesirable, inadequate, and inferior. The less you like the way you look, the lower your self-esteem is apt to be.

In March 1992, *New Woman* magazine did a self-esteem survey of six hundred men and women, respectively. It found that nearly half the women had low self-esteem, while only a third of the men did; and only half as many women as men had high self-esteem (21 percent as opposed to 42 percent). Particularly telling was the survey's finding that the number-one factor contributing to women's self-esteem was satisfaction with their bodies and looks. (This didn't even make the top-four list for men.)

This relationship for women between not liking your looks and not liking yourself is well documented. Research consistently shows that women are less satisfied with their bodies than are men (primarily because women tend to think they're overweight, though most aren't), and that the worse women feel about their bodies, the lower their levels of self-esteem, while men's self-esteem is much less affected by whatever dissatisfaction with their bodies they may feel.

This intimate connection for women between satisfaction with appearance and self-esteem is frequently demonstrated in my self-esteem workshops. When I ask workshop participants to put on paper that mental list we all carry of the ways in which we don't like ourselves—the things about ourselves that make us feel inferior and inadequate—almost invariably high on every woman's list are criticisms of her appearance. This finding is hardly surprising. As women, we know only too well how little it can take to feel unattractive—a little monthly bloating, a new pimple, a bad hair day, feeling out of sorts, not getting a response we want—and how these feelings can deflate our self-confidence and erode our self-esteem.

On the other hand, when we view ourselves as valuable and worthwhile, we tend to both feel prettier and to be seen as more attractive. A nationwide 1994 beauty survey of more than eight hundred women commissioned by *New Woman* magazine found that the majority of the respondents liked the way they looked and that beauty does indeed come from the inside out. The survey found that some women "have the ability to project visually the very best of their inner qualities. Having this power has little to do with traditional standards of physical beauty: a woman may have a plump face, a big nose, or eyes that are too close together. But no one notices or cares, least of all she! There is something about her that draws admiring glances." This something, the survey found, was high self-esteem.

Liking your looks and high self-esteem revolve in a mutually reinforcing circle. Liking your looks helps you to like yourself and makes it more likely that you will have high self-esteem. Liking yourself and having high self-esteem makes it more likely that both you and others will find you attractive. Each reinforces the other and readies you for success. It looks like this:

Liking Your Looks

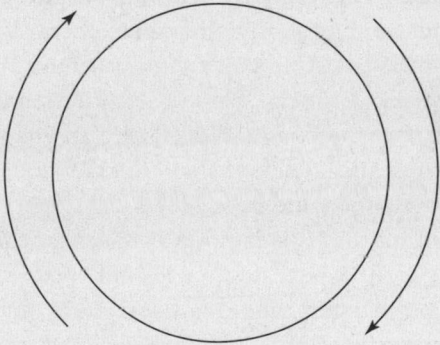

Liking Yourself

You can enter this favorable circle, where you like and value yourself and your looks, from either end. In *Recovery of Your Self-Esteem*, through a step-by-step program, I showed how to enter into it by raising your self-esteem. The exercises in this book are designed to show you how to enter it from the other end—by learning to appreciate and value your appearance, at whatever age and size you are, without having to change anything about the way that you look.

This book is called *Love Your Looks* because self-love really is the key to both body esteem and self-esteem. When you love yourself and treat yourself like a person of value, you raise your self-esteem; and when you love your face and body you enable yourself to appreciate your appearance and yourself.

Let's talk for a moment about what love is and is not. My dictionary defines "love" as "a deep and tender feeling of affection or attachment or devotion to a person or persons." Pay attention to this definition. It says nothing about standards that have to be met, degrees of approval, or contingency agreements ("I'll love you if . . ."). Rather it speaks of *affection, attachment, devotion.* These words seem natural when we think of a mother's love for her children. We expect a mother to feel abiding affection, attachment, and devotion to her children, whether or not they live up to her standards or expectations.

Can you imagine loving yourself and your face and your body in this way? Can you envision giving yourself this love exactly as you look at this moment? Can you picture reaching out to the hurt, wounded part of you with this kind of unconditional love? If not, keep this goal in mind as you read on. There are many exercises in this book, but they all have the same ultimate goal: to teach you how to love yourself and your looks in this way.

You may think that this is not possible, that there is no way you could learn to like—let alone love—the way you look. Like many women, you may feel that unless you alter your face or body, you can't help but be unhappy with, if not ashamed of, your appearance. If so, I can hardly blame you. I spent many years feeling the same way. I hope and believe, though, that by the time you finish this book you will have a very different outlook on attractiveness in general and toward your own looks in particular. Before you start this change process, though, it's important to recognize that powerful societal forces have a strong stake in keeping women obsessed with appearance, and unhappy and dissatisfied with our looks and ourselves.

In her groundbreaking book *The Beauty Myth*, Naomi Wolf

propounds that the backlash response to the revival of the women's movement in the late 1960s and 1970s was to replace the exhausting burdens of homemaking with the equally onerous and more expensive burdens of pursuing an artificially defined, unattainable beauty ideal. The intention and the effect, Wolf argues, are to neutralize women politically by deflecting us from our true goals and by keeping us depleted and feeling deficient and unworthy, so that we have neither the strength nor the confidence to challenge the status quo.

How confident and ready to pursue our personal and political agendas can we be if we feel unattractive, rejectable, and unworthy? And with half or more of the women in the United States at any given time dieting, often stringently, how much energy is left to work toward enlarging women's opportunities, broadening our roles in society, securing our safety, and increasing our incomes? As Wolf explains,

> A cultural fixation on female thinness is not an obsession about female beauty but an obsession about female obedience . . . about how much social freedom women are going to get away with or concede. The media's compulsive analysis of the endless saga of female fat and the battle to vanquish it are actually bulletins of the sex war: what women are gaining or losing in it, and how fast. . . .

> Researchers J. Polivy and C. P. Herman found that "prolonged and periodic caloric restriction" resulted in a distinctive personality whose traits are "passivity, anxiety, and emotionality." *It is those traits, and not thinness for its own sake, that the dominant culture wants to create in the private sense of self of recently liberated women in order to cancel out the dangers of their liberation.* The anorexic may start her journey defiant, but from the point of view of a male-dominated society, she ends up as the perfect woman. She is weak, sexless, and voiceless, and can only with difficulty focus on a world

beyond her plate . . . If a woman can be made to say, "I hate my fat thighs," it is a way she has been made to hate femaleness. The more financially independent, in control of events, educated and sexually autonomous women become in the world, the more impoverished, out of control, foolish, and sexually insecure we are asked to feel in our bodies.

Since 1970, in the wake of the resurgence of feminist activity, the beauty ideal has shrunk. Fashion models, Miss America, movie actresses, and even *Playboy* centerfolds have become thinner and thinner. In twenty years the *Playboy* centerfold lost twenty-five pounds, until she weighed 18 percent less than the medical ideal for her age and height, while the weight of fashion models plummeted even further to 23 percent below that of ordinary women.

Wolf does not suggest that beauty standards are plotted by a sinister secret male corporate cabal; rather that it is to corporate America's advantage to keep women feeling inferior about our looks and ourselves. Big business grows richer as we dissipate our precious resources of time and money trying to look like the impossibly thin beauty ideal. Weight loss alone is a $33 billion industry, and cosmetics, clothes, hair treatments, "anti-aging" products, creams, and other beauty products take additional billions from our incomes.

Big business's agenda is promulgated through advertising and the media, which seduce women into trying to look like the beauty ideal by promising us that if we succeed, we will gain approval, find happiness, and strike it rich. In reality, as we will see in Chapter 2, even if you do manage to be among the scant 5 percent of women who temporarily succeed in approximating the beauty ideal (before you get "too old," which is not very old), you are not at all guaranteed to receive the promised rewards. As for the rest of us, all we really get for all our efforts to look cover-girl gorgeous is to become more dissatisfied with our looks and ourselves as we fall short of this standard. While the Beauty Imperative seems to offer the potential for praise and prizes, it is really a trap that diverts our energies and undermines our sense of self. Still, it's a trap that's hard to resist because its message is so enticing and ubiquitous.

Everywhere we turn we are presented with the directive that it is very important for women to look good, that it is part of our specialness and femininity, and that we can if only we work hard enough at it. These beauty messages have increased exponentially over the last twenty-five years in the wake of the resurgence of feminism. Since the 1950s and the 1970s there has been a large increase in the portrayal of women in purely decorative roles in general interest magazines, and the emphasis on slimness has also increased dramatically. *Ladies' Home Journal* issues published in the 1960s had an average of only one diet article every six months. We all know how much this statistic has changed. The continual message in magazines to women today is to stay in shape and be slim (while at the same time thinking about food and cooking—a good trick).

This societal push for us to spend our time and money pursuing beauty starts when we're still girls. *Seventeen* magazine in the mid-1980s devoted fully 60 percent of each issue's editorial copy, the part of the magazine that talks directly to girls and puts forth the magazine's vision, to beauty, along with fashion, decorating, and cooking.

Magazine ads, with their glamorous models, are important because they deliver a powerful message. Marsha Richins of the University of Massachusetts at Amherst investigated the impact of magazine ads containing beautiful models, as opposed to those without models. She found in two studies that female college students' satisfaction with their own physical attractiveness diminished after looking at advertising with idealized images of physically attractive women.

TV commercials, too, strongly convey the Beauty Imperative by presenting women as beauty objects. In their study of the frequency of attractiveness-based messages in over four thousand network TV commercials, Chris Downs and Sheila Harrison of the University of Houston at Clear Lake found that audiences were exposed to some form of attractiveness message in over a quarter of commercials, and that most were delivered by female performers with male voice-overs, thus promoting the notion that beauty is good, valuable, and of paramount importance for women, and that men—via authoritative voice-overs—approve of and promote this emphasis on beauty for women. Women's role as dependent beauty object is further conveyed by the near absence of women's voices in voice-overs, thus delivering the message that only men are in charge, knowledgeable, credible, and able to judge a woman's worth, and that they will judge it by her appearance.

Television commercials are important because they very much influence what people come to believe. Alexis Tan, a professor in the Department of Mass Communications at Texas Tech University, studied the effects of beauty commercials (those that use sex appeal, beauty, or youth as selling points) on viewers. She showed one group of adolescent girls fifteen such commercials that had been taped from network shows and a second group of adolescent girls fifteen taped network commercials that did not use beauty themes. Girls exposed to the beauty commercials rated beauty much higher when asked which characteristics are most important in being liked by men. And this result occurred after only very short-term viewing of beauty commercials. It is very likely, Tan suggests, that long-term repeated exposure, which accompanies normal TV watching, has stronger and more lasting effects on women viewers' beliefs in the importance of beauty.

Similarly, regular television programming powerfully projects the message that a woman must be attractive, and that only slim and beautiful women are successful and happy. Donald Davis of the University of Georgia examined the demographic variables (age, hair color, marital status, parental status, and provocative dress) of all women on prime-time network TV in action-adventure, comedy, and drama programs. He found as few female characters on TV in the postfeminist era as in the 1950s and 1960s (fewer than 35 percent of all characters), and that these female characters are overwhelmingly young, beautiful, and preferably blonde (outstripping the true proportion of blondes in the general female population by more than two to one), and failing that, redheaded. Conversely, nary a female TV character has gray hair (only about 2 percent), as opposed to 14 percent of male characters. Women are also almost four times as likely to be provocatively dressed, and tend to be younger than their male counterparts by about ten years. Indeed, Davis found few women on the TV screen after age thirty-five until they reach fifty, at which point they reappear as character actresses.

By contrast, the screen value of men in the thirty-five to forty-nine age group becomes greater, as evidenced by their increased numbers.

TV's conveyance of the Beauty Imperative is produced by acts of omission as well as of commission—namely, by the dearth of women who present positive, admirable role models who do not match the beauty ideal. This dearth is particularly noticeable in the television newsroom (a place where reportorial ability should be far more important than beauty), where, as we witness daily, women are generally required to look trim, attractive, and young. When they age, they are often moved out. The few older female newscasters and interviewers who are allowed prominence, like Barbara Walters, normally have to remain trim and often have to resort to plastic surgery while men like Dan Rather, Mike Wallace, and Walter Cronkite are allowed to very visibly age. This double standard of aging and looks discrimination against women in TV news broadcasting is epitomized by the infamous 1980s case in which attractive, thirty-six-year-old TV coanchor Christine Craft was dismissed by Metromedia in Kansas City on the grounds that she was "too old, too unattractive, and not deferential to men," despite the fact that in her nine-month tenure her news program had, for the first time, reached number one. Though two juries agreed with Craft in her lawsuit against Metromedia, male judges overturned their rulings.

Feature films, too, emphasize youth, beauty, and extreme thinness for women. Brett Silverstein of the City University of New York, comparing top box-office actresses in the 1960s and later, found that after the advent of the women's movement actresses became thinner. Nowadays, it is a rare movie that, if it features women at all, portrays them as anything other than young and very thin.

Without other role models and with all this overemphasis on beauty, it is no wonder, then, that many of us have difficulty liking the way that we look in comparison to the sleek, exceptionally thin example held up for us to emulate. Next to this celluloid ideal, how could we feel anything but deficient and dissatisfied with our looks and ourselves?

The irony of women striving to look like the models in the

magazines is that no one really looks like this—not without starving herself, thousand-dollar-plus makeup jobs, artificial posing, two-hour hair-styling sessions, or perhaps cosmetic surgery. A few years ago supermodel Cindy Crawford, in an attempt to help women avoid dangerous breast implants, talked publicly about being taped and contoured to make her breasts look larger and fuller in photographs than they really are. And listen to other top models:

Supermodel Carol Alt: *It takes two hours to put on* natural *makeup.*

Supermodel Kim Alexis: *I remember trying every fad diet. I remember starving myself for four days in a row ... I think I was a normal person before I started screwing around with all those diets. My metabolism got screwed up. I lost my period for two full years.*

Supermodel Beverly Johnson: *In our profession, clothes look better on a hanger, so you have to look like a hanger ... I personally took extreme methods to lose weight and as a result ended up bulimic and, at one time, when I was 27 or 28, anorexic ... One of these days my daughter [age 13] will be in* Vogue *magazine. She will weigh 105 pounds and pose in a dress that a 35-year-old woman then will want to buy. That's really unfair. It does a lot of damage to women's self-esteem because it makes them try to reach a goal that they will never reach. I think that's why there's so much plastic surgery.*

These models are not alone in punishing their bodies and threatening their health because they want to be considered beautiful. According to the National Association of Anorexia Nervosa and Associated Diseases, there are at least eight million women with bulimia and anorexia in the United States today (90 percent of those with these eating disorders are women), with far too many women dying of anorexia each year. This is not a small problem, but an epidemic, with unhealthy dieting (which always precedes bulimia) beginning at younger and younger ages. It is estimated that up to 85 percent of American women diet, many of whom are on diet-binge cycles. Hundreds of thousands of other women are undergoing cosmetic surgery, stomach stapling, and liposuction, enduring considerable pain and risking death, serious illness, and scarring, all in the pursuit of looking younger, prettier, and thinner.

Tragically, the only ones really benefiting from women's efforts to look young and beautiful are corporations and plastic surgeons. We ourselves get very little benefit for all our hard-spent money and efforts. We may not end up looking that much better or younger (because facial appearance and body type are largely genetically determined), and even if we do, often we remain dissatisfied with our appearance and ourselves. Many of us are caught in a vicious cycle in which we feel we can't value ourselves unless we look good, and no matter how good we look, it is never good enough.

> Charlene, forty, is the successful owner of a temporary help agency. She seems to have it all—a loving spouse, two children, and a comfortable lifestyle. Yet she is not happy with herself. While she is aware of her many strengths (intelligence, diligence, warmth, reliability, pleasant personality, sales skills, accomplishments, ability to take risks), she takes little real pleasure from them because she feels so upset by her appearance. She anguishes over her "large" nose, "fleshy" thighs, and especially her weight. For many years she was a size ten, and now, at size twelve, believes that she is too fat, so she is constantly dieting, which makes her irritable, deprived, and prone to bingeing. She says that there is no way she can feel good about herself when she is "so heavy." Her husband, tired of giving her constant reassurance that he likes the way she looks, has stopped complimenting her, leading her to conclude that he no longer finds her attractive.

Charlene is not a narcissistic woman caught up in shallow concerns. She is warm, loving, and caring, but she cannot fully enjoy her accomplishments and relationships and feel good about herself because she is under the sway of the Beauty Imperative; so she believes that she cannot be admirable and of value if her looks don't match society's dictates. Charlene fears that as long as she does not meet these exacting standards, she is, and will be seen as, inferior. The irony is that nobody in Charlene's life values her more at a size ten or less at a size twelve—it is only Charlene's inner voice, her inner critic, that tells her she is more or less valuable according to her weight.

In our beauty-bound society, even young attractive thin women are not insulated from the destructive influence of the Beauty Imperative. In fact, often young women agonize even more about the way they look. A survey of two thousand respondents conducted for *Psychology Today* by psychologist Thomas Cash and his colleagues found that young women were the most dissatisfied of all with their bodies, and the 1994 *New Woman* beauty survey found that women in their twenties, despite rating themselves as more attractive and happier about their figures than older women, feel ugly most often, and spend the most time every day grooming themselves.

> When I first met Brooke she was twenty-five and single, with a satisfying job. With her lively, penetrating black eyes, strong features, beautiful complexion, and size eight figure, she was quite compelling-looking, but not in her own eyes. She felt unattractive and longed to be tall and ultra-thin with a gorgeous face. She thought she hadn't found the lasting relationship she desired because she wasn't attractive or thin enough, and had become thousands of dollars in debt spending money on clothes, cosmetics, creams, and an expensive health club. She only wished she had the money for cosmetic surgery and a personal trainer, as she strove for the beauty she imagined would solve all her problems and make her life wonderful. At the same time, fearing rejection, she had started avoiding social situations where she might find a mate.

In reality, what was holding Brooke back was not her looks, but her lack of self-acceptance and self-assurance. When she learned to accept and value herself and her looks, she gained the confidence she needed to start socializing. She is now in a happy relationship, getting out of debt, and, most important of all, she likes herself.

Many of us, like Brooke, despite frequent examinations of ourselves in the mirror, have no true idea of what we look like. In a 1984 *Glamour* survey of 33,000 women, three-quarters of the respondents—regardless of age, education, income level, or marital status—reported feeling overweight, although only one-quarter could be classified as truly overweight, even according to the stringent definitions used in the study. Furthermore, half of the really underweight women viewed themselves as being too fat, and two-thirds of them wanted to diet! Many other studies have similar findings.

But you don't have to read such studies to know that women think they're fat when they're not. All you have to do is listen to women you know. How many times have you heard an average-size or even quite thin woman complain about how fat she looks? It is very common for a woman who is usually keenly perceptive to lose all sense of proportion when she looks at herself. This distorted self-perception not only undermines women's self-esteem, but it may also be a significant contributor to depression in women. Cash and colleagues found that depressed college students were more dissatisfied with their bodies and saw themselves as less attractive than nondepressed students of equal pulchritude.

Mandy McCarthy of the University of Pennsylvania proposes that our cultural ideal of thinness is a major reason that so many more women than men in Western countries suffer from depression. The emphasis on the thin ideal, she suggests, would account for five depression-related trends: (1) In the West, twice as many women as men are likely to be depressed; (2) this sex difference emerges at puberty (before puberty depression is twice as common in boys; after puberty it is twice as common in girls); (3) this gender distinction is found only in Western countries; (4) there is more depression today than ever; and (5) the average age of onset for depression is lower now than in the past. The first four of these trends, McCarthy notes, parallel trends in eating disorders, which can also be accounted for by the growth of the very thin ideal. McCarthy points out that in all cultures that have the thin ideal significantly more women than men are depressed; and, vice versa, in countries in which the depressed are not predominantly women, the thin ideal does not reign supreme. She suggests that the thin ideal's potential to produce depression has its biggest impact during puberty, when increasing importance is placed on girls' appearance at the very time that their bodies are adding fat stores and going through other physical changes that may cause a discrepancy between their appearance and the beauty ideal. (For information on puberty and fat stores, see Chapter 7.)

Even if you manage to deal with the Beauty Imperative without becoming depressed and emerge with your self-esteem intact, however, it doesn't mean that you're home free. You may still have a hard time knowing how to relate to your appearance, on the one hand wanting to be found attractive, but on the other hand not wanting to be harassed or treated as a sex object. Our culture not only judges a woman's worth and value by near-impossible beauty standards, it also controls women by simultaneously idealizing and exploiting women's sexuality and beauty, telling us that we must be beautiful and then, often, harassing and objectifying us for the way we look. Sexual harassment, like rape, is not about flirting, sex, beauty, or even desire. It is about power. Its implicit "boys-will-be-boys" message is that it is appropriate for men to exert power over women, and that women are not worthy of respect.

In the face of these messages, we women are caught in a no-win situation: If we don't look good, we become objects of derision; if we do look good, we can become objects of unwanted, degrading attention. Either way, our physical appearance may be used to humiliate, demean, and control us. If we object to any of this, we are "bad sports," "exaggerating," or "too strident." (Have you ever noticed that men are never called strident?) The message is that our looks are for men's pleasure, not for ourselves. Men are supposed to enjoy our beauty, while we are supposed to deny and disown it. A woman who dares to call herself beautiful is immediately attacked on all sides for her arrogance and immodesty, lest she and all women discover the power available to us when, rather than looking to others to announce us worthy, we proudly take control of our own bodies, beauty, and lives.

To take charge of your own beauty, you need to be able to recognize and own it—the many exercises herein will teach you how—and to expand your concept of what is beautiful. Despite the pervasiveness of our current beauty ideal, which idolizes youth and extreme slenderness as the one true image of beauty, the truth is that the beauty ideal is not eternal, undeniable, or immutable. On the contrary, it's rather fickle.

As far back as eighteen thousand to twenty-five thousand years ago, our Stone Age forebears sculpted goddesses as very round and voluptuous, with enormous stomachs. Nearer to our times, from around 1400 to 1900 in Europe and America, the ideal woman was pictured by artists as decidedly fat. (If you find it hard to believe that for hundreds of years large-bodied women were the epitome of beauty and sexiness and that fatness and roundness can be a beauty ideal, just go to an art museum or look through art books. Look at the lush, fleshy, sensuous nudes of Titian (about 1490–1576), Tintoretto (1518–1594), Rubens (1577–1640), and Renoir (1841–1919). Be sure to notice Rubens' round, full-bodied, and very lovely Venus, the goddess of beauty.

In nineteenth-century America a heavy and robust "voluptuous woman" was admired, with a waist corseted as tightly as possible. (Such corseting exerted an average of twenty-one pounds of pressure on internal organs, restricting circulation, and causing displacement of vital organs and many miscarriages.) Some women even had a rib removed in their quest for beauty. By midcentury, this ideal was being replaced by a bustier, hippier, heavy-legged woman, culminating in the popularity of 1890s sex symbol, "American Beauty" Lillian Russell, who at her peak weighed just over 200 pounds. In the 1920s, when women got the vote, for the first time the ideal became thin—epitomized by the flat-chested, curveless flapper look. With the Great Depression in the 1930s, hemlines dropped, and the narrow waist returned. In the 1940s the leg was celebrated as an erotic symbol, and garters and high heels were in. The postwar 1950s and especially the 1960s celebrated large breasts, and Marilyn Monroe, who was five five and at times weighed up to 135 pounds—overweight by today's standards—became a sex goddess. Since 1970, in the wake of a resurgence of feminist activity, the thin ideal has reigned supreme. Today, with the advent of the fitness craze, it is seen as desirable for women not only to be very thin, but also to have hard, muscular, tubular bodies instead of softer, fleshier ones.

Different eras and cultures idolize not only different body shapes in women, but also different body parts. For centuries the Chinese admired tiny feet, so upper-class Chinese girls, in the name of beauty, sustained years of incredible pain because their feet were broken at the instep and kept tightly bound until their toes shriveled and fell off, together with a good part of their feet, leaving them only with stumps three to four inches long and two inches wide that they could barely hobble on. Women endured this maiming and perpetrated it on their daughters because without bound feet, women of their class were considered ugly and unmarriageable, a true disaster in a culture in which the only viable life option for women was marriage. As adults, these women prided themselves on the smallness of their feet.

Today, women pride themselves on how good their legs look in high heels—which also often are hobbling and painful, as well as bad for the back—and the thinness of their dieted-down, overworked-out bodies. Both ideals are crippling. How strongly, confidently, and securely can we women stride out in the world in our half-starved, rejected bodies and on those wobbly painful heels? (If you've ever had to work for hours on your feet in heels while your male colleagues stood comfortably in their sensible shoes, or were wearing heels while trying to flee an unsavory character, you know how disadvantageous and hobbling heels can be.)

What body size and part is "in" varies not only from era to era, but also from one society to another, with size preference depending to a great extent on whether food is generally plentiful or scarce in that region. In places where the food supply is often or cyclically inadequate, fat is a status symbol, and a large woman is admired and desired. Her weight is a visible proclamation of prosperity. Indeed, in over 80 percent of the developing societies in the world today, plumpness is viewed as an ideal of feminine beauty, with large hips and legs being especially admired. In traditional African societies, for example, full-figured women are symbols of health, wealth, desire, prosperity, and fertility. Unfortunately, some societies even force their teenage girls into "fattening houses" where they are overfed and allowed no exercise so they will become fat and beautiful.

Even within our culture, ethnic preferences can vary with regard to notions of beauty. For example, studies have found that African-American women are more positive about their weight and body image than their white peers and that they place less emphasis on food and weight control, and on slimness, and that African-American men consider heavier women to be sexier and more attractive than do white men and are significantly less likely than their white peers to have refused to date someone because of her weight. This healthier and more accepting attitude in the African-American community toward weight may be an important factor in understanding why so few African-American women suffer from anorexia and bulimia, despite the fact that African-American women are fatter than any other demographic group in the United States.

Unfortunately, however, as African-American women move up the socioeconomic ladder, they, too, become prey to the eating disorders that are fed by the thin ideal. A recent *Essence* magazine survey of two thousand highly educated, largely affluent African-American women found a preoccupation with food, eating, and thinness that more than rivaled that displayed in their white counterparts. Many women in the survey reported they were terrified of being overweight and were consumed by the desire to be thinner, causing them to diet, exercise, fast, use laxatives, feel guilty when they eat, go on binges they couldn't stop, and for a small proportion, even vomit after eating. Those women with a strong black identity (the poorest and the wealthiest) were less preoccupied with eating and less worried about losing weight, while those in the struggling middle were more likely to de-emphasize their black identities to get ahead, and thus were more susceptible to the dominant culture's destructive emphasis on the thin ideal.

The exponential spread of anorexia and bulimia in the past

twenty or so years, primarily among middle- and upper-class white women (which has occurred only in societies that have the thin ideal), bespeaks a strong connection between these eating disorders and the backlash promotion of the thin ideal. In this regard it is instructive to note that eating disorders also increased dramatically in the 1920s after women got the vote, and at that time also the beauty ideal became thin and masculine, as exemplified by the flapper.

I don't mean to imply that personal and family dynamics and past trauma don't play an important role in the etiology of eating disorders. Clearly they do. Particularly revealing are reports from eating disorders centers that up to 60 percent of the women they see are survivors of sexual abuse, and that bulimic women have unusually high rates of sexual assault in late adolescence and early adulthood. However, it is unlikely that these women's difficulties and struggles would be played out around food if our society did not attempt to control women through the deadly combination of the Beauty Imperative and the thin ideal.

If you are anorexic or bulimic (whether through the use of laxatives and diuretics, overstrenuous exercise, or vomiting) it is important to recognize that when you try to tame your body into submission, you are not really gaining control over yourself or your life; rather, you are being controlled by the culture. Instead, you need to learn how to achieve real power in your family and the world, including how to connect with your feelings and body so that you can speak up for and value yourself. Don't wait till it's too late or you have seriously harmed your body. You can learn how to achieve real power and to like the way you look. Do the exercises in the following chapters, and seek out a feminist therapist at an eating disorders clinic or elsewhere who can help. (See Resources for referral sources.)

You don't have to have an eating disorder, however, to be obsessed with your weight. The general explanation given for women's preoccupation with size and appearance is that we want to look good so that we can get or keep a man (who is presumably mostly interested in how we look—we'll examine the truth of this notion in Chapter 12). However, there is reason to believe that this is not women's main motivation. For one, lesbians (whose potential partners are presumed to be less focused on and judgmental of appearance than men are, both because they are women and because they belong to a subculture that is described as downplaying the importance of physical attractiveness and as challenging culturally prescribed, male-driven ideals of beauty) are no more accepting and appreciative of their bodies than straight women. Three recent studies have found—and my own clinical experience bears it out—that lesbians are no freer than their straight sisters from the invidious influence of the Beauty Imperative. Lesbians, like straight women, are very concerned about their appearance, anxious to keep their weight down, diet to do so, work out, agonize over their faces and bodies, often hang their self-esteem on their appearance, and, in general, are as desirous as straight women of looking young, thin, and beautiful.

Even more suggestive that women's overwhelming desire to be thin—and therefore beautiful—is driven by factors other than wanting to attract a man is the finding of two studies conducted by April Fallon and Paul Rozin of the University of Pennsylvania, which concluded that women want not only to weigh less than they do (although most are of normal weight), but they also want to weigh less than the size they believe to be most appealing to men.

Pursuit of thinness and beauty in our culture has become a goal in itself, divorced from the realities of what it takes to be attractive to potential lovers (male or female), and certainly, as we will see in Chapter 7, from the realization of good health. While society continues to deny women economic and political power, it encourages us to pursue pseudo-power—to be powerful not by gaining real control over our lives but by controlling our bodies, particularly our consumption of food. The more our energies and resources are deflected in the pursuit of this pseudo-power—into shrinking rather than enlarging our presence—the less real power we will gain, as we allow ourselves to be controlled and defined by a societal standard that is detrimental to our health and happiness.

It is time that we obtained real power: economic, political, and personal. When we refuse to blindly accept only one beauty ideal, when we insist on the freedom to look the way that we do—in all our enticing and beautiful multiplicity—when we learn to like our appearance and are not afraid to proclaim it to the world, we develop an inner contentment and pride that is essential to our well-being and that frees us up to acquire real power.

Have you ever avoided going after something you wanted because you didn't feel you looked good enough? Are you postponing your life until you lose weight or otherwise improve your appearance? If so, it's time to stop letting the Beauty Imperative prevent you from pursuing and obtaining the things you want in life. Instead, get ready to start feeling attractive and going after what you want.

The exercises throughout this book will show you in detail how to recognize your true beauty and how to value your appearance whatever your age or size. First, however, let's consider what true beauty is.

CHAPTER 2

TRUE BEAUTY

Contrary to everything you've ever been led to believe, beauty is not a scarce commodity, residing only in the few genetically blessed. Despite the heralding of the beauty ideal by corporate America, the truth is that beauty is not an elusive and ephemeral goal attainable only by the lucky and the truly dedicated, while the rest of us are condemned to exist in that great purgatory somewhere between kind-of-nice-looking and homely.

The reality is that there are many different kinds of beauty and many different ways to be beautiful. A large woman who likes her body and moves with ownership and grace can be very attractive and enticing, just as a petite woman who is at home in her body can be inviting and lovely. Age, too, has a beauty all its own. Some of the most striking women I've known have been women "of a certain age" who have come to like their looks and whose comfort with their appearance radiates an undeniable attraction. In fact, women of all ages, sizes, shapes, and colors can be attractive when we learn to embrace and appreciate our looks.

Attractiveness radiates from self-acceptance and self-appreciation. No, this isn't self-serving sop. It really is true. The more satisfied we are with ourselves and our looks, the more attractive others find us. Remember the *New Woman* beauty survey which found that women with self-esteem have the ability to project an inner beauty, regardless of the details of their appearance. Oprah Winfrey is sexy and exciting at all her various sizes, and Jessica Tandy was attractive at any age.

Of course, this shouldn't really be news to us. After all, women have always known that what we find most attractive in a man is not necessarily the evenness of his features or the size of his muscles, but the glint in his eye and his presentation. A self-confident man who approaches a woman with both assurance in himself and a true appreciation of her is invariably attractive. Conversely, a conventionally good-looking man who is uncomfortable with himself is often less appealing.

While both men and women who are comfortable and satisfied with their looks radiate attractiveness, it is easier for women to recognize this in men because we are so used to being critical about women's looks. To heighten your awareness of the connection between self-esteem and good looks, whether you are straight or gay, consider the men you think are attractive. Are they all incredibly handsome? Think about real men you know, not TV or movie stars (though some stars aren't incredible-looking, either. Al Pacino and Dustin Hoffman, for instance, are often considered to be sexy and attractive though neither is conventionally handsome).

In thinking about the men you find attractive, consider what it is that appeals to you about each of them. Is it the shape of his nose? His well-developed thigh muscles? His flat stomach? Or is it the sexy way he looks at you? His winning smile? The way he can apologize and mean it when he is wrong, and still seem to like himself? When you got to know him better, did he seem better-looking to you than when you met him? This is often the case because once we like a man, we generally start to look at him with our loving eyes, rather than critical ones. Our loving eyes aren't blinders—we can still see faults and shortcomings—but our appreciation of him makes him more attractive to us.

Surprisingly enough, men are not that different from women

in this regard. Their perceptions of beauty, too, are influenced by feelings of affection. Despite the many messages that all men care about is our looks and getting us into bed, there's much more at work. Sure, most men like sex, as do most women, and men do like to look at the women whom they consider attractive (who can blame them? We are lovely in all our multiplicity), but different men find different faces and bodies attractive. Some men like skinny women and others like full-bodied ones. There are men who love a big derriere and those who don't. In fact, men appreciate women across a wide range of features, colors, sizes, and ages. If you doubt this, just look around you at the wide variety of tastes among the couples you see.

The source of women's dislike of their bodies lies less in how demanding individual men are of physical perfection than in what a difficult time we have, because of the Beauty Imperative, in looking at ourselves with loving eyes. Not only are we usually much more critical of ourselves than we are of men, but ironically, women's desire to be what our male-defined culture tells us we must be in order to be admired often leads us to judge our looks much more harshly than our lovers do.

> Julie, twenty, has been going with Al for eighteen months. She thinks he is really handsome and worries that she's not good-looking enough for him. Despite his frequent compliments about her looks and her personality, Julie is not reassured. She spends at least an hour every day fixing her hair, dressing, and putting on makeup. She fears that if she doesn't look her best, some other woman will catch Al's eye. Al is crazy about Julie, loves the way she looks, and doesn't understand why she feels so insecure.

> Ginger, who is thirty-three and has been married for ten years to Tom, has always felt insecure about her appearance. She wishes she were at least ten pounds lighter, her cheekbones just a tad higher, her thighs more than a tad thinner, and her butt smaller. When she looks

in the mirror, these "flaws" jump out at her. Also, now that she is over thirty, she is starting to worry about aging. Tom thinks she's really attractive and tells her so. While his appreciation feels good to her, she tends to disregard it. She feels that because he loves her, he doesn't see her clearly.

Julie and Ginger are not alone in having higher standards for beauty than the men around them. As we will see in Chapter 12, this is quite common, though, of course, not always true. Indeed, some men are very critical of the appearance of the women in their lives; these men may think of "their" women as status symbols—much like expensive cars or watches—and demand the beauty ideal as a paean to their egos. I doubt that this is the kind of man you want to be with. Do you want to diet below your natural and healthy weight; kill yourself working out; overspend on clothes, creams, and cosmetics; or undergo the pain and danger of cosmetic surgery just to get or keep a man who doesn't care about you as a person or appreciate the real you?

Of course not, you're probably thinking. But to develop and maintain a good relationship, don't I have to watch how I look? Perhaps, just as your partner has to watch how he or she looks. However, the question is, what does watching how you look mean? Does it mean having to be ever-vigilant against—and at war with—the inevitable signs of aging? Does it mean never being able to have a healthy relationship with food, in which you feel free to eat what you want when you're hungry? Does it mean having to remain perpetually dissatisfied with how you look, viewing your appearance as a shortcoming that undermines you and gets in your way? Or is there a positive way to care about your looks that also allows room for being natural and growing older? Can you learn to evaluate your looks so that you'll be sure to notice everything pleasing about your appearance, adding continually to your growing store of positive feelings about your looks and yourself?

Let me make myself clear. I'm not against fit bodies or flattering clothes and makeup. It can be fun to use clothes, jewelry, and makeup to adorn ourselves, and create whatever kind of look we desire. I certainly don't advocate giving up this diversity in favor of a colorless uniform analogous to men's suits. What I am suggesting, though, is that if you spend time adorning yourself, you do so because you enjoy it, and not because you can't stand yourself any other way. If you like your eyes and think they look even better with makeup—great! If you're proud of the way your full breasts and hips complement your smaller waist and want to dress to emphasize that—go for it! If you like the way you look and feel when you exercise—wonderful! Just as long as when you're not wearing the makeup or flattering clothes, or you don't have time to work out, you won't start feeling ugly and unattractive.

The real trap of accentuating our good points is that we start to feel that it's the accentuation devices that are attractive, not us. Even worse, many women find that however much they try to improve their appearance, they still feel unattractive and inferior because all their efforts only serve to remind them that they don't look like the beauty ideal.

> Marjory is a well-paid consultant to the fashion industry. She accents her natural good looks by dressing attractively and fashionably, skillfully using makeup, and keeping her thin body in top shape through regular exercise. Men frequently look at her and compliment her. Still, she does not feel satisfied with her looks. She is constantly looking at herself through an imaginary magnifying glass that screams in horror at each line and wrinkle. At forty-two she feels her looks are fading, won't go out without makeup, and hates looking at herself in the mirror. At the same time, she is afraid to take her eye off the mirror, for fear some new blemish will appear.

Even though ostensibly a winner in the lottery of looks, Marjory is not happy with them or herself. The male admiration her beauty brings only confirms for her that her value lies in her face and body, not in her personal qualities and achievements. In our work together Marjory learned how to like her face and body regardless of the changes aging brings, and to understand that her beauty is only one part of the valuable person she is. She now has developed real self-esteem.

How do you feel about your looks? Are you able to admire and appreciate your appealing points and feel good about the way you look? Or do you see mainly your shortcomings, feeling bad about your appearance and yourself? Do the following assessment.

SELF-RATING:

Close your eyes and picture yourself looking your best, and rate your appearance from 1 to 10, with 10 being the highest. Next picture yourself as you normally look most days, and rate yourself again. Lastly, think of yourself in your most natural state (no makeup or special hairdo beyond a quick combing, jeans or some other everyday clothes), and rate yourself a third time. If the range between your everyday and best score is more than 2 points, you are not appreciating your natural beauty. If your lowest score was below 4 or your highest score below 7, you are also not recognizing your true attractiveness.

If you find it hard to appreciate your true beauty, it's probably because you keep measuring yourself against the unrealistic beauty ideal. Later, we will look at the specific steps you can take to recognize your true attractiveness. First, though, broaden your concept of what real beauty is. Come with me on an imaginary trip to a newly discovered galaxy.

A New Galaxy

The first planet we visit is Darkhairland. Here, for a woman to be considered beautiful, she must have dark hair, the darker the better. Women of color, with their very dark hair, are considered the most attractive, along with some white women who have black hair. Next come the brunettes, then women with light brown hair, redheads, gray-haired women, and finally blondes. However, very few women have the courage to remain blonde. Even though hair-dyeing is derided as artificial and tacky, almost all blondes dye their hair to make themselves look more desirable. Usually their mothers began dyeing their hair when they were little children. Men on this planet, on the other hand, can have hair of any color and still be thought desirable because their looks are not considered to be nearly as important as what they do.

The next planet we land on is Roundland. Here the measure of a woman's beauty is determined by the roundness of her body. Sensuality and sexuality are equated with being full and large. On this planet women are forever trying to force more food down their reluctant throats in order to appear rounder and fuller. Of course, some lucky women find it easy to become quite fat, while the major-ity find that no matter how much they eat, and how much they re-strict their physical activity, they simply can't put on weight and keep it on. Through constant effort, they can gain weight, but as soon as they go off their diets the weight just falls off. The women in this country long to be well over 200 pounds, but most can't make it and feel unattractive. Thin women are ridiculed, and everyone thinks they are weak-willed, lazy, undisciplined, morally inferior, and ugly. Thin men, on the other hand, are generally accepted and even sometimes preferred, though most women want to be with fat men.

Next we visit Shortland. The people here admire only women who are under five feet. A woman who is any taller is considered to be unattractive, and a woman over five six is thought to be utterly repulsive. Parents teach their daughters to avoid all foods with cal-cium so they won't grow, and they teach them to walk with bent legs under long skirts so they will appear shorter. Men's attractiveness, by contrast, is not judged by their height.

Our next stop is Ageland, where age and experience is consid-ered to be the hallmark of sexiness. Here the beauty of a woman's face is measured by the lines on it—the more wrinkles, the greater the beauty. A woman who ages prematurely is considered to be es-pecially blessed, as she will spend a greater part of her life admired and sought after. Young men pursue older women or, failing that, contemporaries whose mothers and grandmothers either aged early or have many wrinkles, hoping that their wives will be similarly blessed. Young women often dye their hair gray and buy special creams that promise to hasten the signs of aging, while older women buy these creams in the hope of looking even more attractive. Cosmetic surgery to add wrinkles and sagging skin is becoming more and more common. For men, too, age enhances attractiveness; however, it's not uncommon for young men to be found dashing and desirable. There is no similar word available to describe a young woman as attractive.

Next we visit Thinland, where the measure of a woman's beauty is the thinness of her body. The smaller the circumference of her waist, thighs, hips, arms, and legs, and the flatter her stomach, the more she is admired and desired. Here women unhealthily starve themselves, sometimes even to death, and put undue stress on their feet and bodies through overly vigorous exercise in an effort to appear beautiful. This is a regimen that girls begin as they go into puberty and follow thereafter. Any woman with any fullness to her body is considered fat, unattractive, and morally inferior. By contrast, a more muscular and broader look is preferred in men, and a man has to be rather stout before he is considered to be unappealing.

Lastly, we arrive at Multi-Pleasureland. This is an especially advanced planet where there has been peace for hundreds of years. Here difference is embraced and admired. People pride themselves on their shared ability to find common ground among their many different racial and ethnic groups, and they feel lucky to be continually meeting and dealing with people who are so diverse. Here there is not one beauty ideal, but each shape, size, and color is admired in its own right. Women who are short and wide are admired as having a compact, solid type of loveliness, while those who are short and thin are admired for their petiteness. Tall women are considered alluring and comely; large-bodied women voluptuous and sexy; and thin women pleasing and shapely. Women of different ages and of various eye, hair, and skin colors are each admired for looking exactly as they do. On this planet, men, too, are found attractive in their full diversity. People here are constantly looking at one another with pleasure, and they feel fortunate that they can view so many different types of beauty both in one another and in themselves. Here it is unthinkable for anyone to feel inferior or superior because of her or his looks.

Did you like visiting Thinland? Do you want to be a permanent resident? Does Multi-Pleasureland sound like a fable that is totally beyond realization? Not so. If you want to live in Multi-Pleasureland instead of in Thinland, you can help make this fable into reality.

As women's experience in pursuing equal educational, economic, and political opportunity has shown, when women unite, we can produce significant changes. If we start to look for, respect, and admire the beauty in ourselves and one another, and band together and demand that others accept and admire us as we are, we cannot only learn to like the way we look, but we can also change society's definition of beauty. Later, in Chapter 11, we will see how to further our appreciation for other women's looks, but first we have to learn to like our own appearance. When we do so, we gain the self-esteem that is needed to promote a different, more inclusive view of beauty.

Gaining and maintaining self-esteem, though, is not an easy issue for women. We tend to have lower self-esteem than men for several reasons. For one, we are not in control of our environment (having neither economic nor political power), so we don't experience the sense of self-efficacy that having control brings. For another, we are devalued by society—which views men as the important doers and women as support staff, appendages, and objects—and we internalize this vision of ourselves as lesser. In addition, we are socialized to please others and to judge our worth by how well we succeed in pleasing. This socialization process teaches us to appraise our self-worth not based on our own appreciation of our internal qualities or outer achievements, but on how well we succeed in gaining the approval of others. This puts us in a powerless position in which our self-image falls prey to every passing criticism, no matter how little merit it has. Even baseless criticism can shake our sense of self because we believe we're still at fault, inadequate for failing to please. With this kind of socialization, it's no wonder that so many women have what I call a Swiss cheese sense of self-esteem: Our self-esteem is high and solid in some areas, but full of holes in others, so it takes very little, sometimes as little as an unreturned smile, to make us feel undesirable and unlovable.

Last, but certainly not least, among the reasons women tend to lag behind men in developing self-esteem is the influence of the Beauty Imperative. If a woman doesn't feel inferior due to anything else about herself, she is almost guaranteed to feel dissatisfied with herself because of some aspect of her appearance.

Many of us try to raise our body self-esteem by continually surveying our appearance, searching for areas that need improvement, and straining to look our best. Unfortunately, what typically happens is that the more we look, the more "flaws" we find, and the more critical we become of our appearance and ourselves, berating ourselves for our "shortcomings." This self-belittlement erodes our self-esteem, making us feel worse about our appearance and ourselves, less confident, and, perhaps, even depressed. We may find ourselves in a vicious cycle in which the more we dislike our appearance, the more we criticize it, and the more we criticize it, the more we dislike it and ourselves. Then, instead of having the self-confidence that radiates attractiveness, what comes across are our feelings of being unattractive and unworthy.

If you want to feel more confident about your appearance and yourself, you need to learn to stop beating yourself up. Each time you look in the mirror and condemn what you see, you are lowering your appearance self-esteem. Instead of picking apart your looks, you need to develop a nurturing inner voice, the voice of your inner caretaker which will CARESS you: Show Compassion for whatever you are feeling about your looks and yourself; nonjudgmentally Accept you and your appearance; Respect you for how you look and who you are; Encourage you to take steps and risks to achieve the things you want just as you look now; Support you by believing in you and reassuring you that how you look is just fine; and Stroke you by praising your looks and giving you credit for trying. The more you nurture yourself in this way, CARESS yourself with compassion, acceptance, respect, encouragement, support, and stroking, the better you will feel about yourself and your looks.

Does this sound impossible to you? Are you unable to imagine feeling this way about yourself and your looks? I know how you feel because I've been there. But if the women I've worked with and I can learn to love the way we look, so can you.

Let me tell you more about myself. As far back as I can remember, I was a fat kid. I went from being slightly plump at eight to putting on more weight with puberty to being around fifty pounds heavier than the charts said I should be in high school. Needless to say, I was sometimes teased and made fun of, as fat kids often are. From the fourth grade on, my beautiful average-weight mother put me on diets and took me to doctors in an effort to help me. By college, I was totally obsessed with my weight, and through a series of drastic—what I now know to be unhealthy—diets, I lost a lot of weight. Through my twenties and thirties I hovered at least slightly above what I considered my ideal weight, slowly seesawing up and down the same ten to twenty pounds that on my five-feet-four-inch frame marked the difference between a size 10 and a size 12. By my mid-forties, I was seesawing between a size 10 and 14. My weight losses were always due to strenuous long-term dieting, often on one or another popular program—Weight Watchers, Overeaters Anonymous, the grapefruit diet, Cambridge, Nutri/System, liquid protein. You name it, I tried it. For very brief periods, perhaps seconds, I sometimes even got down to my goal weight and, at a size 8, felt thin and attractive; but mostly I felt fat and dissatisfied with how I looked. Also, like most women, I had no idea of what my true size was. I was forever asking my husband if I was bigger or smaller than some other woman. Often he said that I was much smaller than a woman I thought was close to my size. Needless to say, I religiously weighed myself naked first thing every morning, and even dragged my scale on vacation.

By my mid-forties, I had become increasingly aware that yo-yo dieting was unhealthy and compounded the problem, making it easier to gain and harder to lose weight, but was terrified to stop dieting for fear of ending up like the blimp I saw myself as in high school. Finally, I gathered the courage to quit dieting forever and to learn how to let my own body, not the scale or an eating program, tell me when and how much to eat. I was well aware that this would probably mean a weight gain. Given the fact that I had been fat as a kid, it was likely that my natural weight would be well above our very thin norms (even my thin weights were heavier than that), and that my virtual lifetime of yo-yo dieting had undoubtedly raised my setpoint and lowered my metabolism (if you're not familiar with the concept of setpoint and the metabolic effects of dieting, it is explained in detail in Chapter 7). And, indeed, I did go from a size twelve or fourteen to a size sixteen before leveling off and easily and effortlessly maintaining my weight and size. Throughout this period of weight gain, which took place over a year or two, I exercised regularly, remained quite healthy, and felt great.

But now I had a dilemma. How was I going to feel about the way that I looked? All my life I had equated being attractive with being thin, and even at a size twelve it had been hard for me to feel attractive. Could I be a size sixteen and stand looking at myself, let alone like the way I looked? (I know that for some of you a size sixteen seems very fat while others of you would love to be so thin. I am in no way offering this size as an objective criterion of either largeness or smallness. I'm only sharing my feelings at the time.) First slowly and tentatively, then more and more determinedly, I set out to find ways to like the way I looked. At the same time, in my workshops and psychotherapy practice, I was increasingly working on this issue with other women—some much smaller than I, others considerably larger, and some concerned not with their weight, but other parts of their appearance—developing techniques to help them and myself. Now, despite being no longer either young or thin, I have come to really love my body and like the way I look.

I am glad to share with you what I learned from my own experience and from my work with my clients and workshop participants. By following the exercises in this book, you, too, whether you're a size six or twenty-six, can learn to overcome whatever negative feelings you have about your appearance and learn to like the way you look. Let's start by unmasking some of the societal messages and myths about beauty that keep us fixated on and dissatisfied with our looks.

UGLY MYTHS, BEAUTIFUL YOU

Some of you may be excited at the prospect of broadening your concept of attractiveness. You may have already started to think differently about looks, and may be eager to learn how to see beauty in your face and body in ways that go beyond the very narrow definitions offered by society and family. Understandably, others of you may remain skeptical. After a lifetime of being inculcated with the doctrine of the Beauty Imperative, it is natural to feel that unless you meet society's rigidly defined beauty ideal you may be consigned to a life of unhappiness, disdain, and failure. Well, let me let you in on a closely guarded secret:

> LOOKING LIKE THE BEAUTY IDEAL DOES NOT AUTOMATICALLY BRING SUCCESS AND HAPPINESS. IN FACT, IT MAY WELL NOT IM-PROVE A WOMAN'S LIFE.

The widely held belief that "beauty brings happiness" is really a myth that largely gains its power from the media. On TV and in the movies and magazines, the beautiful woman is the happiest and most successful. Real life, however, is another story.

In real life, except for the relatively few women employed in the glamour industries (models, actresses, and so on), having larger or smaller breasts, a straighter nose, flatter stomach, thinner thighs, or being thin is not likely to help a woman get a good job or promotion, improve her relationships with family and friends, like herself more, or even help her in romantic relationships. If body changes heighten her satisfaction with herself, that self-confidence will undoubtedly help her; however, women do not have to spend huge sums on cosmetics, creams, clothes, diet foods, or personal trainers; mutilate themselves with cosmetic surgery; or be forever half-hungry in order to have this increase in their self-esteem. Let's examine these four areas—work, relationships with family and friends, self-esteem, and getting and keeping a mate—and see what the reality is as opposed to the myth.

In the job market and place of employment—despite the media depiction of the successful career woman looking like a model in corporate attire—the reality is that while being attractive is generally an asset for men, it often works against a woman because attractive women are generally assumed to be feminine and therefore, ipso facto, passive, dependent, emotional, and less competent. Conversely, being viewed as masculine is equated with being capable, competent, and possessing leadership ability.

A study done by Yale psychologist Madeline Heilman with colleague Lois Saruwatari found that while being attractive was consistently an advantage for men in getting hired, whether they were seeking managerial or nonmanagerial jobs, for women being attractive gave them an edge only when applying for nonmanagerial jobs. Women more than lost this edge when applying for a managerial job when being attractive was found to be a decided disadvantage. Physically attractive women were judged more feminine (and therefore, presumably, less competent), which made them less likely to be hired for a managerial position.

Heilman also found that not only is being conventionally pretty a disadvantage for women applying for a managerial position, but that it is also likely to be a liability when a woman tries to get ahead at a firm where she is already employed. Heilman, with colleague Melanie Stopeck, studied the effects of physical attractiveness on performance evaluations and recommendations for promotions, pay raises, and merit raises. They asked male and female MBA students, the very people who would be making these decisions in a few years, to rate employees based on written performance reviews (which were essentially equivalent for all employees), each of which had a photograph attached. Remarkably, the same level of performance was rated significantly lower when ascribed to attractive female managers than when attributed to unattractive women in comparable positions. The study concluded that being attractive (considered more feminine) was always a liability for women in managerial jobs, except in regard to merit raises, in which case looks had no effect.

Similarly, Linda Jackson of Michigan State University found that when professional personnel consultants evaluated employees for jobs generally seen as masculine, feminine, or gender-neutral and made decisions about promotions, special training, and work assignments, decisions about career development were strongly influenced by gender-trait information that had been given to the raters before they made their decisions. Both men and women who were seen as masculine or androgynous were more highly recommended for promotion and challenging job assignments than were men or women who were seen as feminine. Women and men seen as feminine were more likely to be given routine assignments and selected for promotion only in occupations seen as feminine. Interestingly, in this study, physical attractiveness was found to play no role for either men or women, probably because the positive bias toward being handsome (and therefore presumably masculine) that applies to men and the negative bias toward being pretty (and therefore presumably feminine) that applies to women had already been elicited by the gender-trait information the evaluators had received.

When attractive women do succeed, good looks can prevent them from receiving the credit they deserve. Heilman and Stopeck asked adult working men and women to read a short description of a fictitious employee's rise to assistant vice president of a company and to rate the factors responsible for the person's career success.

They found that whether the raters were men or women, when the career description was accompanied by the picture of an attractive woman, success was attributed not to ability but to other than job-related skill or talent. By contrast, attractive men's success was attributed to their ability, and they were rated as more capable than were the unattractive men.

In researching the same phenomenon, Barbara Spencer and Stephen Taylor of Mississippi State University found facial attractiveness to diminish the credit and increase the blame given to both men and women. Using college students as raters, they found that proficient performance by attractive women was more likely than that of others to be attributed to luck or favoritism, while that of attractive males was viewed as occurring with little effort. Conversely, the poor performance of attractive women was blamed on lack of effort, and that of attractive men was blamed on lack of ability. These findings are particularly important, the study points out, because supervisors react more intensely to poor employee performance if it is attributed to internal factors (e.g., lack of effort or ability) than to external ones (e.g., supervisory bias or bad luck).

Even when physical attractiveness does positively influence hiring decisions, research done by David Gilmore of the University of North Carolina at Charlotte with colleagues Terry A. Beehr and Kevin G. Love at Central Michigan University, using both students and professional employment interviewers as raters, found that such influence is negligible, accounting for only 2 percent of the variance in hiring decisions. Paula Morrow and colleagues at Iowa State University found the same negligible effect (2 percent) of attractiveness both on hiring and on promotion decisions. After reviewing the research on the effects of physical attractiveness on employment hiring and promotion, Morrow concluded that:

> physical attractiveness is generally an asset for men. . . .
> For women, the findings vary with the type of job. For
> managerial (masculine) jobs, physical attractiveness is
> probably a handicap for women. Unattractive women,
> who might be regarded as less feminine, and therefore
> more appropriate for the job, are preferred.

But it is not only in managerial positions that being attractive is disadvantageous. Women working in nontraditional areas, such as the construction trades (as carpenters, electricians, and plumbers) and firefighting, report that sexual harassment is rife, and that being pretty only makes it harder to be respected as a worker.

As for those jobs seen as feminine where conventionally pretty women may have some slight advantage, often these are dead-end or underpaid jobs. Of course, when you desperately need the income, as many women do, any job is desirable and any edge you may have is welcome, but it's not as though approximating the beauty ideal is a ticket to a great-paying, fabulous position.

If you still think looking like the beauty ideal is a passport to riches, spend some time at a welfare center, walking around a very poor neighborhood, and around a working class neighborhood. You'll find the same 5 percent or so of women who approximate the beauty ideal as you find anyplace else.

Not only is beauty not an advantage when trying to get ahead in the work world, it is usually not an asset in forging and cementing friendships and family relationships either. Very attractive women most often experience envy and resentment from their earliest years. If they grow up in families that make a big fuss about their beauty, as is common, their less favored siblings usually deeply envy and resent them, not only in childhood, but often throughout their lives.

In adolescence, a girl who is both pretty and popular (and not all even very conventionally pretty girls are popular) usually finds that other girls are eager to be her friends, hoping to ride the coattails of her popularity. She quickly learns that it is hard to tell who really likes her and who is just trying to use her, especially when she hears that some of her "friends" are putting her down behind her back. If she tries to avoid being used by hanging out only with other popular girls, she may well be seen as a snob and resented even more. Moreover, these popular girls are not necessarily the girls she would like most if allowed to freely choose. All of this envy, jealousy, and resentment make it harder for the pretty and popular teenage girl to find true friends who like her just for herself.

In college, too, it may be harder, rather than easier, for conventionally pretty women to be liked and accepted. Dennis Krebs and Allen A. Adinolfi asked same-sex dormmates to rate each other on various measures of personality and sociability, and based on these ratings divided their subjects into three groupings of socially accepted, rejected, or isolated. They found that the women in the rejected group were the most attractive. Other studies have found that very attractive women college students tend to be seen by their female peers as more egocentric, egotistical, snobbish, and materialistic.

In adulthood, this problem often continues. The more attractive a woman is, the more likely other women are to envy and resent her. People may even try to dismiss her as a bimbo no matter how smart she is. Not that very attractive women can't, and don't, have close friends. Of course many do. But it is usually harder, not easier, for them to forge these relationships and to be respected.

As for self-esteem, Yale psychologist Alan Feingold found, after reviewing hundreds of studies, that our stereotypes of very attractive people don't match reality: They are not categorically more confident, intelligent, social, dominant, or mentally healthier, nor are they more confident about their appearance. On the other hand, he found that people who see themselves as attractive (whatever their objective appearance) because of their good self-esteem do have many of the traits commonly (and wrongly) ascribed to very attractive people.

In reality, the woman who is very attractive as defined by society not only doesn't have an easier time feeling good about herself, but often has a much more difficult time learning to value herself as a full human being. Very attractive women learn early in life that their "value" lies in their looks, and this dogma becomes more and more strongly enforced as they move through adolescence and into adulthood, buttressed by continual praise for their appearance. Consequently, beautiful women often hang their whole self-image on their looks, and any flaw rocks their confidence and inner security. Whatever their other talents and achievements, they often feel, even more than other women, that their real worth lies in their looks, and so fail to integrate a positive sense of themselves based on their full personhood. When aging distances them from the beauty ideal, they often go to great lengths to remain young-looking, trying to battle feelings of inadequacy and inferiority.

Miranda, five feet seven, naturally thin, full-breasted, with clear skin and compelling features, is the type of woman that both men and women stare at because she is so attractive. Many women have told her that they would "kill" to look like her. On the one hand, she loves this attention (though she hates being hassled on the street), and it makes her feel really good. On the other hand, she feels that no one knows the real her, and that if they did, they wouldn't like her. She sees her looks as a gorgeously adorned shield that both attracts others and deflects them away from really seeing her. She has spent many hours fantasizing about what it would be like to be plainer, imagining that then she would know what people really think about her. At the same time, she is terrified of aging, afraid of becoming invisible. Much of the time, despite the smile she puts on for everyone, she is depressed.

Okay, you may be thinking, maybe being really great-looking isn't as helpful as I thought it was in the workplace, with family and friends, and in building self-esteem, but I know it has to be crucial in getting and keeping a mate, especially a male one. Well, yes and no.

No doubt about it, men like attractive women. However, and this is a big "however," their concept of beauty is not transmitted on the Y chromosome. What men may be biologically programmed—or culturally conditioned—to want (and even this is questionable) is to win out over other males, to get the prize. So, if society says very fat women are the most beautiful (as 81 percent of traditional cultures do today), men want fat women. If society says it is women with tiny, malformed feet who are the most good-looking (as upper-class Chinese society maintained for thousands of years), men want women with tiny feet. And if society says it is very thin women who are the epitome of beauty, these are the women whom many men, and some lesbians as well, desire.

However, being sought after as a prize has its drawbacks. For one, it makes it harder, not easier, to find a mate who truly values you for the whole person you are. For another, being with a partner who views you as a trophy means you run the risk, as you start to tarnish, of being replaced by a newer, shinier one. A recent example that jumps to mind is that of Donald Trump, who left his wife, Ivana, for a woman whom many see as a younger version of her.

The reality is that there is not a whit of evidence that very attractive women end up with relationships that are any better, longer-lasting, or more satisfying than the rest of us. Ray Bull and Nichola Rumsey extensively reviewed the research on the relationship between facial attractiveness and marital satisfaction. They concluded that "no consistent relationship between facial appearance and marital adjustment has been found."

In fact, noted physical attractiveness researchers Ellen Berscheid and Elaine Walster found just the opposite to be true. They looked at women's college yearbook photographs and interviewed the same women in midlife. They found that "in each of the instances in which a relationship between attractiveness and satisfaction was found, the more attractive a woman was judged to be from her college photos, the less happy and the less well-adjusted to her current life she was." They found no such relationship for men.

What ultimately holds true is that the better a woman's self-esteem, the more likely she is to find a satisfying relationship—and the more she likes her looks, no matter how close or far they are from the beauty ideal, the better her self-esteem is likely to be.

Not only does beauty not bring happiness, but most other generally held beliefs about beauty are also myths. Let's look at these myths and the concomitant realities.

Myths	Realities
Beauty for a woman is everything.	Your looks are only one of many valuable qualities you possess. The more you focus on your looks, rather than appreciating and emphasizing your other qualities and achievements, the more insecure you are likely to be, and the more likely you are to have low self-esteem.
Your appearance is the measure of your worth. The less attractive you look, the less worthy you are.	Your worth is based on being the good and valuable person you are. Your looks are only window dressing.
Whatever you have accomplished in life doesn't matter as much as how you look.	Your accomplishments reflect the real you. Your looks depend largely on genetics.
You must look young.	You are going to age. Each age has its own kind of beauty that you can learn to embrace and enjoy. (See Chapter 10.)
There is no such thing as being too thin.	Mortality is higher for people who are too thin than for people who are fat. (See Chapter 7.)
It's your own fault if you're fat, so it's okay to look down on and make fun of yourself or other fat women because its your/their own fault and you/they deserve it.	Being fat is largely due to genetics (and is made worse by dieting, as we will see in Chapter 7), not to lack of willpower or moral fiber.
A woman should have pert, ample breasts.	Has anyone ever met a woman whose breasts are naturally both pert and ample, and if so, was she over twenty?

(continued on page 60)

The ideal look of the moment is something you should strive for.	However you look, that's the ideal for you. That's the way Mother Nature made you. Learn to celebrate it, and others will celebrate it, too.

Are you starting to see what a bill of goods we women have been sold about beauty? Remember, the more we focus our money and energies on beauty work, the less time and money we have to do the things and make the changes that can really make us happy. So let's start learning how to like our looks and ourselves without all that beauty work.

BEAUTIFUL ME:

Write down everything you like about your looks, starting each item with "I have," and label this list "BEAUTIFUL ME." Be specific. For example, in addition to writing "I have a pretty face," say what you like about your face, such as:

I have wide, penetrating, enticing eyes.
I have a chin with character.
I have rich black hair.
I have full lips.
I have a face on which everything is in harmony.

In making this list:

Think of everything you have ever found pleasing about your looks, no matter how inconsequential you may consider it to be. For instance, "I have great toes."
Don't leave little things off as too unimportant.
Think of everything about your looks that others have ever praised, every compliment that you have ever received about your appearance.
Ask others whom you trust what they like about your looks,

and add it to your list. If you strongly disagree with something, put it in a "maybe" grouping. For instance, if people tell you they really like your rear, even if you think it's too big, add it to your list. If you've always hated your rear, put it in "maybe."

In completing this exercise, don't look in the mirror. This is not the time to stare critically at every part of your body, as if under a magnifying glass, and become critical rather than appreciative. It's too easy to begin thinking, Well, now that I'm looking at it, I think my left eyebrow isn't full enough. Hmmm. . . . Yep, I definitely don't like my left eyebrow. If your left eyebrow hasn't bothered you up to now, leave it alone. On the other hand, it is the time to mentally notice those pleasing parts of your appearance that you normally either don't notice or take for granted, such as: Now that I'm thinking about it, my eyebrows do have a great natural arch.

Make your list as long as possible, aiming to enumerate at least five traits. If you have trouble thinking of five things you like about your looks, consider such areas as the color or texture of your hair or complexion; the shape or color of your eyes; the appearance of your mouth, chin, cheekbones, eyebrows, ears; the shape of your shoulders, arms, legs, breasts, fingers; your brow line; posture; smile; waist; or walk. As you go through the various exercises in this book, keep adding to your BEAUTIFUL ME list as you develop new positive regard for other aspects of your appearance. By the time you've done all the exercises, you should have at least five items on your list. If you have more, congratulate yourself.

From now on read your BEAUTIFUL ME list slowly out loud with conviction two or three times a day. At the end say:

I am [your name], and I am uniquely beautiful in my own way.
I am [your name], and I have an inner beauty that shines through.
I am [your name], and I look just the way I am supposed to look, and that's beautiful.
I am [your name], and I love my body, which is a woman's body.

I am [your name], and I am a sexy woman.
I am [your name], and I am beautiful at my weight.
I am [your name], and I accept and love myself and my body.
I am [your name], and I love the way that I look.
I am [your name], and I am uniquely beautiful in my own way.

Don't worry if at first these affirmations feel foreign or like blatant lies. You are not used to CARESSing yourself and feeling good about the way that you look. With time, though, as you continue to recite these affirmations, you will experience the power of self-acceptance and self-praise. More and more, these affirmations will sink in, and you will feel a new sense of self-worth and self-liking. If any of these affirmations are not right for you, of course omit them, but be sure to replace them with affirmations that communicate what you really need to hear.

If you are not sure what you would like to hear, ask your inner child. Do the relaxation exercise in the Appendix, then imagine that you are talking compassionately with the wounded child within you. Ask her what she would like you to tell her about the way she looks that would make her feel better about her appearance. Be open and nonjudgmental as you listen to her, and be prepared to tell her whatever she needs to hear to feel good about the way she looks. It doesn't matter if what she wants to hear is very far from the way both you and she presently view your face and body, but don't say things that don't match your body. For instance, if you are four feet ten and your inner child wants to hear that she is very tall, don't say, "I am very tall," but rather say, "I am a good height, and I am beautiful at my height." The same thing with weight. If you weigh 280 pounds, don't tell yourself, "I am very thin," but rather say, "I have a sensuous, sexy, cuddly body, and I am beautiful at my current weight." (In Chapters 7 and 8 we will deal in detail with learning to feel attractive at whatever weight you are.) Then add these affirmations to your BEAUTIFUL ME list.

Now that you have started to recognize some of your real attractiveness, let's confront those negative self-appraisals that keep you from really liking the way you look.

WHAT I DON'T LIKE ABOUT MY LOOKS:

Make a list of everything you don't like about your looks, and label it WHAT I DON'T LIKE ABOUT MY LOOKS. Again, be specific. Don't write something general such as "I hate everything about my looks" or "I'm just awful." For example, you might write:

Thighs too wide
Nose too long and flaring
Shoulders are square

and so on.

When you're done, see how many items are on your second list, compared to your first. Generally, the longer your second list the more important the beauty ideal is to you, the more insecure you feel about your looks and yourself, and the less you like yourself. Sometimes, however, just one item can make a woman hate her whole appearance, such as thinking she is too fat. If you are disfigured or disabled, it may be especially difficult for you to think that anything else about your appearance matters. We will work with this body hatred as we go along, so save this list.

MY BEAUTY IDEAL:

Write down how you believe each body part should look, and label this list MY BEAUTY IDEAL. For instance:

Thighs should be narrow and firm.
Noses should be short and bobbed.
Shoulders should be long and sloping.

By the time you finish, you will have a list of "shoulds" that, along with your list of what you like about your looks, narrowly and precisely defines your beauty ideal. Now, try expanding it.

DIFFERENT WAYS OF BEING PRETTY:

Take your list of "shoulds" and compare them to the traits of real women whom you think are attractive. You can look for attractive women among your family, friends, acquaintances, coworkers, or just women on the street or in the supermarket—but not women on TV, in magazines, or in movies. (Remember that because of camera angles, taping, contouring, cosmetic surgery, makeup, and airbrushing, you really don't know what they look like.) Consider each attractive woman you find. Does she match your list in every detail? Likely not. Some attractive women may meet most of your criteria, while others some, or few. If these women can be attractive without meeting all your criteria, why can't you?

Some of you may find that the women whom you consider to be attractive closely match your lists. If so, this is a sign that you really are very rigidly defining beauty. Take this opportunity to expand your vision. Can you purposely find a woman with, say, wide thighs, a long nose, or square shoulders whom you find attractive? Start by just slightly expanding your criteria—say, thighs just a little fuller, a nose just a little longer, or shoulders a little less sloping. Next, find a number of women whom you consider attractive who do not possess at least two of your "shoulds." Once you can do this, look for attractive women who do not match three of your "shoulds," then four, then five. By then you will have come a long way in recognizing the variety inherent in perceptions of beauty. As you do so, modify your MY BEAUTY IDEAL list to fit your expanding experience of attractiveness. Next to each body part, write down the new ways you are discovering that that body part can be attractive. For instance:

> ~~Noses should be short and bobbed.~~ Noses are attractive short and bobbed. They are also attractive wide and broad, long and narrow, turned up, and turned down.

If you are having difficulty widening your view of beauty, it may be because you are wedded to the beauty concepts that were emphasized in your family. Let's see how different types of parenting affect our feelings about how we should and do look.

CHAPTER 4

FAMILIAL MESSAGES, INFLUENCES, AND MODELS

The way we feel about our looks, like much of our self-concept, is shaped in our childhood years. While society dictates what a woman "should" look like, it is in the family that our self-image is first formed. If our parents like the way we look and find us attractive, without overemphasizing our appearance, we internalize a positive body image that helps us weather the pressures of adolescence so that we can emerge into adulthood with a positive regard for our appearance and ourselves.

Many parents, however, are unable to give their daughters this acceptance and approval of their appearance. Fathers, having been socialized to see beautiful women as status symbols, often overemphasize their daughters' looks as a way of adding to their own status; while mothers, struggling themselves with their own body images, often want more than anything for their daughters to grow up thin and beautiful so that they will have the success and happiness that society promises beauty will bring.

Unfortunately, the more parents try to shape and mold their daughters' bodies and appearance, the more miserable girls become. They learn that their body is their enemy—too skinny or too fat, too tall or too short, too full or too flat, too dark or too light—and not to be trusted. Rather than learning to identify with and love their bodies, girls learn to view them as betrayers that proclaim to the world their inadequacy and unworthiness.

Although mothers usually are blamed for whatever problems their children have, when it comes to appearance self-esteem, fathers play a big role. Through their views, actions, and reactions they powerfully transmit and present societal norms of beauty to their daughters, who generally accept these notions as the male concept of beauty.

For instance, if a father habitually praises, say, large breasts, long legs, a trim butt, or light skin, the growing girl learns to see these features as especially attractive. If she possesses them, she may feel particularly proud. If she doesn't, she learns to feel deficient. If a father ogles women on the street and TV or flirts with casual acquaintances, his daughter learns that women are valued as objects, not people, and that it is necessary to be flirtatious and pretty to be liked. If Dad continually appraises women by how they look—talking about how this one looks good, and that one old; this one is too heavy, while another has a great body—he further transmits the Beauty Imperative, teaching his growing daughter that there is nothing more important for a woman than how she looks because that is primarily how she will be judged.

How Dad treats Mom also very much influences his growing daughter. If Dad's expressions of affection to Mother are usually tied to comments about her appearance, daughter learns that you get love from men mainly by looking good. If Father frequently disparages Mom's looks, nagging her to lose weight or to "fix herself up," again daughter learns that looks are all important and that it is hard to please. In adolescence, she may even become anorexic or bulimic. Eating-disordered women often report that appearance was overemphasized in their families, and that their fathers disparaged and shamed their mothers for gaining weight or being heavy, while praising them for losing weight and being slim.

For the sake of clarity, I have broken down paternal responses to daughters' appearances and their effects into six main categories. These categories, like any categories, will not fit everyone, and will fit no one exactly. Your father may not precisely fit into any of these groups, or he may fit into more than one. Use these categories to increase your recognition of how your father has affected your appearance self-esteem, without trying to pigeonhole him in a way that doesn't fit.

Your "father," of course, may not have been your biological father, but a stepfather, adopted father, grandfather, uncle, cousin, much older brother, or some other older male who functioned in the father role. Some of you may have no father whom you knew while others of you had more than one fathering man in your life, either at different times or at the same time. It is important to consider how each of the fathers you knew influenced you and your view of yourself.

The Endorsing Father

This is the father whom every woman wishes she had had— the dad who really loves and values his daughter for herself; the kind of dad who thinks it's neat that at age two or ten you took the alarm clock apart to see how it works; the father who will toss a ball around with you or take you to the ball game and who also wouldn't miss one of your recitals. He likes to hear about what you've been learning in school, your opinion of your friends, movies, TV shows, politics, and anything else that interests you. This dad thinks you're really pretty whether you're dressed for a dance or washing the car. When you were little, he spent time with you, held you on his lap, put you to bed when he could. As you grew into adolescence he hugged you when you were celebrating, or disappointed, or just whenever you wanted a hug. While he was not necessarily gushy with compliments, you always knew that you were tops in his eyes, and that he genuinely thought you were beautiful as a person and as a woman.

If you have a dad like this, you undoubtedly know what a wonderful influence he has been in your life. You realized growing up that even if you messed up in some way, while he would be disappointed in you, he would also love you. He understood that messing up was sometimes part of growing and maturing. And you also knew that while he loved the way you look, he also didn't think this was the most important thing about you; that he saw your beauty as being much more than the way your hair looked or what the scale said. As you grew, you internalized this sense of beauty and felt really attractive. Although in adolescence—as peer and social values pressed down on you—you may have felt very self-conscious about your looks, longed to look like a model, and picked at your "flaws," still you carried within yourself a sense of satisfaction with your looks that helped shape how others saw you. As an adult, while not impervious to the lookism of society (this is much too strong not to affect almost every woman), at any age or size you continue to have an inner core that allows you to feel attractive, and you have little difficulty dealing with the changes that aging brings.

Unfortunately, many of us did not have an endorsing father and grew up feeling very different about our looks.

The Adoring Father

The adoring dad dotes on his daughter. This is the father who goes on and on about how cute and pretty she is. He constantly shows her picture to all comers, and frequently tells her how gorgeous she is. He likes to give her little trinkets and toys, like hair ribbons and Barbie dolls, that have to do with dressing up and looking beautiful. As his little girl grows, he loves watching her practice dance or gymnastics in her leotard or tutu and seeing her dress up. He discourages her from activities that require her to get dirty, telling her that she's much too pretty to get messy.

When his daughter becomes an adolescent, his attitude toward her may change. He may become more physically distant—no longer hugging her because of potential impropriety. Or he may be critical of those she dates, feeling that no one is good enough for his daughter. Or he may just remain there as her number-one cheerleader, telling her how great she looks and how glad he is that she is popular.

While some of the adoring dad's actions may be similar to those of the endorsing dad (endorsing dad, too, likes showing off pictures of his daughter and thinks she's wonderful-looking), the message is very different. While the endorsing dad values his daughter's beauty as one of her many admirable qualities, the message from the adoring father is that a big part of what makes her so special to him is the way she looks.

The daughter of the adoring father may well internalize good feelings about her looks from all his adoration, but she typically also strongly internalizes the Beauty Imperative and firmly feels, even though her head may tell her otherwise, that nothing is more important than how she looks. Both in adolescence and adulthood she is likely to put a great deal of time, money, and effort into looking good, while never feeling secure about her attractiveness. The daughter of an adoring father has a particularly difficult time with aging, feeling that as her looks diminish (according to our culture's view), so does her desirability and her value.

> Cassie, who is twenty-eight, had an adoring father. She was a very cute and pretty little girl, resembling her beautiful mother. Her father continually oohed and aahed about her looks, telling her how pretty she was. When she bought new clothes, he loved seeing her dressed up in them. While Cassie is very bright and made excellent grades in school, it was clear to her that what her father most valued about her was how she looked.

As an adult, size 5 Cassie put great effort into her appearance. She was always beautifully dressed, made-up, and coiffed. She worked out regularly and was in top shape. However, she had very conflicted feelings about her looks. On the one hand, she knew she was attractive and was proud of it. On the other hand, she never felt attractive enough. If a man wasn't interested in her, she always assumed it was because she wasn't still more attractive. She also felt that her natural looks were not good enough. She made sure she would never be seen without makeup and counted every calorie that went into her mouth. If she gained a few pounds, she felt fat and undesirable. Though a well-respected professional, her self-esteem plummeted when she felt she didn't look good. In our work together she learned how to value her looks as just one aspect of herself. Now she has gained new freedom and happiness with her appearance. She is no longer fanatical about exercise and diet, comfortably goes without makeup away from work and social functions, and feels happy with herself.

The Narcissistic Father

The narcissistic father needs to prop up his ego at all costs because deep down he feels fragile and is unsure of his own worth. He may be very into his own appearance or take great pride in having an attractive wife. Or he may be resentful toward his wife for not looking as good as he thinks the woman who reflects him should. He may have affairs as a way of feeling desirable and admired, or leave his wife for another woman whom he sees as more attractive or who is more admiring of him.

The narcissistic father views his daughter, like his wife, as a reflection of himself and wants her to look good as proof of his own worth. He may pick at certain aspects of her appearance that particularly matter to him, or push her to make changes he thinks would improve her appearance. While he may say this is for her own good, in reality he assumes that what pleases him is what is good for her, and has little idea of what her real feelings, needs, and wishes are, let alone how they could best be met. If he likes the way his daughter looks, she may grow up feeling pretty but rather empty because his praise does little to satisfy her need for real caring. If he is generally displeased with her appearance, she likely feels unattractive and undesirable, as well as empty.

Monica's father, a successful accountant, was narcissistic. After her parents divorced when she was eight, she continued to have ongoing contact with him in the small town where she grew up. As Monica grew into adolescence, she remained slim, almost boyish, in figure. Still, her father thought she had a large rear end and continually commented on it. Beyond that, he had little to say about her looks. Monica was mortified, believing she had this enormous failing that she could do nothing about. She knew that looks were important to her dad. He dressed smartly, was always flirting with attractive women, and had one younger girlfriend after another.

Though Monica had little respect for her father and increasingly dreaded her time with him, she still longed to be beautiful, imagining that then she would gain his true interest and concern. In high school, college, and afterwards, Monica generally had a boyfriend and felt somewhat attractive. Yet she was continually plagued by images of her "tremendous" rear end (which was not large, but a bit bigger than the rest of her slim body), and it took little to make her feel unattractive, sad, and empty.

The Distant Father

This father pays little attention to his daughter. He may be absent and have little or no contact with her, or his contact with her may be haphazard and disinterested. If he lives at home, he may seldom be there or spend his time staring at the TV. Alternatively, he may be totally immersed in his wife, son(s), another daughter (sometimes a man is narcissistically or adoringly involved with one daughter but distant from or critical of another), or some activity of his own, largely ignoring his daughter unless he wants her to do something for him.

Of course, not all fathers who work long hours do so to distance themselves. Some fathers, like some mothers, have no choice but to work two jobs or lots of overtime to make ends meet or to provide a decent standard of living for themselves and their families. Others, though, especially workaholics, use the need to provide for their families as an excuse, when really they are avoiding intimacy.

By contrast, fathers who are capable of endorsing their daughters manage to do so in the time available. Even though they may be out of the home for much of the day, they are eager to find out what their daughters are up to, talk with them about these interests, and in general convey their liking for and appreciation of them as young women and as individuals.

Truly distant fathers convey very different messages to their daughters. They seem never quite able to remember their daughters' interests, friends, concerns, or activities. While they may make the requisite appearance at events important to their daughters, it may be because they were "dragged" there by their wives, or because of a sense of obligation, and paid only perfunctory attention.

If a distant father likes his daughter's looks, she naturally figures that if only she were prettier, she would get more of the attention she longs for, so she blames herself and her looks for Dad's distance and feels inadequate. If her father ignores her looks, or makes occasional negative comments (such as "Why don't you stand up straighter? You'd look so much better"), she feels even more that the problem is that she isn't attractive enough, and that if only she were prettier (i.e., following the media myth), he would pay her more attention. Of course, no matter how much she may improve her posture, her father still doesn't give her the attention she needs. Daughters of distant fathers typically grow up feeling inadequate about their looks and themselves, and long to be beautiful while believing they never can be.

> Trish had a distant father. He worked long hours during the week and spent weekends glued to the TV. The only attention he paid her was when he asked her to bring him things, do the dishes, or perform some other chore. She grew up with a sense of herself as unattractive and insignificant. In her teens she immersed herself in music and her orchestra friends. In college she slowly became aware of her attraction to women, and in her twenties established a stable lesbian relationship.

When I met her at thirty-five, Trish was very happy in her relationship of ten years, but unhappy with herself and her looks, feeling insignificant and unattractive. She felt her lover was interested in her despite—not because of—her looks. While she felt dissatisfied with various aspects of herself, her looks were high on her dissatisfaction list. She longed to walk down the street, or go to a party, and feel all eyes on her, or just stay home and look in the mirror and feel pretty and desirable. While I saw her as lovely-looking, she saw herself as plain, too heavy, colorless. In our work together she learned how to see herself differently, and now is aware of her true attractiveness.

The Highly Critical Father

Some fathers are very critical. Whatever their daughter does is never good enough. If she gets a B+, it should have been an A; if she cleans her room, it's never done right; when she buys him a gift, it's the wrong color. A man like this is almost inevitably also very critical of his daughter's looks. No matter how attractive she might be, he is sure to harp on her failings, not happy with anything less than his version of perfection. His daughter learns that she has to be perfect to measure up, that there is no room for flaws and that she is inadequate.

> Julia, a thin, attractive, serious-minded, very likable seventeen-year-old who had not yet begun to date, had such a father. As she was preparing to go off to a prestigious college, he suddenly decided that she should get a nose job. He said this would increase her chances for social success. Julia, who had never thought that anything was wrong with her nose, was outraged at this suggestion, but she also began to become self-conscious about her nose. Although she did not have the operation, her father's suggestion to her undermined her confidence in her looks, just at a time when she could most have used some positive reinforcement.

A man like Julia's father believes he is acting in the best interest of his daughter, but is blind to the highly negative effect his standards, demands, bossiness, and perfectionism have on her developing sense of self. In reality, his daughter's not dating is not about her looks but stems from her unconscious fear of entering into the kind of controlling relationship she has experienced with him.

The Abusive Father

An abusive father's actions teach his daughter that she is worthless. A girl who is beaten usually believes that if she weren't bad and without value, she wouldn't be treated that way. To make things worse, often while her father is beating her, he generally also berates her and blames her, telling her that she is bad, no good, worthless, ugly. He may belittle many things about her, including her looks, or say he is beating her because of her "loose" behavior (which may be no more than coming home a little late, having a dreamy look on her face, or sitting with her legs uncrossed).

In adulthood, an abused daughter usually continues to feel worthless and often ugly.

> Sandy, a redhead, was raised in a family where physical abuse by her middle-class, college-educated parents was a common occurrence. Because she was the only redhead in her nuclear and extended family (except for her father's mother, who was an alcoholic and ne'er-do-well), her looks were considered to be trashy. Growing up, she was constantly called ugly and told that she was too skinny and had no shape. Even though from early adolescence until she married in her late twenties, she was almost never without a boyfriend, she still felt ugly. Now a very attractive thirty-three, she will not leave the house unless her hair and makeup are perfect, for fear that people on the street will stare at her homeliness. She has even had minor cosmetic surgery, hoping to correct the ugliness she alone views in her face.

Particularly horrific is the father who sexually abuses his daughter. He makes his daughter feel like damaged, worthless goods. Frequently her whole life is permeated with the lingering effects of abuse. Some of the common feelings she—as well as a physically abused daughter or other trauma survivor—may experience, as documented by Harvard psychiatrist Judith Herman, are shame, doubt, guilt, self-blame, feelings of inferiority, helplessness, defilement or stigma, and a sense of being completely different from others. Ways in which she may react to these feelings, Herman explains, include the exhibition of compulsive or extremely inhibited sexuality or explosive or extremely inhibited anger (these types of anger may alternate). She may also experience flashbacks to the trauma or inability to remember it; depression; hypersensitivity to external and internal stimuli; suicidal thoughts; an urge for self-injury; dissociated states in which she feels disconnected from herself and her body; multiple personality disorder; feelings of persistent mistrust; isolation, withdrawal, or search for a rescuer; repeated failures at self-protection; loss of sustaining faith; and a sense of hopelessness and despair.

Needless to say, a sexual abuse survivor's relationship with her body and her looks is often filled with tension and unease. Perhaps wrongly believing that her looks brought on the abuse, she may be afraid to look good so she downplays her appearance. If her father (or other abuser) praised her looks while he was abusing her, she may be even more afraid to look good. Some survivors are ashamed of their bodies and are exceedingly modest, though others are not. Still others go to the other extreme and treat their bodies like a barterable commodity. In doing so, a woman may act as if she knew that she is attractive and sexy, but it's all a facade. In truth, she believes that men want her not because she's beautiful and valuable, but because they're lustful and she's an available object. If any pleasurable body sensations were associated with the abuse, these may add to the tremendous guilt the survivor typically feels, and may make it even harder for her to allow her body to give her pleasure. It is common for survivors to dissociate themselves from their bodies, which were the medium of so much pain, humiliation, and betrayal. Some survivors of sexual abuse experience sexual difficulties, though others do not, and up to 60 percent of women with eating disorders have been found to be survivors of sexual abuse. If you are a survivor, you may have an especially difficult time liking the way you look or being comfortable with your body because your body has been the site of trauma.

> Amy is a forty-five-year-old woman who was sexually abused by her father repeatedly between the ages of seven and ten. He then deserted the family and she never saw or heard from him again. As an adult Amy remembered the abuse, but thought of it as something that was far behind her. In her teens and twenties she dated little, avoided sex, and immersed herself in her work and her

friends. She dressed stylishly and attractively, but when men flirted with her she felt dirty. At thirty she married a very sweet and supportive coworker with whom she had worked closely for some years and to whom she was drawn because he was gentle and understanding. He also respected her desire to wait until after marriage to have sex. They developed a mutually supportive marriage, with infrequent sex that Amy did not enjoy. After a couple of years they had a son.

When I met Amy in her mid-forties, she continued to dress attractively, wanting to look right and fit in, but underneath she distrusted her body and saw it as separate from the real her. She consulted me after reading books for survivors of sexual abuse that led her to hope that she could feel different about sex. Much of the work we did together involved her learning how to own and like her body, as well as her working through the sexual trauma. She needed to repair her relationship with her body and learn to love it and feel in charge of it; only then could she use it to feel pleasure.

Although I am addressing sexual abuse by fathers, any sexual abuse, which unfortunately is rife in our society and may be perpetrated on as many as one out of three women, has similar damaging effects. A single incident of abuse that occurs in adulthood, such as a rape, can be highly damaging. Childhood sexual abuse can be even more traumatic and harmful and generally, the earlier the abuse, the more severe it was, and the longer it went on, the worse the trauma, with ritual abuse being especially traumatic.

Abuse by fathers is particularly damaging not only because it was likely to have started at an early age and been repetitive, but also because it involves betrayal and violation by the very person who is supposed to protect you and help you develop a healthy appreciation of what it means to be a girl and a woman.

While the treatment of sexual abuse is beyond the scope of this book, if you are a survivor, it is important to know that you have been affected in ways that in all likelihood are strongly influencing your life, that it is not your fault, and that you can heal. If you are experiencing difficulty in your life, it can be very beneficial to consult with a mental health professional experienced in working with survivors, as well as to participate in a group for survivors. It can also be helpful to read some of the excellent literature available, some of which is listed in the Suggested Readings section.

Fathers, of course, are not the only parents who strongly influence their daughters' sense of attractiveness; mothers do as well. Mothers serve as exemplars to their daughters of how to relate to their looks and the beauty culture. If a mother is comfortable with her face and body, her daughter learns that she can like the way she looks without being perfect or continually at her best. However, this is often not the case.

Given the immense impact of the Beauty Imperative in our culture, it is common for mothers, like other women, to hate their bodies, and thus to have a difficult time presenting a positive role model for their daughters. In the 1984 *Glamour* body-image survey of 33,000 women, only 13 percent of the respondents thought that their mothers had liked their own bodies.

Mothers may agonize about their appearance, be ashamed to be seen without makeup, diet continually, or diet and binge, be anorexic or bulemic, fervently use face creams, fanatically exercise, have cosmetic surgery or liposuction, devote a significant portion of their precious resources of time and money on beauty enhancers and clothes, or in some other way express undue concern with their looks. The growing girl learns, through example, that looking good is essential and takes tremendous effort, and that she can never be satisfied with how she looks because beauty can quickly slip away.

In addition to serving as role models, mothers directly affect their daughters' body self-esteem by the degree of appreciation, acceptance, or criticism they express toward their daughters' looks. Unfortunately, as the *Glamour* body-image survey documented, mothers who dislike their own bodies are more likely to be critical of their daughters' appearance. This is no surprise. When a woman is dissatisfied with her appearance, it's usually because she believes, à la the Beauty Imperative, that looks are everything, so if she doesn't look like the beauty ideal, she's inferior. Wanting her daughter to be successful, and perhaps also wanting her to make up for a disappointment in her own looks, she regards her daughter with an ever-vigilant, critical eye, hoping to immediately spot and correct any beauty flaws her daughter may have. While generally well intentioned, this kind of overemphasis on beauty, combined with hypercriticism, is destructive, leaving a daughter feeling bad about herself, excessively focused on her appearance, and believing that whatever she does she will never be pretty enough. The *Glamour* survey found that "a respondent's perception that her mother's attitude toward the respondent's body was mainly negative was associated with numerous measures of poor body image, self-consciousness, and severity of dieting techniques."

A study of girls in junior and senior high school found that over 30 percent had been told by their mothers that they needed to lose weight, though fewer than 5 percent were overweight. Undoubtedly these mothers were judging their daughters with the same hypercritical eye through which they view themselves, since over two-thirds of all the girls interviewed also reported that their mothers frequently dieted, and it is highly unlikely that all these mothers were of more than average weight. The same connection between a mother's criticism and her daughter's dieting (and therefore presumed body dissatisfaction) was found in a cross-sectional study of more than 2,000 girls ages eleven to eighteen and almost 1,300 of their mothers. Half the girls who were dieting were encouraged to do so by their mothers, while only 14 percent of the nondieting girls had been urged to diet by their mothers.

Psychologist Judith Rodin, founder of Yale University's Eating Disorders Clinic, reports that mothers of daughters with eating disorders are usually themselves longtime dieters who started dieting at a younger age than mothers of daughters without eating disorders. Though both groups of mothers in her study had similar weights, the mothers of eating-disordered daughters were much more dissatisfied with their own bodies and with their daughters' bodies as well, wanting their daughters to be thinner than other mothers did and rating their daughters as even less attractive than their daughters rated themselves.

In another survey of college women, researchers found that

while almost all (92 percent) of the college women rated their mothers' attitudes toward them as people as "mostly positive" or better, considerably less than half (43 percent) rated their mothers' evaluation of their bodies this high. In cases where mothers were perceived as viewing daughters' bodies negatively, these college women were found to have scores on eating disorders inventories which are predictive of bulimia and body dissatisfaction.

On the other hand, the good news is that many parents are not critical of their daughters' look. A majority of the 33,000 women polled in the *Glamour* survey reported that their parents had either neutral or positive feelings about their daughters' bodies. Significantly, when mothers had positive attitudes toward their daughters' bodies, these daughters were much more likely to be happy with their own bodies than were daughters of critical mothers (68 percent vs. 42 percent).

While mothers are not as easy to classify as fathers, given the detrimental effect the Beauty Imperative and the beauty ideal have on most women, clearly the attitudes mothers have toward their daughters' looks have an important impact. Let's consider the following categories of mothers.

The Nurturing Mother

A nurturing mother CARESSes her daughter. That is, she is Compassionate to her feelings; lovingly and proudly Accepts her as she is and how she looks; Respects her for the person she is; Encourages her to reach for what she wants; Supports her whatever her level of achievement; and Strokes her with loving hugs and words of praise.

The nurturing mother, like the endorsing father, loves the way her daughter looks, whether she is dressed for the holidays or playing in the mud. While the nurturing mother may enjoy taking her daughter shopping, she enjoys equally playing a game with her, discussing a book, or talking about whatever her daughter is interested in. She genuinely likes her daughter's looks and is comfortable expressing this approval, without overemphasizing this one part of who her daughter is. The nurturing mother is content to let her growing daughter develop according to her own body's plan, without trying to squeeze her into a mold. If her daughter doesn't in some way match the beauty ideal, mother is content with and appreciates how her daughter does look. The nurturing mother does not supervise her daughter's diet beyond a basic concern for nourishment. She allows her daughter to learn when to stop eating by listening to her own body, not some outside authority or the scale. Most important, the nurturing mother does not try to live vicariously through her daughter, using her as a mirror for her own successes or failures.

The Merging Mother

The merging mother sees her daughter as an extension of herself. If her daughter is happy, she's happy. If her daughter is sad, she's sad. For her, "love" means feeling and thinking alike. She wants her daughter to be able to tell her everything, and feels hurt and injured when her daughter seeks privacy. If she is considered beautiful, she wants her daughter to look just like her. If she always wanted to be better-looking, she desires more than anything for her daughter to look the way she always wanted to. The merging mother is willing to spend a lot of time and money helping her daughter look beautiful, no matter how meager her resources, and she is deeply disappointed if her daughter does not became a social success.

The daughter of the merging mother has great difficulty differentiating her looks from her mother's ambitions and loving herself as she is. On some level, she's aware that her mother's vicarious gratification and sense of vindication is riding on how she looks, and she greatly fears failure. If she is socially successful, her popularity further reinforces for her that looks are everything, and dreads any change that may mar them. If she is not popular, she's convinced that it's because she isn't pretty enough, and feels unattractive, inadequate, and deficient. Later, she has a hard time dealing with the changes that age brings.

Susan, shy and quiet both as a child and adult, had a mother who longed for her to be Ms. Popularity. From the time Susan was a toddler, her mother spent hours fixing Susan's hair, making her clothes, and dressing her "just right." As a teenager Susan had a group of good friends but was not part of the popular crowd. This would have been okay with Susan, except that she knew it really bothered her mother. Her mother was always offering to take Sue shopping, though money was tight, and telling Sue how pretty she was, hoping to build her confidence. Each time her mother complimented her, Sue inwardly cringed and felt less attractive, reasoning that if her mother really thought she was pretty, she wouldn't have to constantly go out of her way to build her up. As an adult Sue continued to feel plain and dreaded calling attention to herself. It wasn't until midlife that she began to develop positive feelings about her looks.

The Narcissistic Mother

The narcissistic mother needs to feel extraordinary in order to cover deep-seated and unrecognized feelings of emptiness and inadequacy. She is often extremely concerned with her own appearance, and sees her daughter not as an extension of herself but as a reflection. She may require her daughter to dress impeccably and engage in a lot of beauty maintenance; or she may go to the other extreme and neglect her daughter's appearance, wishing to be the only star, with her daughter as part of her adoring and admiring audience. Either approach leaves her daughter unable to truly like and appreciate her own looks. If her daughter is required to look perfect, she learns that beauty is everything and that no deviation from the ideal is allowed, leaving her no solid foundation of self-approval. If mother neglects her daughter's looks, her daughter gets the message that she can never (and should never) measure up. In this case, the daughter often (consciously or unconsciously) feels that it is wrong and dangerous to approve of her own looks.

Elena had a mother who was considered by everyone to be a great beauty and who was doted on by her father. Elena did not look particularly like either of her parents, and both her parents were disappointed that Elena did not resemble her mother. Clearly looks were very important in her family, and Elena always felt that she did not measure up to her mother. When she entered adolescence, her mother, who strictly limited her own food intake, became very watchful of whatever Elena ate. When she was twelve, Elena went to sleep-away camp for two months and came home five pounds heavier (she also grew three quarters of an inch). Her mother immediately put her on a diet and watched even more carefully what she ate. After this Elena always felt fat (though she never was), and saw her body as her enemy—something that had to be tamed and thinned lest it reveal the fat, ugly person she believed herself to be. In high school, and later in college, she avoided possible rejection by staying with the same boyfriend throughout. She later married a man she met at her first job. Now, after eight years of marriage and two children, Elena still sees herself as not pretty enough, and her body as her enemy. She carefully supervises her food intake, swims regularly, and dresses meticulously, but whatever she does she always feels one step away from being ugly.

The Highly Competitive Mother

The highly competitive mother is unconsciously in competition with her daughter because she needs to surpass others to feel good about herself. This competition is usually quite subtle and takes place in many different areas. While the competitive mother typically encourages her daughter to compete with peers in many areas (academics, music, sports, arts, dance), and is genuinely pleased at her daughter's successes, at the same time she subtly undermines her daughter's pleasure in these successes. It's as though the competitive mother's very attempts to build her daughter up also have an element of tearing her down. A mother may do this by praising others, by never seeming entirely pleased, or by reacting to her daughter's successes with stories of her own triumphs. The overt message is: Do your best and be great. The covert message is: Don't outshine me.

This double message leaves the daughter in a quandary: To please Mother she has to excel, but she also has to be subservient to her mother and her ideas, methods, and beliefs. The competitive mother encourages her daughter to express her opinions and stand up for what she believes in vis-à-vis others, but not with her, because she firmly believes that Mother knows best.

Needless to say, this two-sided message is also prevalent in a competitive mother's attitude toward her daughter's looks. She presses her daughter to look good, and frequently comments on her appearance with a mixture of compliments and criticisms. "That's a pretty outfit, but I don't think that hairstyle suits you." Many mothers might make a comment like this one, but with the competitive mother they're constant. Here again the double message is: You must be pretty, but don't surpass me.

Some daughters respond to this competition by bowing out and becoming underachievers. Others excel, then find that no matter how much they try to please, and despite whatever their mothers may say, their mothers never seem entirely satisfied. The daughter of the competitive mother frequently has very conflicted feelings about her looks. She may try her best to please and work hard on her appearance or rebel and seemingly disregard her looks, taking herself out of the competition. To the degree that she is praised, she may incorporate positive feelings about her appearance; however, she also learns that it is very important to excel at being beautiful (as with everything else), yet no matter how good she looks, it is never good enough.

Elissa, a bright, accomplished, fifty-six-year-old woman, grew up in a very competitive household, with an older brother and a younger sister. Her mother, an attractive woman, was a devoted homemaker who cooked, baked, went on class trips, did volunteer work, and was well liked by Elissa's friends. Everyone wanted a mother like Elissa's. As a teenager Elissa

couldn't understand why she herself so often felt wary
and angry.

In our work together Elissa came to understand that despite
all the ways in which her mother gave her genuine support, she also
subtly undermined her. For instance, while many of her mother's
overt messages about Elissa's looks were positive ("You look
pretty"), they were often followed by a question that implied criticism ("But do you think that's the best color for you?"). The rare
times Elissa tried to express her pain over this constant but subtle
criticism, her mother told her that she was exaggerating and misin-
terpreting her comments, and that she wasn't appreciating her good
will. Upset by Elissa's "ingratitude," she would start to cry. Elissa
soon learned to keep her pain to herself and pretend everything was
okay. To this day, whenever her mother first sees her, she scrutinizes
her appearance and makes a comment on it. Each time Elissa inwardly braces herself, knowing that she's about to be judged and inevitably will not quite measure up. Needless to say, Elissa spent
most of her life feeling that she's not as pretty as her mom, and that
she would never be really attractive. Now, however, she learned to
recognize her true appeal.

The Highly Critical and/or Abusive Mother

The highly critical mother, like the highly critical father, has
standards that daughter can never meet and is constantly criticizing
or belittling her daughter, whether out of hostility, jealousy, or in a
misguided attempt to shape her up. The abusive mother combines
her verbal attacks with physical ones, and in some cases even with
sexual molestation. Such treatment from a mother, as from a father,
is deeply damaging to the growing girl in a multitude of ways; however, the impact on how she feels about her looks may be different
from that of similar treatment by her father.

The daughter of the highly critical mother is less likely to
make a direct link between her feelings of unworthiness and her
looks, unless a mother specifically finds fault with her daughter's appearance. However, this is quite probable. Given the tremendous
overemphasis put on women's looks in our society, the hypercritical

mother is very likely to focus on and be dissatisfied with her daughter's looks. This leaves the daughter feeling that she has a face—or body—that even a mother can't love. If a mother is physically or sexually abusive, the daughter is left with the same legacy of problems as those generated by being abused by a father that were detailed on pages 73–77.

> Melba's mother seemed to be on a constant improvement plan—and her project was Melba. Whatever Melba did, there was something wrong with it. If she got an A, it should have been an A+. When she did the dishes, they were never done right. The same for how she cleaned the house, drew, danced, talked, and looked. Her mother complained about how she wore her hair, the clothes she chose to wear, and many things about her face and body—from her posture and the shape of her lips to the fullness of her hips and most especially her weight. Perhaps because Mother was a large woman herself, she could not stand Melba's full body. The more her mother complained, the harder Melba tried to please—and once in a great while her mother really did seem pleased. These small successes kept Melba trying. It was only after she grew up that Melba realized that her mother, who had had a very hard life, was a basically unhappy person and next to impossible to satisfy.
>
> As an adult Melba remained very focused on pleasing. She married a man who is very fussy about a great many things and dedicated herself to keeping him happy. The more she catered to him, the fussier and more critical he became. In addition to all the other ways in which she tried to please him, she did her best to look good, even though she felt that she was basically fat and unattractive. On weekends she would have liked to be comfortable in jeans or sweatpants, but she always made it a point to put on makeup and dress in the clothes he preferred, and she did her best to keep her weight down, but it was a losing battle, and after three children she

weighed thirty pounds more than she had when they got married. Her husband never ceased reminding her of how fat and disgusting she looked, though he had put on weight himself. Melba had already felt unhappy with her looks, but now she really hated them and herself as well. She imagined that if only she were prettier and thinner her husband would truly love and appreciate her.

After a lot of hard work in therapy, Melba learned to stop evaluating her worth, value, and attractiveness through her husband's and her mother's eyes, and to recognize, appreciate, and value the person she is and the way that she looks. Ironically (but not unexpectedly), as she focused on pleasing herself instead of her husband, and has even begun to question whether she wants to remain with him, he has become more eager to please and keep her, and less demanding.

The degree of influence each of your parents or parenting figures exerted on your appearance self-esteem is undoubtedly different for each of you. Some of you may have had two narcissistic parents who influenced you equally, or you may have had a nurturing mother who influenced you much more than your distant father. You may have had a narcissistic mother and adoring father, or a distant mother and critical father, or a nurturing mother who presented a poor role model because she hated the way she herself looked, or parents who fit several or none of these categories. Perhaps you were raised by only one parent or another relative or guardian, or lived in a series of foster families.

In addition, how your parents treated each other, and the level of conflict between them (whether overt or covert) may also have had a significant effect on you. Moreover, for some of you, there may have been major problems in your family that greatly colored your growing-up experiences: alcoholism or other substance abuse, an eating disorder, major illness or disability, loss of a nuclear family member, repeated dislocation, or other trauma or dysfunction. Don't try to pigeonhole familial influences on how you feel about your appearance into any of the categories if they don't fit. In the next chapter, you will learn to specifically identify how your family affected the way you feel about your looks. For now, just use these general categories, as applicable, to better understand the ways your parents' attitudes might have affected your self-image.

Mothers and fathers, of course, are not the only family members who shape a growing girl's self-image. Siblings, grandparents, and other close relatives can have a significant effect for good or harm. Other adults, too, can greatly influence how a developing girl views herself. Messages and treatment from teachers, Girl Scout leaders, coaches, clergy, and other significant adults can have a powerful effect.

> A friend of mine has a fifteen-year-old daughter who is a size 7 and very attractive. In her gym class the girls are required to have the percentage of their body fat measured and are then given a readout that tells them whether they are "just right," "average to pleasingly plump," and so on. Her readout said that she was average to pleasingly plump. When she asked her thin and athletic teacher about it, the teacher said that her problem, much like the teacher's own, was that she has a big behind.

My friend and I were horrified to hear about this practice. Here was a teacher who was passing on distorted notions of body size to her students, without any idea of the permanent damage she could be causing. My friend's daughter, on the one hand, thinks her readout is ridiculous, but on the other hand, she has started to think of herself as too fat. I can only imagine the damage caused to students larger than a size 7. Thankfully, after my friend protested, the principal put an end to routine body-fat measurements.

The 1990 American Association of University Women study "Shortchanging Girls, Shortchanging America" documents a loss of self-confidence in girls that is twice that for boys as they move from childhood to adolescence. While this is true for a variety of reasons, certainly an important contributing factor is the heightened power of the Beauty Imperative as girls enter adolescence. The increased emphasis on their looks—which occurs at precisely the time that girls are biologically programmed to add body fat (see Chapter 7 for information on adolescence and body fat)—primes girls to see themselves as "too fat" and therefore unattractive and unworthy.

Adolescence is a crucial period because as girls and boys are struggling to find their own identities, they desperately want to fit in with their peers and to be at least accepted, if not admired. How popular a girl is or isn't in high school can very much affect how attractive she feels thereafter. While we are exploring parental influences in this chapter, I in no way mean to imply that peer group experiences are not of equal, if not sometimes greater, influence. However, if you are raised by a nurturing mother and endorsing father, it is more likely both that you and your self-esteem will stay intact during these difficult years, and that you will have the confidence in yourself and your looks that radiates attractiveness and makes for popularity.

Sometimes, though, our looks are met with such expressions of cruelty by our peers that almost no amount of positive parenting can prevent scarring. This happens most often to girls who appear appreciably different: the disfigured, the disabled, the fat, and sometimes the early or late developer. If, during your growing-up years, you were teased, taunted, or called names by some of your peers, you know the deep scarring that this kind of rejection can cause, especially during adolescence. If adults stared at you when they thought you weren't looking, and then quickly glanced away when you tried to meet their eye, you know how this only confirmed your feelings of being freakish and hideous-looking. If you continually experienced such cruelty, and maybe even ostracism, in your formative years, it can take many years to heal your pain and begin to see yourself through different eyes.

While as an adult you most likely have come to understand that the adolescent castigation of those who are different stems from the insecurity of those who are doing the taunting, it may be hard to stop seeing your body through your tormentors' eyes. And some of you may be continuing to experience derision, especially if you are quite fat. The exercises in this book are designed to teach you how to view your body and yourself through your own loving eyes. In the next chapter you will learn how to identify the ways in which individual family members influenced your view of appearance in general and of your own looks in particular, and how to take steps to exorcise negative introjects and messages.

CHAPTER 5

CHALLENGING FAMILIAL MESSAGES

An important step in letting go of body hatred and unrealistic standards is to recognize the degree to which you have been inculcated with others' concepts and prejudices, so that you can let go of unhelpful attitudes and judgments you incorporated from your family and others that are stopping you from liking the way you look.

Identifying the Importance of Beauty in Your Family

Get a piece of lined paper and fold it in half vertically, then fold it in half vertically again, so that you have four vertical columns. In the first column, list the names of everyone who lived in your household while you were growing up. If other close relatives or adults had an especially big impact on you while you were growing up, list them, too. Last on this list write, "Family as a whole."

Next, in the second column, enter a percentage that represents how important looks were to each person on your list. This may be easy for some of you to identify and difficult for others. Or you may have an easy time assigning percentages to some family members, but not to others. If you have difficulty, close your eyes, take a few slow deep breaths to relax, and go into yourself.

As you continue to keep your eyes closed, ask yourself, How important were looks to this person in my family? and wait to get a sense. Then try to attach a percentage to this value. See if it feels right. It's not important to be precisely accurate, just get the best sense that you can. When you're ready, open your eyes and write the percentage in the second column.

Repeat this procedure with each person you listed. For your family as a whole, just get a general sense that feels right to you. Don't try adding up all the percentages and averaging them. Often the whole is different from the sum of the parts because some family members influenced you more than others.

When you finish, your sheet should look something like Kitty's:

Family Members	Importance of Beauty
Mom	75%
Dad	75%
Older sister	85%
Younger brother	35%
Grandma (lived with us)	50%
Family as whole	70%

Now, again using percentages and the same slow deep-breathing method, think about how satisfied each person in your family was with his or her own looks, and enter this in the third column, so that your chart now looks like this:

Family Members	Importance of Beauty	Satisfaction with Own Looks
Mom	75%	40%
Dad	75%	85%

Older sister	85%	40%
Younger brother	35%	95%
Grandma (lived with us)	50%	75%
Family as whole	70%	N/A

Next, relax again, again using the slow deep-breathing process, then identify first how important looks are to you, and then how satisfied you are with the way you look, and add it to the bottom of your chart, so your chart now looks like this:

Family Members	Importance of Beauty	Satisfaction with Own Looks
Mom	75%	40%
Dad	75%	85%
Older sister	85%	40%
Younger brother	35%	95%
Grandma (lived with us)	50%	75%
Family as whole	70%	N/A
Myself	75%	40%

Lastly, relax once again, then ask yourself how satisfied each of your family members was with your looks as you were growing up. When you're done, write these percentages in the last column, so your chart now looks like this:

Family Members	Importance of Beauty	Satisfaction with Own Looks	Satisfaction with My Looks
Mom	75%	40%	70%
Dad	75%	85%	60%
Older sister	85%	40%	55%
Younger brother	35%	95%	85%
Grandma (lived with us)	50%	75%	85%
Family as whole	70%	N/A	65%
Myself	75%	40%	N/A

Now evaluate your chart. As you can see from Kitty's chart, usually the more important looks are to people, especially to women, the more likely they are to be dissatisfied with their appearance. On the other hand, the less emphasis they place on beauty, the more apt they are to like and appreciate the way they look; though men, across the board, are more likely than women to feel satisfied with their appearance.

Perhaps you are surprised in looking at Kitty's chart that even though no one was under 55 percent satisfied with Kitty's looks, and several people really pretty much liked the way she looked, Kitty still feels only 40 percent happy with her looks. Actually, it's quite common and understandable. The major message Kitty got from her family as she was growing up was that looks were important for women, and that Kitty wasn't nearly pretty enough. Yes, Grandma and her little brother liked her looks, but this was more than offset by her father's disappointment that she wasn't a great beauty like his brother's daughter, her mother's only lukewarm acceptance and approval, and her sister's critical appraisals. In her family, where emotions were rarely directly expressed and judgments were conveyed more by what wasn't said than by what was, Kitty grew up feeling that she just wasn't very pretty. It wasn't till much later that Kitty discovered her true ability to be attractive.

In our society, in which looks are so important, anything less than an 80 percent rating from your family is like being panned. The same thing is true of intelligence. If your family thought you were only 65 percent smart, you probably grew up feeling you were stupid. If you are less than 80 percent satisfied with your looks, you are undervaluing your looks and yourself and undermining your self-esteem. If you are less than 50 percent satisfied with your appearance, you probably have low self-esteem and find it difficult to feel good about yourself in general. Let's look more deeply at how these feelings about your looks developed in your family.

Compare your scores on the chart with those of each family member. How much does your score in the first column, "importance of beauty," match that of each family member and that of your family as a whole? Are your ideas about the importance of beauty truly yours, or are they really just replications of some or all of your family's attitudes? Have you been particularly influenced by one family member more than others? For instance, Kitty's feelings about beauty and her own looks exactly mirror those of her mother. This indicates that her mother may have been a big influence on her in these areas, and that this relationship is particularly important for her to explore. How does it make you feel to reflect, or differ from, your family's concepts?

Some women feel guilty when their values differ from those of their families, believing that by having different ideas and feelings they are being disloyal, wrong, or bad. Other women are glad to be different and are upset when they discover similarities. In truth, though, we are all similar to our families in some ways and different from them in others. Families are an important place where values are taught, and we all learned some of our values there. However, there's a difference between values that make you a better person and values that simply make you unhappy with yourself, without benefiting anyone else. The Beauty Imperative espouses just such values. It is important to let go of family values that are undermining your self-esteem with regard to appearance, but first you need to identify what negative values you have absorbed.

Visualizing Your Self-Image

Get comfortable. . . . Then close your eyes, and put your thumb and index finger together on each hand. . . . Take a deep breath, deep into your diaphragm and abdomen, and hold it for five seconds, . . . then gradually let it out to a slow count of five. . . . Now, take five SLOW deep breaths . . . and when you finish, let your fingers open, and continue breathing normally and comfortably. . . . While you are breathing slowly and deeply, or in any way that is comfortable for you, maybe you can let yourself become a little more peaceful and comfortable, . . . letting go of tensions in any way that you know how, . . . with every breath that you take being able to become more relaxed. . . . Letting go of the cares of the day, . . . going inside yourself to a secure place of comfort . . . and peace, . . . or any place that feels right to you. . . . Knowing that there are many different ways to become relaxed, . . . and it really doesn't matter what ways you find to perhaps let go a little bit more in the way that is right for you, . . . without even having to know that you're doing it. . . . And knowing, too, that if whatever is said, either now or later, isn't right for you, you can disregard it, or change it into whatever you need to hear to relax in the way that is best for you, . . . and to benefit in the ways you need to benefit. . . . Finding your own way to deepen your relaxation, and to feel a lovely sense of peace and comfort, . . . perhaps relaxing your muscles just a bit, . . . or going deeper into yourself, . . . or letting your breathing carry you into a beautiful sense of calm and safety, . . . a lovely peacefulness, . . . or maybe just remaining as you, as you relax in whatever way is right for you, . . . knowing that you really do know what is best for you.

As you continue to relax, visualize a large circle that represents your self-image. It's made up of different pie-shaped pieces that represent all the various appraisals you have about yourself, both good and bad. See what the different pieces are, and how large each piece is. Notice how much of your self-image is taken up by feelings about your looks. Then examine that wedge of the circle more closely and see what percentage represents good feelings about your looks and what percentage represents bad feelings. When you have a firm sense of this, make a mental note of it, then consider the other wedges. What other general areas are there, and how much of each is made up of positive and negative feelings? Other general areas may include personality, intelligence, talents and achievements, and relationship abilities, but of course you don't have to stick to these. Choose whatever general areas apply best to you. In each area, see how much of your feelings about yourself are positive and how much negative. Take as much time as you need. Get a firm sense of how your self-image divides up. Then, when you are ready, open your eyes and come back to the room. Immediately draw your self-image circle.

Flo, a woman in one of my workshops, produced the following self-image circle. In looking at Flo's circle, you'll see that I have entered the exact percentages that each wedge makes up of the total circle. You don't have to bother doing this. What's important for you is not that you put in exact numbers, but that you get the general proportions down in a way that reflects how you really feel.

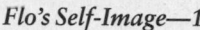

Flo's Self-Image—1

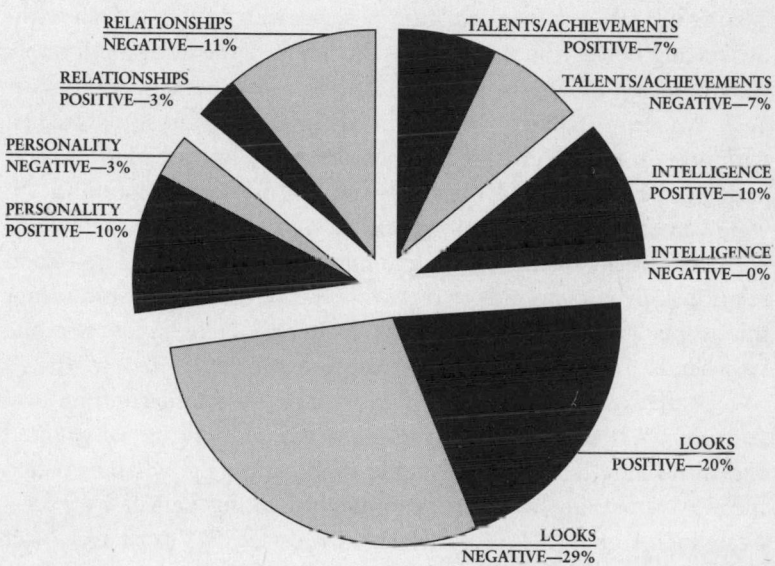

As you can see, looks made up about 50 percent of Flo's self-image, with her feelings about her looks being more negative (60 percent) than positive (40 percent). Beyond looks, the other major areas were about of equal importance to Flo in her self-assessment. She felt totally good about her intelligence and mostly good about her personality. She felt negatively about her abilities in relationships and fifty-fifty about her talents. Her overall self-image was exactly evenly split, with as many negative as positive feelings about herself. However, with the exception of her looks, her feelings about herself were decidedly more positive than negative.

It was clear to Flo from looking at her chart that her feelings about her appearance were taking up a large part of her self-image, leaving less room for positive feelings in other areas, and decidedly contributing to her feelings of dissatisfaction with herself. This came as a real surprise to her because she thought her looks were only of average importance to her, and that her low-level depression had more to do with feeling she had not achieved enough in life, and with the difficulties she was encountering as a single parent. In discussing her self-assessment diagram, she readily saw that even without feeling better about her looks, if they became even moderately less important to her, she would feel better about herself.

We also discussed the area in which she was most dissatisfied with herself—relationships. She felt like a real failure. Her ten-year marriage had ended in divorce; her two children, ages eight and six, were constantly bickering no matter what she did; and her dealings with her critical and demanding family were stressful. She had good relationships with friends and coworkers, but she did not consider this as much of an accomplishment. "After all," she said, "everyone has friends, and it's not hard to get along at work."

Rather than seeing herself clearly, Flo was undermining herself in ways that are common to many women: taking for granted and dismissing her successes while focusing on the ways in which she was not doing well, and ultimately judging herself by excessively high standards. Actually, it's untrue that "it's not hard to get along at work." Many people find work relationships to be very stressful. Flo's excellent work relationships with a wide variety of people are a real tribute to her. Similarly, the fact that she has good, close, enduring, and dependable friends is much more a reflection of who she is than is the stress she experiences with her family. As for her children, she has a very good relationship with them, and their bickering is something that most siblings of their ages engage in.

In the area of Talents/Achievements, Flo was also being too hard on herself. She is a well-respected supervisor in an insurance company, well liked and proud of her work, but she felt she hadn't achieved enough. Some people she had gone to school with were further ahead in their careers or were making more money. Instead of taking well-deserved credit for what she had accomplished, she focused on what she had not accomplished, seeing herself as mediocre. She also gave herself no credit for her talents for gardening, fixing things, and crafts, since she thinks of these as hobbies, not abilities. After some discussion she began to see that she was discounting her successes and focusing on her self-perceived deficiencies and "failures."

I suggested that she again close her eyes, get comfortable, relax by using the slow deep-breathing technique, and then revisit her self-image circle. Once she visualized it, I asked her to make the looks portion of her pie chart shrink, while allowing her positive feelings about herself to expand and fill the vacated space, letting her good feelings about being smart, personable, and adept at cultivating and nurturing relationships to grow and spread out, filling the space left open by her decreased emphasis on "looks"; adding appreciation of her talents for gardening, fixing things, and crafts to further fill out the circle. When she had finished, Flo was surprised to find herself feeling better about herself. Her self-image circle chart now looked like this:

Flo's Self-Image—2

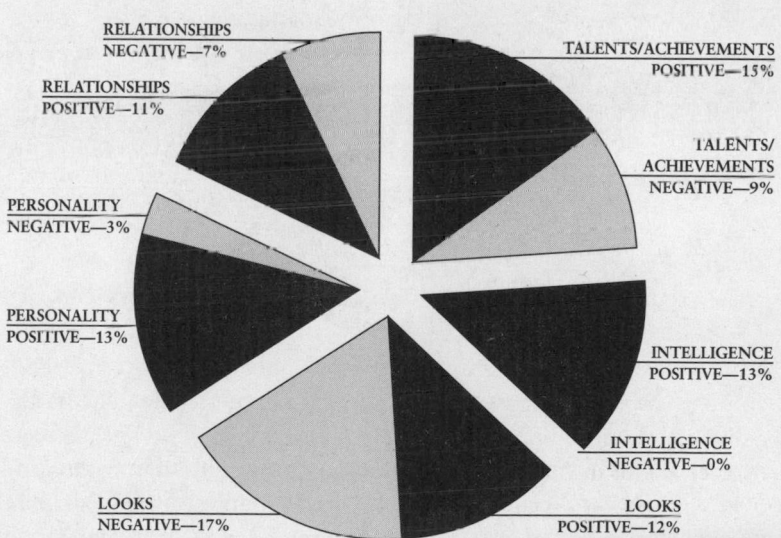

RELATIONSHIPS NEGATIVE—7%

RELATIONSHIPS POSITIVE—11%

PERSONALITY NEGATIVE—3%

PERSONALITY POSITIVE—13%

LOOKS NEGATIVE—17%

TALENTS/ACHIEVEMENTS POSITIVE—15%

TALENTS/ACHIEVEMENTS NEGATIVE—9%

INTELLIGENCE POSITIVE—13%

INTELLIGENCE NEGATIVE—0%

LOOKS POSITIVE—12%

Even though Flo's feelings about her looks were still divided sixty-forty percent, negative to positive, by shifting her emphasis and recognizing and appreciating her achievements, talents, and positive qualities, she was already starting to like herself better. Now her positive feelings made up nearly two-thirds of her self-image.

This change is even more dramatic for women who have lower self-esteem. Fran, another woman in this workshop, started out feeling bad about almost every aspect of herself. Her original self-image circle looked like this:

Fran's Self-Image—1

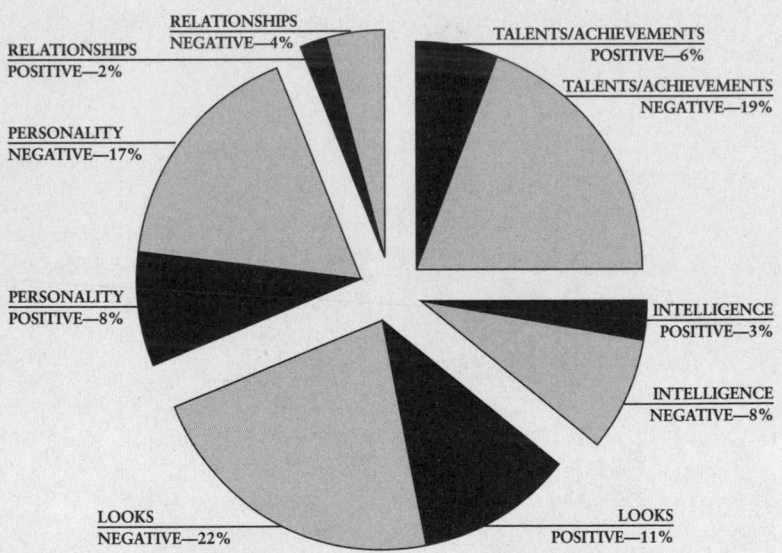

In all areas Fran felt her liabilities outweighed her assets. Indeed, her positive feelings contributed less than a third to her self-concept, while negative feelings made up 70 percent. Appearance took up the most space on her chart, with negative feelings about her appearance taking up double the space of positive ones. She spoke longingly of wishing she looked like a model, and she felt that her whole life would be wonderful if only she could.

In reality, Fran was an alluring woman who would be quite attractive once she learned to appreciate her true appearance, but for the moment I put this aside, knowing that she was not ready yet to see her looks in a positive way. Instead, we worked on identifying some of her other assets, talents, and accomplishments, followed by the exercise to shrink the appearance wedge of the circle. After this exercise her self-image circle looked like this:

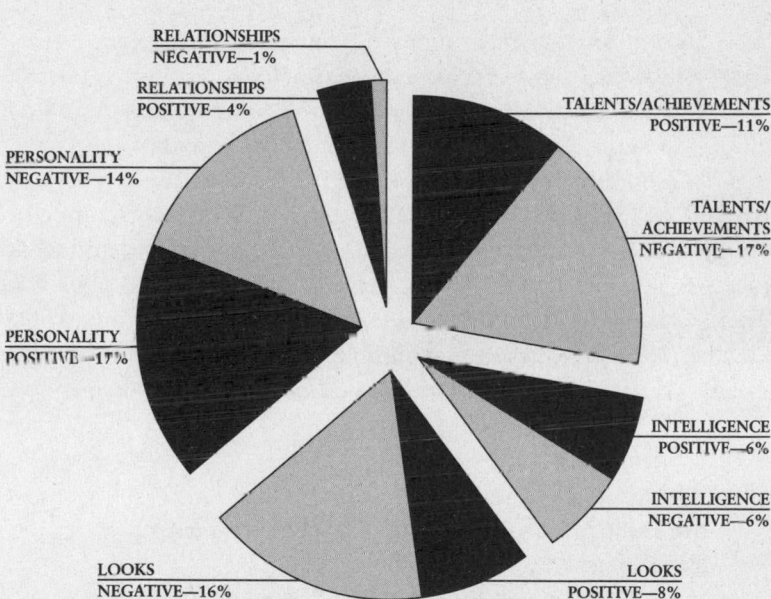

Fran's Self-Image—2

While looks remained important to her self-concept, making up almost a quarter of it, by shrinking their importance she now had room in which to expand some of her growing positive feelings about herself. She had identified some of her ignored talents and achievements, felt a little smarter, begun to recognize that she had a likable personality, and felt a little better about her relationships. The things she had previously disliked about herself took up almost the same amount of space, but the overall picture had changed. Now her positive feelings about herself made up almost half of her self-image, while negative feelings had receded from 70 percent to 54 percent. She was amazed at how helpful it was to her to de-emphasize beauty, and how much better she had already began to feel. Try it for yourself.

WHAT I LIKE ABOUT MYSELF:

Start by identifying as many of your assets as you can, including personal qualities (such as being warm, loyal, or funny), talents, intelligence, achievements, personality, and communication and relationship skills. Write down everything you like about yourself, making your list as long as possible, and call it WHAT I LIKE ABOUT MYSELF. Don't dismiss anything as being too common or unimportant. Ask other people what they like about you, and what they see as your strong points, and add these things to your list. Then expand your list, in each of your major areas, by asking yourself the following questions, continually adding newly discovered valuable qualities to your list as you go along:

I. Intelligence

Am I able to learn new things when I am relaxed?
Have I learned some complicated things?
Have I ever helped someone else figure something out?
Do I have common sense?
Am I able to understand books?
Am I ever able to realize what others are doing wrong?
What kinds of things have I learned or figured out that have helped me at home? At work? With friends? With children? In relationships?

Do I sometimes have an intuitive grasp of a situation?
What things am I able to help other people with?

In answering these questions, remember that you are not look-ing for perfection. You don't have to have all the answers to be smart. And many very bright people did not do well in school. You are probably more than intelligent enough for most situations. Take this in, and let your good feelings about your intelligence expand.

II. Personality

What do other people like about me? (For instance, are you compassionate, friendly, understanding, adventuresome, reliable, funny, generous, spiritual, warm, or caring?)
What qualities do I have that make me a good worker? (For instance, are you responsible, persistent, hardworking, or creative?)
What qualities do I have that have helped me get through rough times in my life?
What qualities do I have that enable me to have fun?
What qualities do I have that make me a good friend? Partner? Mother? Worker? Daughter? Grandmother?
Do I have a sense of humor?
What sensibilities do I have?

In answering these questions and adding to your list of what you like about yourself, be sure not to dismiss positive qualities you may normally take for granted, such as being warm, loyal, kind, nurturing, understanding, honest, earnest, straightforward, tactful, organized, reliable, responsible, creative, zany, fun-loving, respon-sive, attentive, adventuresome, and good-hearted.

III. Talents/Achievements

What am I good at?
What do I enjoy doing?
With what kinds of things do other people turn to me for help?

What things at work (whether a paid job, homemaking, or
    both) am I good at?
In what ways have I grown?
What things, small or large, have I accomplished? (Accom-
    plishments can range from cooking a good meal to
    preparing a banquet—and everything in-between.)
What things have I done that I once thought I would never be
    able to do?
Have I done things that others admire?

In thinking about your talents and achievements, it is especially important to give yourself credit for whatever you have done.
Don't undermine yourself by thinking that anything short of the
apex in your field doesn't count. If, for example, you want to be a
writer but haven't been published yet, give yourself credit for having
the courage to write and for producing what you have. If you've
been published, all the more reason to give yourself credit. You
don't have to win a Pulitzer Prize before you can feel you have accomplished something.

Take credit for accomplishments, no matter how little. For instance, I feel proud of having a vegetable garden, even though it is
small, its output meager, and some plants never make it. At least I'm
doing it. Every time I look at my little garden, I feel a sense of accomplishment. Here I am, actually making things grow!

IV. Relationships

Do I have any good relationships? If so, what do I contribute
    that makes these good relationships?
Do people I like ever call me up or seek me out?
In difficult relationships, are there parts that are good? If so,
    what am I contributing that makes these parts good?
In areas where I feel disliked (such as with family, socially, or
    at work), are there some people who like me (some fam-
    ily members, friends, coworkers)? What do they like
    about me?

> If I feel bad because I am not in a love relationship, have I been in one in the past? Can I recognize that I have the ability to be in a relationship, even if I never have or currently have not found the right person? What qualities do I have that would make anyone lucky to be with me?

Relationships are an area where many people feel troubled. It is very common to have all kinds of difficulties with your family of origin. You may also be in a difficult relationship with your spouse or lover or having a hard time with your children. Or you may be in a stressful work situation where you are constantly being hassled. Or you may be single and desperately looking to be in a relationship. In any of these situations, it is common to unfairly blame yourself for what is not your fault or largely beyond your control, and to believe that these relationships are troubled because of your inadequacy. In reality, you may be dealing with difficult people who will remain difficult no matter what you do. Or you may be doing much better than you give yourself credit for. If you are single despite wishing to be in a relationship, it's probably a result of a variety of factors that have nothing to do with your worth, likability, or attractiveness.

In all of these situations, it is important to recognize and take credit for the good relationships you do have and the valuable qualities you bring to a relationship. The more you do so, the more you will like yourself, and the more you like yourself, the more others will. It is well known that people with self-confidence tend to be well liked by others.

After you have made your WHAT I LIKE ABOUT MYSELF list as long and as full as possible, you are ready to continue with the "shrinking looks" exercise. But if you are trying to improve your self-esteem, don't use your list only for this exercise. Keep it handy and read it aloud twice daily. Read it SLOWLY, and start each item with "I really am . . ." or "I really have. . . ." Take full credit for all the valuable qualities you have and the things you have and are doing, or trying to do, in your life. The more you recognize and focus on your positives, the more you will like yourself, and the better you will feel.

Shrinking Looks

(See the Appendix for full relaxation instructions.)

Get comfortable. Then close your eyes, and put your thumb and index finger together on each hand. Take a deep breath, deep into your diaphragm and abdomen, and hold it for five seconds, then gradually let it out to a slow count of five. Now, take five comfortable SLOW deep breaths, and when you finish, let your fingers open, and continue breathing normally and comfortably. As you breathe in any way that is natural, let yourself become perhaps a little more peaceful, maybe a little more relaxed, letting go of tensions in any way that you know how, and going inside yourself to a secure place of comfort and peace, or any other place that feels right to you.

As you continue to relax, again visualize your self-concept as a circle, as you did before. Take your time, and wait for it to be clearly in your mind. Now let the looks section start to shrink. See it getting slowly smaller, till it is as small as you can make it. At the same time, see your good feelings about yourself growing and expanding, filling the vacated space. Let your new feelings of appreciation for your intelligence, personality, talents, achievements, and abilities in relationships come in, spread out, and fill in the open space, filling your self-image circle with good feelings about yourself. Let these good feelings continue to grow and enlarge and take root within you. And as they take their place and spread out, it will be interesting to notice in what ways you start to like yourself better, and to see what special ways you find to let these good feelings about yourself spread throughout your being, and center themselves within you and flourish. Perhaps now, or in a little while, you will feel a new sense of positiveness, or a deeper appreciation for yourself and all that you have been through, all that you have done, and what you have to offer. And it will be interesting to see in the future, when you think back on this exercise, what you will have learned about how to like yourself. And right now, you don't have to do anything but let yourself know, in any way that you wish, just how very special you are. Take in this feeling, and enjoy it for as long as you wish. Then, when you are ready, open your eyes and return to the room.

How do you feel? Has anything changed? Have you started to feel even a little bit better about yourself? Many of you will have, but others of you may not have. If so, that's okay. Everyone changes in different ways. Just read on and continue with the exercises. You may find yourself wanting to redo the "shrinking looks" exercise at a later point, after you have dealt more directly with specific issues having to do with your looks, or you may prefer other exercises. What's really important is that you are making a commitment to feel better about how you look. Now that you have shrunk the looks portion of your self-image circle, let's examine that portion directly.

Original Critics: Where Did I Learn That How I Look Is Not Okay?

Take out your BEAUTIFUL ME and WHAT I DON'T LIKE ABOUT MY LOOKS lists that you made in Chapter 3. Which list is longer? Is the balance the way you visualized it in your self-image circle? Maybe not, because how you feel about your looks may be much more complex than adding up the number of items on each side. You may consider some items to be much more important than others. For instance, in our culture any woman who thinks she is fat may hate the way she looks even if this is her only negative item and she has eight positive ones. To get a more accurate picture, rate the importance to you of each item on both lists from 1 to 3, with 1 being least important and 3 being most important. If something really, really, really bothers you or really, really, really pleases you, then give it a 4. Add up the numbers on each side. You should now have a fairly accurate representation of how you feel about your looks.

For example, here is Flo's chart. Flo's chart reflects her forty–sixty percent split between liking her looks and not liking them.

Like About My Looks		*Don't Like About My Looks*	
Nice smile:	2	Too fat:	4
Shapely lower legs:	2	Big butt:	2
Pretty eyes:	2	Unclear skin:	3
Full breasts:	3	Curly hair:	1
		Square shoulders:	1
		Big thighs:	3
Total =	9	Total =	14

Next, consider which of your negative attitudes toward the way you look stem from your family. Examine your list of what you don't like about the way you look, and consider:

Where did you learn that these particular characteristics were important?

How did you decide how these characteristics should look?

When did you start to feel that you didn't measure up in these areas?

Were any of these characteristics emphasized in your family? If so, by whom?

Was anyone in your family particularly concerned with this aspect of her or his appearance?

Did anyone in your family ever criticize or disparage this part of the way you look or suggest that it needed improvement?

Next to each item on your list write down who in your family influenced you to dislike the way this part of your looks. When you have finished with all your items, group them by the person who influenced you, and label this your ORIGINAL CRITICS list.

Flo had no trouble recognizing that her father always told her that her behind was too big and her hair too curly, while her mother agonized over every pimple Flo got and was forever dieting. Flo realized that it was precisely these "defects" that she herself hated in her looks. Her WHAT I DON'T LIKE ABOUT MY LOOKS list now was like this:

Don't Like About My Looks		Person Learned From
Too fat:	4	Mom, Dad
Big butt:	2	Dad
Unclear skin:	3	Mom
Curly hair:	2	Dad
Square shoulders:	1	Sister
Big thighs:	2	Dad, Sister

Original Critics:
Dad: Too fat, big butt, curly hair, big thighs
Mom: Too fat, unclear skin
Sis: Square shoulders, big thighs

Ella, on the other hand, while she was not directly criticized by her parents, grew up with a father who placed great emphasis on women's looks and "critiqued" the looks of every woman he saw. Her mother, meanwhile, was obsessed with her own looks, especially her face. She never sat in the sun for fear of wrinkling and refused to let anyone outside the immediate family see her without makeup. Ella, too, is obsessed with her looks, especially her face, and refuses to be seen without makeup.

Many of you, like Flo and Ella, will see direct connections between your family's attitudes toward beauty and your own. Others of you may have been less influenced by your family and more by peers, media, and society at large. If so, consider yourself fortunate because it is easier to let go of attitudes that were acquired after your earliest years, and that were not, and are not, reinforced by your family (unless, of course, you have been crucified for your looks by your peers). However, given the tremendous "lookism" in society, it is rare to find a family that has not been influenced and controlled by it.

It is important to figure out what influence your family has had on your feelings about how you look, so that you can combat these powerful negative messages. The point is to be able to empower yourself to change these messages which have become your internalized beliefs, not to blame your family, who in most cases were doing the best they knew how, no matter how deleterious their influence turned out to be.

This is not to say, however, that in going through the process explained in the next section it is not okay to be angry. It is natural to be angry when you recognize that you have been harmed, and owning and experiencing your anger can often be freeing and en- abling. Ultimately what's most empowering is to focus your anger toward the society we live in, which promulgates the Beauty Imperative, and toward the corporate powers that profit from it. First, though, you need to deal with your feelings toward your own family and to reevaluate your WHAT I DON'T LIKE ABOUT MY LOOKS list.

Reconsidering My Looks

Look at your list of things you don't like about your looks. How many of these items are really valid? For instance, I asked Flo to reconsider whether she really had a big butt, unclear skin, curly hair, square shoulders, and big thighs. She insisted that her butt was round and full, and stuck out. I pointed out that this is the nature of butts. Do people other than her father also dislike her butt? Well, she had to admit, many men had told her they liked her butt, but her response was always to feel, Yuck. How can he like this? The same with her thighs. They had extra fullness, as women's thighs ordinarily do, but they were not the monstrosities she imagined them to be. As for her skin, it was unclear and she was convinced it made her ugly. The women in her workshop told her that her skin wasn't nearly as unattractive as she perceived it and, in fact, was just one small part of the way she looked. (Later, when we did the exercises in Chapter 6, she developed better feelings about her face and complexion.) The same with her shoulders. While they were indeed square, they balanced well with her body, and, in any case, were as intrinsically attractive as sloping shoulders. As for her curly hair, the other workshop participants all loved it.

As for her being fat, while at five six and 140 pounds she was considerably larger than the beauty ideal, the other workshop participants and I found her curvaceous body very attractive. We also discussed the whole concept of fat, and how it is only recently, and only in the West, that weight is considered unattractive. (If you think you are too fat, pay special attention to Chapters 6 and 7.) When Flo finished re-assessing her WHAT I DON'T LIKE ABOUT MY LOOKS list it appeared like this:

Don't Like About My Looks		Person Learned From	True or False
Too fat:	4	Mom, Dad	F: Curvaceous and sensuous
Big butt:	2	Dad	T: Sexy!
Unclear skin:	3	Mom	T: Not that important
Curly hair:	2	Dad	T: Good!
Square shoulders:	1	Sister	T: Looks fine
Big thighs:	2	Dad, Sister	F: Womanly

As you can see, Flo began to understand that some ways in which she perceived her body parts were inaccurate, while others were accurate, but wrongly judged as unattractive. She now added her reframed positive view of her body to her BEAUTIFUL ME list, so that it looked like this:

Flo's BEAUTIFUL ME list:

I have wide, penetrating, warm, exciting eyes.
I have nice eyebrows, with a wonderful arch.
I have very shapely legs.
I have long tapering fingers.
I have a fabulous smile that lights up my whole face.
I have full sexy breasts.

[Added]

I have a sensuous, full-figured body.
I have wonderful curly black hair that people love to run their fingers through.
I have a full, round, sexy butt.

I have square shoulders that go well with my body and let people know that I'm no pushover.

I have round, full, womanly thighs.

I generally have a nice face.

Now it's your turn. In evaluating whether some aspect is (1) as you see it, and (2) attractive or not, use the following guidelines:

1. If you believe some part of your body is too big or too small, or not the right shape, REALLY THINK ABOUT IT. For instance, are your thighs extraordinarily large, or are you just so focused on them that they seem tremendous? Check it out with family or friends who are generally supportive. Don't ask people who are generally critical or who have very critical standards for their own looks because they are likely to be negative for reasons that have nothing to do with the truth. Don't try to compare your thighs or any other body part to that of other women because you're too likely to misjudge yourself. As we saw in Chapter 1, women almost always see themselves as larger than they really are.

2. If the body part is truly as you see it (for instance, if your friends tactfully agree that your thighs really are considerably larger than most women your size, and are disproportionate to the rest of your body), think about whether this necessarily makes it unattractive. On what are you basing your idea of how this body part "should" look? In Chapter 3 we saw how women you find attractive can have body parts just like the ones you don't like on yourself. Remember, any beauty ideal is arbitrary. Some societies adore large thighs. Become more accepting and approving of your body through the following exercise:

Liking Your Body

(See the Appendix for full relaxation instructions.)

Get comfortable. Then close your eyes, and put your thumb and index finger together on each hand. Take a deep breath, deep into your diaphragm and abdomen, and hold it for five seconds, then gradually let it out to a slow count of five. Now, take five com-

fortable SLOW deep breaths, and when you finish, let your fingers open, and continue breathing normally and comfortably. As you are breathing in any way that is natural, let yourself become perhaps a little more peaceful, maybe a little more relaxed, letting go of tensions in any way that you know how, and going inside yourself to a secure place of comfort and peace, or any other place that feels right to you.

As you continue to relax, imagine, now, that you live in Multi-Pleasureland, or Africa, or Samoa, or Tonga, or eighteenth-century Europe, or some other culture that holds to different standards of beauty, or no standards. Imagine people in that culture loving the way you look. Imagine them really admiring your thighs, and the shape of your legs, arms, breasts, rear, torso, facial features, and hair. See them crowding around looking admiringly at you, taking pleasure in each one of your features, and body parts. Take in the good feeling of having your looks admired, and let it flow around your body, and as it flows, let it bring a sense of comfort, contentment, and pride to every part of your body, till all of you feels proud of how you look. Let those good feelings continue to flow, so that they seep into you and become embedded in your very core, and in each and every part of your body, filling all of you with a sense of contentment and pride in how you look. Stay there, and enjoy that sense of contentment and pride knowing that bodies come in different shapes and sizes, and your shape and size are just right for you. Recognize that you really are attractive in all your uniqueness. And know, too, that you can bring these beautiful feelings back with you, and tap into them whenever you think the word "love," or any other word or image that feels right to you. Continue to enjoy the lovely feeling of liking the way you look. Then, when you're ready, open your eyes and come back to the room.

How do you feel? Is your body self-image starting to change? Can you at least feel that it can change? Now go back to your list of what you don't like about your body and reevaluate it. Regard your appearance as though there were no beauty ideal, and encourage yourself to be positive. If you find it hard to view certain aspects of your appearance in anything but a negative way, don't worry. There are many more exercises in the next chapters that will offer you concrete help in dealing with the parts of your face and body you don't like, as well as with your size. As you continue reading, keep out your list of what you don't like about your looks, and continue to reevaluate it. As you change your view of different aspects of your appearance, keep adding to your BEAUTIFUL ME list.

When you're ready, do the following exercise, and experience the freedom that comes when you let go of the beauty frames of reference you learned in your family, symbolically confront your original critics, and assert your own attractiveness. Before doing this exercise, you may want to wait until you've completed the exercises in Chapters 6 to 10, as those exercises will concretely help you to feel positively about the various parts of your face and body as well as your body size.

ASSERTING YOUR ATTRACTIVENESS WITH YOUR ORIGINAL CRITICS:

Start with one of the people on your ORIGINAL CRITICS list. Some of you may wish to start with the person who made you feel the worst about your looks. Others of you may wish to start with the person you find it easiest to confront, or the person you feel closest to or most distant from. It doesn't matter whom you start with, as long as you do it in the way that feels preferable to you.

Imagine that you are having a talk with this critic. You are doing the talking. Your critic has been temporarily struck dumb and paralyzed, so he or she cannot move away, interrupt, or speak unless you ask him or her to. You can talk with this critic in writing or out loud. If you're doing it in writing, imagine you are recording a scene that is going on in front of you, and get all of it down, writing as fast as you comfortably can. If you are doing it out loud, place two seats opposite each other. Imagine your critic sitting in one seat, then sit or stand opposite him or her.

Look this critic in the eye and explain how his or her actions, reactions, or lack of response has hurt you, and left you feeling that you aren't pretty enough, or are plain, homely, or even repulsive. Explain how these feelings have affected you and your life. Perhaps your critic doesn't want to hear this from you, but he or she has no choice. This is your day. Express whatever you genuinely feel. Perhaps, for instance, you feel compassionate toward your mother for urging you to diet because you understand that she meant well, and you also feel sad that both of you have been so controlled by the Beauty Imperative; maybe you're angry as could be at your father or brother for constantly criticizing your appearance; maybe you feel eager for your critic to understand; or know that he or she never will; maybe you're mostly glad that you are developing a different view of your attractiveness, and just want this original critic to know. Whatever you feel, express it.

Speak to your critic for as long as you wish, until you have fully expressed what is in your heart and on your mind. End by telling this critic about the positive feelings you now have about this aspect of your appearance, and about your appearance in general, and recite your BEAUTIFUL ME list to him or her. If you want to hear what your critic has to say, grant him or her the power of speech. Otherwise, don't. Some of you may see an admiring, compassionate look in your critic's eye. Others of you may see only scorn and derision. If so, let yourself know that scorn and derision are fed by feelings of inadequacy, jealousy, and the fear of being outshone. Don't let your critic put you back under his or her thumb. Stand up for yourself, knowing that you are attractive and learning to love the way you look, and that no one can take that from you. Tell your critic so. End by telling your critic that though you would like to have his or her acceptance and approval, you no longer need it because you are learning to give it to yourself.

How do you feel? Confronting your original critics can evoke many different feelings. Some of you may feel exhilarated at standing up and championing yourself. Others of you may feel intimidated by the derisive looks you received or saddened by your critic's defensiveness, or guilty and angry that your critic responded by feeling wrongly blamed and sorry for him- or herself. Whatever you feel, know that you are doing something courageous and good for yourself, and that in time you will become aware of the healing power of asserting yourself, your attractiveness, and your worth. Give yourself well-deserved credit for asserting yourself as you have done. When you're ready, today or another day, repeat this exercise with your other original critics or the same one if you have more to say. Know that the more you assert yourself and give yourself credit for doing so, whatever your critic's response, the better you will feel about your looks and yourself. Now let's see specifically how to accept and like your face.

CHAPTER 6

"*I* JUST DON'T HAVE A PRETTY FACE"

Irene hates her face and always has. When she was sixteen she read *Seventeen* and longed to look like the models. In her twenties she fervently wished she had a face like the women in *Glamour* and *Cosmopolitan*. Now, in her thirties, her magazine subscriptions have changed again, but her feelings about her face remain the same. She would consider plastic surgery but she doesn't have the money; besides, she doesn't even know what to fix because as far as she's concerned her whole face is just wrong. She longs to be beautiful and admired, like the women in the magazines, and feels second-rate.

Do you, like Irene, feel like a loser in the genetic lottery of facial beauty? If so, you have lots of company. Many women long for a face like those displayed on magazine covers. We're taught from the time we're little that "your face is your fortune," as though this were a good thing. We learn that our value lies not in the kinds of people we are or what we accomplish, but rather in the bargaining power of our looks. We're told that if we're pretty enough, we can land ourselves a rich husband and/or a glamorous job. The media surround us with unrealistic images of how we should look. No wonder so many women hate their faces because they're not Hollywood-perfect. Cosmetic surgery is big business, and though it carries real risks, is painful, expensive, and often needs to be repeated every few years, women turn to it in droves for nose jobs, face-lifts, and other facial and body alterations, searching for a way to improve their fortune and their self-esteem.

The beauty ideal is just as stringent in its requirements for facial beauty as it is for body size and shape: You must be young, with smooth clear skin and regular features, and it's best to resemble the dominant culture (unfortunately, the Western ideal, through its domination of advertising and other media, is fast becoming supreme, not only in the West, but throughout the world). So Western double-lidded round eyes are generally preferred over Asiatic almond eyes with single lids and a "Cupid's bow" mouth over the fuller lips typical of black Africa. Sometimes, though, it is the rarer look that is more admired. For instance, there are fewer blue eyes and blondes than brunettes in the United States, so there is a certain value applied to these features. All of this indicates how much beauty is culture-bound and, ultimately, in the eye of the beholder.

Philosophers and academic researchers have long been in a quandary trying to define facial beauty. In any given culture it is easy to obtain a general consensus on which facial photographs are more attractive than others, but no one has been able to accurately describe the components that invariably make up facial beauty. Now Judith Langlois and Lori Roggman at the University of Texas at Austin have come up with an amazing answer to the question of what makes a face beautiful: It is to be most ordinary! They digitized on computers the photos of ninety-six men and ninety-six women (breaking down each picture into a grid of squares), made composites consisting of up to thirty-two same-gender faces (all the faces were of young, mostly white university students from the Southwest), then showed the real and the composite pictures to raters. Amazingly, raters almost invariably found composites made up of sixteen or more faces more attractive than the real people, and the more faces that went into a composite, the more attractive raters found them.

If you don't like your face, perhaps it is because you are distinctive instead of merely average. While it is true that in many ways our culture pursues the ordinary (fast food and TV fare are two examples that pop into mind), this is by no means the best we have to offer. Instead of longing for commonness, perhaps you can begin to widen your appreciation of the whole range of human features and faces, and accept and pride yourself on how you look, whether your features are common or distinctive.

In the following exercises you will learn how to change the way you regard your face, gaining a more realistic, accepting, and positive feeling about it. I say "realistic" because if you hate your face, you're not being realistic. No matter how different your face may be from the beauty ideal, it has its strong points—components of it that you can learn to like and admire. And any face becomes significantly more attractive when your eyes glow with pride and confidence. We all know both women and men whose features are not classically attractive but who are considered intensely alluring by all who meet them because their faces are lit up from the inside.

The first step in learning to light your face from the inside is to associate it with positive feelings about yourself. Take out your WHAT I LIKE ABOUT MYSELF list that you made in Chapter 5. Look at these items, each of which describes something about your character, personality, or achievements, and consider which part of your face does, or could, convey this sense about yourself to other people. Is it the way you hold your head? The look in your eye? The tilt of your chin? The structure of your face? The smile on your lips? The decisiveness of your nose? The strength of your cheekbones? The shape of your brow?

This may sound strange to you. If you pride yourself on being, say, responsible, warm, caring, good at arts and crafts, creative, loving, resourceful, persistent, calm, getting promoted at your job, being a good partner, or being a good mother, all this may seem to you to have nothing to do with your face. And that's true enough. On the other hand, all these qualities and achievements can be projected onto your face.

Think of your face as your communicator with the world. It takes your inner feelings of worth and extends them into your physical presentation. Of course, your body does this, too, especially in how you stand, hold yourself, and walk. But your face is your communicator par excellence. You can convey a myriad of messages by the look in your eye, the expression on your face, or the set of your mouth.

Your face is communicating all the time—whether you want it to or not. You can't stop it—that's the nature of faces—but you can control the messages it projects. If your thoughts are centered on self-criticisms and feelings of inadequacy and inferiority, these are the images it will project. On the other hand, when you focus on your own worth—on all the things that make you a terrific person— this is what gets projected. Let's see how to do this by looking at Irene's WHAT I LIKE ABOUT MYSELF list:

Responsible
Reliable
Warm
Caring
Smart
Good at arts and crafts
Creative
Loving
Resourceful
Persistent
Tenacious
Curious
Adventuresome
Calm
Consistently getting promoted
In some ways a good mother

Looking at Irene's list you may think she has really good self-esteem, but she doesn't, though it is improving. It was a struggle for her to recognize her positive attributes instead of maintaining her usual focus on what she doesn't like about herself. She has been unhappy with her face for years, suffering over her complexion (she has oily skin, which tends to break out) and her nose, which is slightly larger than average and which she sees as grotesque. I suggested that Irene first center herself in positive feelings about herself by reading her "WHAT I LIKE ABOUT MYSELF" list over slowly, starting each sentence with "I really am . . .," and pausing to take each one in. Then I asked her to close her eyes and imagine that her body and face were reciting this list, item by item, and to experience where in her body these feelings were expressed.

Irene discovered that her pride in being responsible was expressed by lifting and straightening her shoulders, lengthening her neck, raising her head, and putting a hint of confidence in her eyes. Reliability was expressed similarly, as well as with a little thrusting out of her chest and a loosening of her facial muscles. Warmth, caring, and lovingness emanated from the smile on her lips, the raising of her cheekbones, the expansion of her chest, and the glow in her eyes. Her intelligence was expressed by her perceptive glance and the upward tilt of her chin. Her ability at arts and crafts she felt first in her hands and arms, and then in her head, which made her head and neck feel comfortable and loose. Her creativity and resourcefulness were two qualities she felt in her whole body—sensing that she could turn, twist, move, think, or react in whatever way was necessary to meet the situation at hand—and particularly in a loosening of her face muscles and a burst of confidence in her eyes. She felt her persistence and tenaciousness in the determined set of her jaw. She expressed curiosity with a slight widening of her eyes, in her nose for discovery, and with a gentle swiveling of her head as she looked around. She embraced adventure by widely opening her arms, ready to welcome new things, and by simultaneously opening her face, so all of it felt lit up. In contrast, she sensed calmness as a peaceful feeling in her body and a relaxation in her face. Her pride in getting promoted brought a huge smile to her face, together with a look of self-respect to her eyes and facial expression. Last came her appreciation for herself as a mother. This she felt first in her heart, then in her arms, with which she embraces her children, and then in her face, which added an aura of quiet satisfaction. When she finished, she already started to feel different about her face, now that she had experienced firsthand its power as an active communicator, rather than a passive object waiting to be judged.

Pretty Thoughts—Pretty Me

Try it for yourself. First go over your WHAT I LIKE ABOUT MYSELF list to see if there is anything you can add to it. Be sure not to dismiss anything as too small or insignificant. Then recite it slowly out loud, starting each item with "I really am" or "I really do," as appropriate, and pausing to fully take in each item. When you are done, repeat your list again, this time pausing after each item to close your eyes and go into your body. With your eyes closed, think about this admirable quality, talent, or achievement of yours, and see where in your being you experience it. Then imagine that you are a mute, needing to express this feeling about yourself without words. How can you project it even more into your presentation, and especially into your face? Concentrate on experiencing your face as your communicator and press agent, telling the world about all the valuable qualities you possess. Deal with each item separately, and take as much time as you need. Write down what you discover.

How do you feel? Have you started to experience how positively you can regard your face when you view it as your communicator? The more you repeat this exercise, the easier this will become. With practice, you will find it easier and easier to light up your face from the inside by focusing on the things that make you a valuable, desirable person.

Some of you may have a hard time viewing your face as a positive communicator because you are so convinced that its appearance can't help belying your true worth. If you are disfigured, this may be especially so, but it may also be true if you have severe acne, facial discoloration, a particularly large nose, or some other feature that you think is both unattractive and very noticeable. Often in these cases we are so focused on these distinctions that it is difficult for us to nonjudgmentally accept our faces as they are, let alone view them in any positive way. If this is true for you, it is especially important to engage in the following exercises designed to change your perspective on your face. If you are disfigured, you may also find it helpful and inspirational to read Lucy Grealy's moving and wonderfully honest *Autobiography of a Face,* in which she recounts her experience with being disfigured and her journey toward self-acceptance and self-appreciation.

PRETTIER THAN A PICTURE

Identify at least two things you like about your face. In looking for these things, don't search for perfection—just things you find likable. Perhaps it's the look in your eyes, your smile, teeth, hair, brow, cheekbones, complexion, nose, chin, or ears. Write these two or more things down, and list what you like about them. For instance:

> *Hair:* I really like the way my hair frames my face, and the texture of it. It's really pretty.
>
> *Lips:* I really like my full, wide, luscious, sexy lips. (Or my thin, narrow, inviting, warm lips.)
>
> *Eyes:* I really like the color and shape of my eyes, and the way they sparkle.
>
> *Mouth:* I really like the way my mouth looks in different expressions. And I have a great smile.
>
> *Chin:* I like the shape of my chin. It's distinctive, and it fits my face.
>
> *Nose:* I really like my nose. Its shape is right for me.
>
> *Cheekbones:* I really like my high prominent cheekbones (or my low cheekbones). They add interest to my face.

These examples are just a few of the many positive ways you could feel about these features. Or perhaps you like a different facial feature, such as your eyelashes, eyebrows, forehead, complexion, dimples, or ears. Choose whichever you like, and as many as you can. Again, remember that you're not looking for perfection, just appreciation.

If you are having trouble finding two of your features that you like, you are being too critical. We all have at least two nice features. Put away the magnifying glass and consider which of the following positive ways you could regard your features:

Eyes: *Everyone has beautiful eyes. They're where your vitality, depth, interest, and exuberance show through. When your eyes twinkle, your whole face lights up. Recognize that twinkle, and praise yourself for it. Color and shape are frosting on the cake. The more you approve of yourself, the brighter that twinkle becomes, so give yourself the approval you need.*

Mouth: *Mouths, like eyes, are lovely and exciting. Your mouth is where your smile is, and when you smile from the inside it's captivating. Beyond that, lips are sensual. We use them to eat, kiss, nuzzle children, form words, and express ourselves. Whatever the shape of your mouth or the size of your lips, mouths and lips are inherently sensual. Give yours the approval it deserves. Tell yourself that your mouth is large and inviting, or small and enticing, and that your lips are full, rich, and tempting, or thin, fascinating, and alluring. Give yourself the admiration you need and merit.*

Hair: *I don't have to tell you how important hair is to most women. It's our "crowning glory." We often spend lots of time and money on it, and dread having a "bad hair day" (though, often, the difference is noticeable only to the woman herself). Hair is easy to like because it is so malleable. It can be permed, straightened, set, blow-dried, braided, weaved, covered with a wig, and worn short, long, or in-between. Happily, this is one area in which fashion embraces diversity. Hair is alluring, frames faces nicely, and looks good at all lengths, with each color lending its own charm. It can be very sexy, and often people love to run their fingers through it.*

Nose: *If you think the only pretty shape for a nose is small and slightly turned up, be aware that this is an ethnocentric view. It's no accident that nose shapes associated with being, say, Semitic or African, are considered ugly by some people. When you accept and value your nose just as it is, you are also saying that you value who you are. If you embrace the racial or ethnic background apparent in the shape of your nose, you are also saying that you are proud of your heritage. A large nose can be viewed as noble, regal, and distinctive.*

Chin: *Chins are usually more important to men than to women (because the ideal says men are supposed to have square, well-defined chins. Another silly beauty standard). Well, we women, too, can be proud of our chins. Each shape chin has its own allure. Round, square, pointed, or soft chins can all be attractive in their own way, and each can convey character. Give yourself a chance to appreciate yours.*

Facial Structure: *Facial structure includes the shape of your face, your forehead, and cheekbones. No one face shape (round, oval, square, rectangular, or heart) is inherently more attractive than another, nor is having a high or low brow, or more or less prominent cheekbones. Yes, I know; we've all heard that having a heart-shaped face is ideal. Don't believe it. Look around you. Attractive women have many different shaped faces. Each can be animated and express character with a charm of its own. Appreciate yours.*

Complexion: *The beauty ideal dictates that being pretty means having flawless, wrinkle-free skin. Few can meet this ideal, and none can meet it as they move into and beyond middle age. Many women can't imagine feeling pretty with crow's-feet, laugh lines, freckles, blackheads, or any other kind of complexion imperfection. Don't ac-*

cept the notion that your complexion has to be perfect before you can like it. Does your skin feel smooth? Soft? Does it have an attractive hue or color? Is there an aliveness to its tone and texture? Does its weather-beaten look bespeak experiences you have had? Do its laugh lines portray the fun you've had in your life? Appreciate your complexion for the way it looks, and as a positive reminder of your life experience. (See Chapter 10 for how to like the way your face looks as you age.)

Eyebrows: *Eyebrows are easy to like—or to shape differently if you desire. They go nicely with your eyes and help protect them.*

Ears: *Ears, like eyebrows, are usually easy to like, as they generally easily and quietly complement our faces. And, unless you're deaf, love your ears for bringing you the joys of speech and music.*

Hopefully, by now you've identified at least two, if not more things you like about your face. Add these to your BEAUTIFUL ME list, which you are reciting at least twice daily. Next:

PRETTIER THAN A PICTURE, PART II

(See the appendix for full relaxation instructions.)

Get comfortable. Then close your eyes, and put your thumb and index finger together on each hand. Take a deep breath, deep into your diaphragm and abdomen, and hold it for five seconds, then gradually let it out to a slow count of five. Now, take five comfortable SLOW deep breaths, and when you finish, let your fingers open, and continue breathing normally and comfortably. As you are breathing, in any way that is natural, let yourself become perhaps a little more peaceful, maybe a little more relaxed, letting go of tensions in any way that you know how, and going inside yourself to a lovely place of comfort and peace, or any other place that feels right to you.

As you are continuing to relax, imagine that you are in the country on a beautiful day. The weather is just as you like it. The birds are singing prettily. There's a gentle and pleasing breeze. Gorgeous flowers are all around you with their wonderful bouquet. And near where you are comfortably sitting is a magnificent waterfall. The water roars down and crashes on the rocks, then runs on, creating a panoply of images that delight your eye. There is the dramatic drop, rushing water, spray, splashes, eddies, current, and all around the waterfall the peacefulness and beauty of the countryside, and the soothing warmth of the sun. Somehow, the unusual force of the waterfall makes its surroundings seem even more peaceful and lovely, and the peacefulness of the countryside adds to the delightful force of the waterfall. And it really doesn't matter whether it is the waterfall's force and distinctiveness that creates more peace, or if it is the peace and beauty of the countryside that accents the waterfall's magnificence. Each complements the other, and you know it really is nice to have so many different things to look at and enjoy all at once. Or perhaps you prefer to rest your gaze on only one or a few of the sights around you—perhaps the waterfall, or the sun, or the flowers, or the birds, or whatever else is most pleasing to you. And as you are doing so, you can enjoy feeling the warm sun on your face, and the gentle caress of the breeze. As the breeze caresses your face, you, too, may want to caress it—gently stroking your face—with caring, acceptance, and love. As you do so, let all the warmth and love that is in your heart travel into your fingers and from them to your face, so that as you caress your face you take it into your heart, and love and accept it as yours. While doing this, allow yourself to think of the things that you like about your face that you have already identified, and any other positive feelings about your face that may now come into your awareness. Really let these things you like about your face enter into your heart, and anchor them into the core of your feelings about your face, so that from now on, whenever you think of your face you will think of your enticing lips, beautiful eyes, lovely cheekbones, terrific smile, or whatever other parts of your face you like. You may even find now, as you focus on these positive aspects of your facial appearance, that you experience a new sense of acceptance and appreciation for your face, recognizing that your face is attractive, and

*that accepting and appreciating your face helps your inner beauty
shine through. Stay where you are for as long as you like, gently caressing your face, enjoying the scenery, lovingly accepting and appreciating your features. Then, whenever you are ready, open your
eyes and return to the room.*

How do you feel? Are you starting to realize how much more
attractive you feel when you accept your face as it is and focus on its
pleasing attributes? Your aim is to let the things you like about your
face bring a smile to your lips and pride to your eyes, and to add
these feelings to the inner beauty that your face projects. The more
you practice this, the easier it becomes.

I Love You More Today Than Yesterday

Gently caress your face, as you did in the visualization, for at
least five minutes. As you do so, concentrate on sending it loving
messages. These messages can be expressions of appreciation, such
as "I love how pretty my eyes are" or "I love the way my eyes can
express confidence and tenderness." Or they can be affirmations of
acceptance and appreciation, such as:

> This is my face, and I love it for being mine.
> My face looks just the way it is supposed to look.
> I appreciate my face for telling the world what a terrific person
>   I am.
> My face proclaims my inner beauty.
> My face is unique and attractive.

Continue with this exercise once or twice a week until its message becomes firmly implanted, so that whenever you look at your
face instead of focusing on whatever aspects may displease you, you
actively concentrate on the features that you like and your face as
the communicator of the terrific person you are.

FAT: FEARS, FABLES, AND FACTS

Deborah has been dieting practically all her adult life, countless times losing and regaining the same weight. She has spent literally thousands of dollars on diets, weight reduction programs, diet-plan foods, liquid protein, and diet doctors. When her weight is down, she feels slim, glamorous, and wonderful about herself. When her weight is up, she feels fat, ugly, inferior, undesirable, and undeserving.

Does Deborah sound familiar to you? If so, it's not surprising. For many women, whatever their size, their weight is the most troublesome aspect of their appearance. I don't have to tell you that most of us are obsessed with our weight. While some few of us believe we are too skinny and bony, the overwhelming majority of us are terrified of becoming larger or hate ourselves for not being thinner, and hang our whole self-image on what the scale says. Years ago when Cher had her own TV show, I remember her telling the audience that her fate was in their hands because when she feels appreciated, her weight stays down and she weighs something like 101; but when she feels she's doing badly, she gets fat and weighs something like 106.

While the idea of Cher feeling fat at 106 pounds, or thereabouts, may sound ludicrous, the reality is that she has lots of company. We saw in Chapter 1 that most women, even women who are underweight, see themselves as larger than they really are, and that huge numbers of women who are of normal weight or less diet. Much of this size dissatisfaction is due to the fact that since the 1970s the beauty ideal has become increasingly out of sync with what most women look like. The ideal has kept shrinking while American women have grown larger. The average American woman today is five four and weighs 144 pounds, and over half of the women in the United States now wear a size fourteen or larger. As we women keep trying to cram our bodies into the much too small mold of the beauty ideal, we have become obsessed with our size, so that the compliment a woman most wants to hear, whether she's a size five, ten, eighteen, or much larger is, "You look as if you've lost weight."

This fear of fat causes tremendous stress and strain in many women's lives, and often produces self-loathing. In this chapter we are going to examine the fables that surround the fear of fat and replace them with the facts. Then we will move on, in the following chapter, to learn how to appreciate the way that we look at the size that we are.

Fable: The slim are good and the fat are bad, so the fat deserve to be discriminated against and scorned.

Slimness in the second half of the twentieth century has become equated with goodness. Slim women are seen as admirable and morally superior because they are assumed to be in control of their eating and themselves, while fat women are thought to be slothful, self-indulgent, gluttonous slobs. We women—fat, thin, or in-between—have absorbed and internalized these judgments. When a woman restricts her eating, she says, "I've been good," and when she eats what she feels like eating, she says, "I've been bad." Nowadays when a woman shamefully confesses her transgressions to her best friend, rather than revealing that she's been having an extramarital affair, she is more likely to be admitting to having had a banana split or perhaps two cookies.

Because slenderness is equated with goodness, women who view themselves as overweight typically blame themselves, believe that society's scorn is just, and feel inferior. In fact, part of the reason women want to be slim is so as not to be disdained or stigmatized.

Fact: There is no correspondence between moral character and body size; but there is real discrimination against fat people, especially fat women.

Fat people are no lazier, sloppier, self-indulgent, or out of control than any other group. (If anything, fat women may be less self-indulgent because they are made to feel so contemptible they sometimes have a hard time feeling entitled to give to themselves.) But they are under considerable stress due to the disdain and discrimination they experience based on these stereotypes.

Fable: If you're large, it's because you have a self-esteem problem.

Pop psychology says that people become fat because they don't value themselves and eat out of unhappiness.

Fact: Fatness is not caused by low self-esteem.

That low self-esteem is not the cause of being fat is evidenced by the many even quite fat people with good self-esteem (as well as by the many thin people with poor self-esteem). A recent study published in the prestigious *New England Journal of Medicine,* reporting on how the fattest 5 percent of a nationwide sample of young people fared over seven years found that despite telling indications of fat discrimination, these decidedly fat young people had good self-esteem both when they were teenagers or young adults and seven years later.

Investigating weight discrimination in employment, psychologist Esther Rothblum of the University of Vermont surveyed nearly four hundred women and seventy-eight men who are members of the National Association to Advance Fat Acceptance (NAAFA). She found that the very fat in the survey (most of whom were double their ideal weight according to the charts) had indeed experienced significant employment-related discrimination. Nevertheless, these very fat respondents did not earn lower salaries or hold jobs with less prestige than did average-weight or mildly to fairly fat respondents. It is reasonable to suppose that these quite fat NAAFA members, because they belong to a group that actively promotes size acceptance, are more accepting and appreciative of their size and themselves than most very fat people, and that this increased self-esteem makes them better advocates for themselves at work. A strong indication of the power of liking the way you look!

However, if you think you're overweight, you may not think as well of yourself as these people do. One of the impediments that makes it hard for people who consider themselves overweight to approve of themselves is the common belief that:

Fable: Being fat is a sign of emotional disturbance, so if you're fat you must be neurotic or dysfunctional.

Fact: Study after study shows that the fat are as mentally healthy, or healthier, than people who are of no more than average weight.

William McReynolds of the University of Florida extensively reviewed the research on the relationship among personality, level of adjustment, and body size. He found that fat people are at least as mentally healthy as everyone else. Furthermore, Anita Stewart and Robert Brook of the Rand Corporation found that the fat are significantly less depressed, less anxious, and score higher on the Mental Health Index, an instrument measuring mental health.

Fable: Fat people become overweight because they eat not out of hunger, but in response to emotional stress.

Fact: Fat people are no more likely than thin people to eat when under stress, but dieters are.

Some people may indeed consistently overeat in response to various types of emotional stress—life problems, trauma, inner conflicts, or other circumstances—but they probably make up only a small proportion of fat people. Researchers Janet Polivy and Peter Herman found that fat people as a group are no more likely to eat under stress than their thin peers. Rather, they found, what determines whether people respond to anxiety, depression, or other emotional stress by eating or fasting is not their weight, but whether or not they are dieters. Dieters (whatever their weight) eat when stressed; nondieters fast. This indicates that people do not eat as a way of handling stress or disturbing feelings but rather that anxiety, stress, or depression can break the iron resolve that dieters need to ignore hunger. For the same reason it is primarily dieters (of whatever size) who binge, while fat people who don't diet generally don't binge either.

The association of being fat with being weak, bad, troubled or gluttonous is based on the next several myths:

Fable: Anyone can be slender, or at least of average weight, if she just eats normally and healthfully, and practices a little self-control; therefore, the fat must be weak-willed people who are continually "stuffing their faces."

Fact: Fat people don't eat more than anyone else.

That's right. As unbelievable as it may seem to you, fat people as a group don't eat more than average-weight or thin people. Noted obesity researcher Albert Stunkard reviewed 144 studies and found no relationship between food intake and body weight in adults and infants. Susan and Wayne Wooley, noted authorities on eating disorders and codirectors of the Eating Disorders Clinic at the University of Cincinnati College of Medicine, reviewed twenty studies and found the evidence to be overwhelming that "obese people do not, on the average, eat more than anyone else."

Not only do the fat not eat more than their average-weight and thin peers, but several studies have found that many fat people eat less. A study of almost 2,500 French children, ages seven to twelve, found that upper- and middle-class fat children ate less than their lean peers, and that lower-class fat children ate less than both slim and average-weight children in their socioeconomic class. This revealing finding could not be accounted for by the kinds of calories the children consumed because fat children did not eat either more fat or more carbohydrates than their thinner peers.

Fable: Fat people have bad eating habits. They would lose weight if they learned to eat like thin people.

According to this theory, promulgated by a behavior therapist and espoused by various weight-loss programs, the fat have distinct eating styles—they take fewer and larger bites, eat more rapidly, snack more, eat on the run or while watching TV—and can reduce by learning to eat like thin people.

Fact: The fat do not have a distinct eating style.

Despite the popularity of this theory, two separate researchers at the University of Pennsylvania have documented that fat people do not have different eating styles than thin people. Michael Mahoney, in four separate experiments, verified that fat people do not eat more rapidly or take different bite sizes than thin ones. K. S. Kissileff, after reviewing two-week food-mood-activity diaries filled out by a large number of overweight and thin volunteers, found no differences between the two groups in how long they ate, where they ate, the physical position they ate in, what else they did while eating, with whom they ate, their mood around eating, or their degree of hunger. All the participants reported eating when not hungry, eating quickly, and snacking frequently—ways that are considered typical of only fat people. A government health survey of over 40,000 people nationwide came up with the same finding: There is little difference in the snacking habits of thin and fat people.

The fact that fat people don't eat more or differently than the thin may come as a surprise to you, whatever your size, even if you've been battling your weight for years and protesting that you really don't eat that much. Women who have a tendency to gain weight, while they may staunchly maintain to others that they really don't eat that much, often secretly believe that they must. Why else, they reason, does the scale go up? To answer this we must examine another myth.

Fable: *Caloric intake is what primarily determines weight gain.*

Many people are under the misapprehension that because weight gain is governed by a simple equation:

Energy stored (fat) = Energy In (calories) - Energy Used

It is primarily overeating, perhaps coupled with lack of exercise, that causes weight gain.

Fact: *"Energy used" in metabolic burning of calories is a major determinant in weight gain, and is very variable from person to person.*

There are three ways calories are burned by the body, with by far most calories being burned in the first two ways:

1. your basal metabolism, which is the number of calories your body burns when you are resting, just to keep your body going.

2. additional calories burned fueling normal sedentary activities and metabolizing food with its associated heat loss.

3. calories burned in exercise.

In all these ways, people are not created equal. Some people burn calories much more slowly than others while at rest, in sedentary activities, after eating, and while exercising. Differences in resting metabolic rate alone can account for individual differences in daily energy expenditure of as much as 400 to 500 calories, with the maximum variation being 770 calories. This means that if two people just sit around all day watching TV, one may burn up 400 to 770 more calories than the other. These differences in metabolism result in great individual variance in how many calories an individual needs to maintain her or his weight. A classic study found that individual consumption ranged from 1,600 to 7,400 calories a day, yet none of the subjects gained or lost weight. Furthermore, when these subjects were put in pairs matched for gender, weight, age, and activity level, often one member of the pair was eating twice as many calories, while both were maintaining their weight, and the large eaters tended to weigh less. These metabolic differences lead us to another common myth.

Fable: *A woman's ability to keep her weight down is mostly determined by how much willpower and self-control she has.*

Fact: *A woman's ability to keep her weight down is to a large degree determined by her luck in the genetics lottery.*

The reality, as researchers have been discovering more and more, is that both the amount and the distribution of fat on the body is largely genetically determined, and it changes with age. Adopted children are much more like their biological parents than their adoptive parents in body size and composition, and this similarity continues in adulthood. Likewise, identical twins have closely related weights, over two times as similar as those of fraternal twins or other siblings. And when identical twin pairs are equally overfed, twins are similar to each other with regard to the amounts and distribution of weight gained. Some twin pairs gain a lot and others relatively little. In families, 40 percent of children with one obese parent become obese, while fully 80 percent of children with two obese parents become obese.

There are three important interconnected areas in which genetics determines or influences weight control: metabolism, fat cells and setpoint. Let's consider each of these separately.

Metabolism: There is increasing evidence that people inherit their rate of metabolism. Dr. Susan Roberts of Cambridge, England, tracked babies born to thin and fat women until they were one year old. She found that half the babies born to the fat mothers burned nearly 21 percent fewer calories than the other infants and became overweight by their first birthday, though they ate no more than the other babies. None of the lean mothers' infants were overweight when they turned one.

Fat Cells: Fat in your body is stored in fat cells. Fat cells can expand and contract to some degree, depending on how much fat is stored in them. When your fat cells fill up, new fat cells may be formed, especially in people who have a genetic tendency to create new fat cells. Once created, fat cells are permanent, and the more fat cells you have, the greater your tendency to gain weight. A while back the theory was trumpeted that having excessive numbers of fat cells was caused by having been overfed as an infant or young child. This theory, which has since been disproven, led many mothers to fear satisfying their children's appetites. We now know that new fat cells can be created at any age, and the propensity to create them is largely genetic. They are also more likely to be created after dieting.

Setpoint: Much evidence indicates that everyone is born with a control system dictating, within a range and changing with age and perhaps with hormonal shifts, how much fat she or he is genetically programmed to carry. Your setpoint is the weight you would normally maintain, give or take a few pounds, when you are not thinking about it. Some people are genetically programmed to carry a lot of body fat, while others are programmed to carry relatively little. Our bodies actively seek to maintain the desired level of fat by balancing food intake, physical activity, and metabolic efficiency in order to maintain that amount. If we diet below our setpoints, our bodies respond by slowing our metabolisms (so we burn fewer calories), creating lethargy to discourage physical activity, and by making us hungry in the hope that we will eat. This means that a woman who naturally weighs, for example, 122 pounds can eat a lot more while maintaining her weight than a woman whose natural weight is 135 and who diets down to 122, because the slimmed-down woman's body is burning off fewer calories. In response to overfeeding, too, our bodies again try to maintain setpoint, this time by speeding up our metabolisms and burning off more calories. Setpoints, in some people, appear to be moderately lowered by regular exercise and raised by diet composition, especially by one high in fat.

Until recently, scientists were ignorant of the mechanism by which the brain is informed of the body's fat stores. Now, however, a protein has been discovered by a research team at Rockefeller University led by Jeffrey Friedman that likely does just this. You've probably heard about this "obesity gene." This peptide (small protein) hormone called leptin is secreted by the fat cells into the bloodstream, then travels to the brain, where it conveys the message about the amount of fat in the body, so that the brain can arrange for the desired level of fat storage by orchestrating changes in appetite, metabolism, food storage, and perhaps even some aspects of physical exercise. Perhaps some people have a defective version of this gene, or a defective receptor for it, misleading the body into increasing body fat. Because the body views its desired level of fat stores as vital, it protests loudly and forcefully when you try to remove them by dieting. This leads us to our next myth.

Fable: If you want to lose weight, you can compensate for a sluggish metabolism by exercising more.

Fact: Exercise plays a very limited role in weight control.

The role of exercise in weight loss is largely misunderstood. It is true that regular mild to moderate aerobic exercise can help people lose modest amounts of weight and/or to stabilize their weight, but its effects are limited. You don't burn up a whole lot of additional calories when you exercise. We've all heard that you have to walk thirty-five miles to burn off a pound. The real contribution of aerobic exercise to weight loss and weight stabilization is that it seems to moderately lower setpoint while increasing metabolism. Usually these results are experienced mainly in the first year of regular exercise, and are modest, resulting in a weight loss of perhaps fifteen to twenty pounds. Further, dieters burn fewer calories when exercising than nondieters. Intense exercise can also sometimes have the opposite effect. Your metabolism may actually slow down the more you exercise intensely as your body struggles to conserve energy, especially if you are below setpoint; and suddenly undertaking intense exercise in people at high risk for heart disease can lead to a heart attack.

Fable: Once you adjust to a diet, you should feel fine, be able to stop thinking about food, and easily continue with your life.

Fact: When you deprive yourself of food and diet below your setpoint, your body forces you to think about food, and your mood and personality can change.

The body's violent reaction to being deprived of the fat stores it deems necessary is dramatically illustrated in a classic study of semi-starvation done with conscientious objector volunteers during World War II. Within a few weeks of being on a 1,600-calorie diet, these healthy, emotionally stable, intelligent, highly motivated young men became preoccupied with food (even collecting recipes, studying cookbooks, and licking their plates clean at meals). Within three months, as the men lost 20 percent of their normal weights, their personalities and energy levels dramatically changed. Whereas initially they had been full of altruism, enthusiasm, and energy, they became tired, edgy, irritable, and argumentative, then slipped into lethargy, becoming apathetic, moody, depressed, undisciplined, and unable to either work together as a group or function in work or social situations. They gave up their activities, lost all interest in sex, and were constantly cold, even in July. Despite their high motivation, some broke the diet. Those who succumbed ate garbage, raw rutabagas, or infinitesimal amounts of food, trying to minimize their transgression and expiate their guilt, and blamed themselves for lacking discipline and self-control.

The preoccupation with food exhibited by the conscientious objectors is undoubtedly familiar to you if you're a dieter. When dieting, no matter how much you may want to forget about food and concentrate on other things, your body, wanting you to eat, continually tempts you with tasty images. These thoughts may get steered into approved diet channels: planning your next meal, thinking about shopping for ingredients you need, deciding what to order when you eat out, drooling for that low-calorie treat you can have in another two hours. Often, though, the dieter is flooded with continual images of "forbidden" foods—the very foods she would most like to eat, and try as she might, she just can't make these images go away.

For much of my married life, I had been unable to understand why my husband, who is naturally thin, waited until he was hungry, or I or our children said we were, before he thought about what he was going to make for supper. By then, in those days before we had a microwave, it was too late to start defrosting meat (a staple of ours in those blissful days gone by when people thought eating red meat was healthy). Often we ended up eating late, or very hit or miss, when it was his turn to cook. Even though this continually happened, he never learned to plan ahead. I might just have attributed this to a tragic flaw in his otherwise sterling character, except this was the man who was always ready early with whatever was needed for all other endeavors, while I was the one who was fully capable of arriving at the theater without the tickets. I finally just gave up trying to understand (and nagging about) his last-minute cooking, and resigned myself to the way things were. Imagine, then, my surprise, after ceasing to diet, to find myself, too, not thinking about meals until I get hungry, and then desperately trying to figure out what I can prepare. I now understand that when chronically dieting, I never failed to plan dinner well ahead of time because I was thinking about food all the time anyway, and what I had for dinner was vitally important to me in a way that now it no longer is.

Preoccupation with food doesn't just disappear, either, as soon as you finish a diet.

Fable: *When you finish a diet and return to sensible and moderate eating, you should be less hungry because you're eating more than you were during dieting, and you should feel fine.*

Fact: *After dieting, your body pushes you to eat while keeping* *your metabolism down, so you will regain lost fat stores. In this process you may feel far from fine.*

Pay attention to the experience of the conscientious objectors. During three months of controlled refeeding they remained ravenous and insatiable—even though they were ingesting ample calories—and they remained depressed, irritable, weak, tired, and in pain. After the three months, when allowed to eat as they wished, many men ate more or less continually, yet they still complained of hunger and suffered from the irrational fear that food would be taken away from them. It was only eight months after refeeding began—at which point the men had regained 10 percent more weight and 40 percent more fat than they had had before the experiment started—that the men recovered their old personalities and lost their preoccupation with food. Eventually, after more than a year, the men returned to their original weights and fat compositions.

But, you may be thinking, those men were of normal weights. What about really fat people? Don't they have more than sufficient fat stores so that they can easily stand to diet? This brings us to our next myth.

Fable: *Fat people don't need to eat. They can live off their stored fat.*

Fact: *Whatever your weight, when you go below your setpoint, your body goes into starvation mode.*

If you're fat, don't let anyone tell you that you don't need to eat and that you can live off the "fat of the land." The truth is that even if you're over 300 pounds, if you severely restrict your caloric intake, or go below your setpoint, you will start to feel as if you are starving because you will be! The heavier you are, the more fat cells you are likely to have, and fat cells take up nutrients. When you underfeed yourself, you are not providing enough nutrients for both your fat cells and the rest of your body, so you are being undernourished.

With this myth goes another.

Fable: The fat are slobs who will eat anything.

Fact: Strict dieters are driven by their hunger to slacken their standards and manners.

Hearing about the conscientious objectors licking their plates and eating garbage may not sound totally unfamiliar to you, if you are a dieter. Many chronic or strict dieters have been known to eat food left over on their families' plates or food in the fridge that may be starting to go bad, lick a plate clean when no one's looking, and even occasionally fish something out of the kitchen garbage. This similarity of behavior indicates that these actions are not the result of a lack of willpower, or of deficient sanitary standards, but of the force of the body's insistence on getting the nourishment it desperately wants and needs.

Okay, you may be thinking, maybe all that happens to you when you practically starve yourself. But isn't sensible dieting a good idea and effective? The answer to this question is connected to our next myth.

Fable: Sensible dieting is likely to produce long-term weight loss, or at least to prevent weight gain.

Fact: Dieting of any kind generally leads to long-term weight gain, with 95 percent of dieters regaining the weight, and then some, within one to five years.

In 1992 the National Institutes of Health Technology Assessment Conference on Voluntary Weight Loss and Control (the same group that in 1984 labeled obesity a "killer disease," thus setting off a wave of diet mania) officially announced the failure of all weight-loss techniques. After reviewing over a thousand research papers, they concluded that all forms of weight-loss treatment (diets, diet programs, drugs, behavior therapy, and so on) have failed abysmally, with almost all lost weight regained within one to five years. As an alternative, they recommended focusing on improving health in ways other than through weight loss.

Weight-loss attempts don't work because when you diet, your body believes you are living in a time of famine and tries to protect you so you won't die of starvation. A couple of weeks after you begin a diet (it usually takes about two weeks before your body decides a change in eating is more than transient and reacts), your body, whatever your starting weight, lowers your metabolism so it can use calories more efficiently. Usually after only a few weeks on a low-calorie diet, resting metabolism slows down by 15 to 30 percent. When dieting, your body also burns fewer calories during activities, and uses lean muscle mass, including heart muscle (rather than fat), as fuel in an effort to preserve body fat (which is its major long-term source of energy), so that your body burns not only fewer calories but less fat, making it more difficult to lose weight where you want to.

To make it even more unfair, fatter people, who generally have lower metabolic rates to start with, have been found to have the biggest drop in metabolic rate while dieting. That's right, unfair as it is, fatter people are precisely the people whose metabolisms slow down the most when dieting and who therefore burn the fewest calories. To make it even more unfair, dieters use less energy to digest their food immediately after a meal and burn fewer calories during exercise. Because of all these metabolic adjustments, after an initial period of weight loss (usually ten to twenty pounds) many women find that they reach a "plateau" at which no matter how little they eat, they just can't seem to lose more weight.

If you manage through heroic willpower to sustain this plateau, maybe even somehow summon the energy to exercise, and—despite the constant messages from your body begging you to eat and evoking images of food—stick to your diet, you probably will continue to lose weight (there's only so much your body can adjust metabolism—either up or down—to defend its setpoint). However, you can't sustain this forever. The point will come when either you can't take it anymore and binge or you think you are thin enough, and you go off your diet (unless you are anorexic, and then you risk death). Then comes the really unfair, though inevitable part. However little you increase your caloric intake, your body seizes on it and more rapidly stores it as fat (during refeeding there is an increase of lipid [fat] synthesis by the liver, and the ability of fat cells to absorb lipids increases tremendously), while continuing to burn calories slowly.

When the famine is finally over, your body wants to rebuild its depleted resources and start saving for the next period of scarcity, just as after a long period of involuntary unemployment in which part or most of your savings were depleted, you probably would want to sock away more money than you had before and continue to spend sparingly. So frightened by what it has just been through, your body doesn't just want to go back to the fat levels it had before you started dieting. It wants to store more fat as a reserve. Now you have a higher setpoint. You also have more fat cells because as you regain weight after a significant loss, your body forms new fat cells (and the more fat cells you have, the greater your tendency to gain weight).

Fable: While one-shot dieting doesn't work, you can keep your weight down by chronically dieting.

Fact: Chronic or yo-yo dieting causes long-term weight gain.

If you are a chronic or yo-yo dieter, as many women are, gaining and losing the same weight over and over again, the chances of keeping the weight off become even more stacked against you because each time you cycle, it takes longer to lose weight, less time to gain it back, and more time for your body to get back to its normal metabolism.

We women are often caught in a vicious self-defeating cycle. In reaction to the weightism in our society—whether or not we are actually large—we start to diet. The more we diet, the more our metabolisms slow down, the higher our setpoints become, and, while we may temporarily lose weight, the fatter we ultimately become. This, in turn, leads to disgust with ourselves for failing to keep the weight off and to repetitive attempts to diet.

Evidence that dieting leads to long-term weight gain is reflected in the fact that Americans are getting fatter, even though we are consuming fewer calories and eating less fat. In the 1960s, 42 percent of the average American's calorie consumption consisted of fat. Currently, fat consumption has been reduced to 34 percent, close to the American Heart Association's recommendation of 30 percent. Still, the prevalence of fatness for Americans has been rising consistently since 1960, with a sharp increase since 1980 (when diet mania took over), so that fully a third of our population is deemed to be overweight. Despite this evidence women and young girls are dieting in droves. If you are the mother of, or close to, a young girl, make sure you explain to her the facts that counter this and the following myth.

Fable: To avoid a lifetime of being fat, it's important to start off on the right foot by dieting when you hit puberty.

Fact: A large percentage of women who report strenuous dieting during puberty later develop problems controlling their weights.

Women are designed to carry more body fat than men and to carry it in different parts of their bodies. Even before puberty girls have 10 to 15 percent more fat than boys. At puberty both girls and boys tend to experience a weight spurt, but while boys gain primarily in muscle and bone, puberty, for girls, brings an increase in body fat that is 15 to 100 percent greater than that of boys. That fat goes primarily into rounding women's breasts, hips, and thighs. By age twenty, girls have about twice as much fat as boys, but only about two-thirds as much lean tissue. In adulthood normally 28 to 30 percent of a woman's body consists of body fat.

While it is natural for girls to gain body fat with puberty, it is a particularly unfavorable time to diet. Psychologist Judith Rodin, founder of Yale University's Eating Disorders Clinic, reports that "dieting at the time when the sex hormones are being established and regulated appears especially destructive for normal body-weight regulation. A large percentage of women who report strenuous dieting during puberty later develop problems controlling their weight." Perhaps this at least partially explains why girls who are early maturers—who have been found to be more likely to diet and to use extreme dieting measures, such as frequent fasting, than their later blooming peers—tend to be fatter than their peers and to remain so once they have completed their pubertal growth.

Fable: Women have no more reason to gain weight than men do.

Fact: Women's hormonal changes are associated with weight gain, and we also usually have lower metabolisms than men.

Besides puberty, there are two other times when hormones are associated with a woman's tendency to gain body fat: at pregnancy and at menopause. Naturally, women put on weight at pregnancy. In contrast to the weight prejudice of the 1950s and 1960s, which decreed that women should limit their weight gain during pregnancy to no more than 20 pounds, it is now recognized that it is beneficial to gain weight during pregnancy, and that dieting during pregnancy produces smaller babies who are more at risk. In fact, fat is so necessary for pregnancy that a woman cannot even get pregnant unless she has a certain minimum amount of body fat.

Not only is it natural and healthy to gain weight during pregnancy, but many women also find that weight gained with pregnancy is hard to lose. This may be because the vast majority of American women don't nurse their children, or do so only briefly, so they don't experience the natural burning of calories that comes with breast-feeding. However, hormonal changes or the raising of setpoint may also be involved. It would seem likely that there is some beneficial reason for such a common phenomenon. Investigators at the Centers for Disease Control, in a study of thousands of Americans, found that over a ten-year period the incidence of major weight gain was twice as high in women as in men, and highest in women ages twenty-five to thirty-four, the prime childbearing years. However, women were no likelier to end up overweight, as they started out thinner.

Women's naturally higher percentage of body fat than men's

explains why, in addition to differences in body size and hormonal changes, it is generally harder for women than for men to maintain or lose weight. Women typically have lower metabolisms than men because fat is less metabolically active than lean body tissue, so the higher the percentage of body fat, the lower the basal metabolism.

Fable: If you eat right and exercise, there is no reason to gain weight as you grow older.

Fact: Almost everyone gains weight as they grow older, and women tend to gain more weight than men.

Both men's and women's basal metabolisms slow down with age, so that people generally put on weight in midlife, especially between the ages of forty and sixty. However, midlife women's metabolisms slow down more than those of men, so that women tend to gain more weight than their male peers. This added poundage tends to be redistributed primarily around the stomach, so that women's waists thicken out, even with little or no change in eating or exercise. After sixty, the weight trends go in the opposite direction, with people tending to lose a few pounds a year.

Perhaps all of this information about the futility of dieting may be upsetting or depressing to you because you fear that if you were to stop dieting, your eating would become completely out of control and you would gain a lot of weight. Well, read on and cheer up.

Fable: I need to follow a diet because I am a compulsive eater. Without a diet to guide me I would lose all control, and just pig out and become really fat.

Fact: Only dieters are compulsive eaters or bingers. When you stop dieting and listen to your body, you can effortlessly maintain the weight that is right for you.

The fact that dieting doesn't work doesn't mean that you are destined to be out of control. Our bodies are exquisitely sensitive instruments that, left to their own devices, automatically balance energy needs, metabolism, and desired fat stores with food consumption, so that we easily maintain the stable weight that is right for us. Now, if you're a dieter, this may sound totally unbelievable. You may be convinced that if "left to your own devices," you would stop eating only when you were too exhausted to keep your mouth moving, and maybe not even then. Many dieters have this belief because dieters are often chronically hungry, like the conscientious objectors, and truly never know when they have had enough.

When we diet, we learn to disregard our bodily sensations of hunger and eat according to what our heads or, more accurately, our diets tell us: so much of this, none of that, exactly ½ cup of this and 3 tablespoons of that, and one of those only on Saturday nights. After years of this we no longer know when we are hungry, or when we've had enough. Studies of appetite, as measured by conditioned salivary response to the sight of food, found that nondieters adjusted their appetites after taking in as few as 150 calories, while dieters of any size showed no change of appetite after 900 calories.

When a woman abandons dieting, learns to listen to her body, and gives herself full permission for life to eat and enjoy whatever and how much she wants when she is hungry, in time she stops bingeing, as her fat stores are restored and her body no longer fears renewed famine. In time she will find herself eating when she is hungry and stopping when satisfied. While she may initially gain weight, over the course of a year or more as her metabolism returns to normal she may find herself losing weight if she is above her setpoint. On the other hand, if through severe restriction she has been maintaining a weight below her setpoint, she may level off at a weight that's not as low as her present size. If so, she's also likely to live longer because despite all the hype about how fat is unhealthy and thin is healthy, the facts tell a different story. Let's examine the fables and facts around weight and health.

Fable: Fat is a killer disease, and being even a little fleshy is unhealthy.

Fact: Unless you are very thin or very heavy, your weight is either irrelevant to your health or (if you are moderately heavy) may even prolong your life.

Epidemiological studies show that for people in the middle 80 percent of the weight range, either weight is irrelevant to their health or it helps prolong life. For example, the Seven Country Study, coordinated by Ancel Keys, begun in 1960 studied nearly 13,000 relatively healthy middle-aged men living in Japan, Yugoslavia, Finland, Italy, the Netherlands, Greece, and the United States over many years. Dr. Keys concluded:

> no indication of increasing death rate with increasing frequency of overweight or obesity could be found . . . the tendency in all regions was for the death rate to *decrease* with increasing relative weight and fatness. . . . Except for men in the extreme upper end of the distribution, overweight is not an important risk factor for coronary heart disease nor for premature death.

Dr. Keys further concluded, after examining thirteen different studies on obesity and mortality, that for women, too, mortality increases only at the weight extremes, but that otherwise weight poses no hazard for the large majority of women.

> Both extreme under- and overweight seem likely to entail risk, but there is no acceptable evidence that relative body weight has any relevance to future health for women in the middle 80 percent of the relative weight distribution.

Many other studies and experts, including Dr. Reubin Andres, clinical director of the Institute for Aging of the National Institutes of Health, support these conclusions. And even for the fattest 10 percent of the population, as Dr. William Bennett, past editor of the *Harvard Medical School Health Letter* and Joel Gurin, past editor of *American Health,* point out in their excellent book *The Dieter's Dilemma,*

> . . . As you might expect, no one has ever proved that the obesity is in itself responsible for the poor health of people affected. . . . Nor has anyone managed to demon-

strate that the life expectancy of morbidly obese people
is improved by weight loss.

The fact that mildly to moderately fat women are not at increased risk is particularly significant in light of the fact that it is
precisely these women who are the major consumers of weight-loss
products.

Biomedical researcher Paul Ernsberger, a professor at Case
Western Reserve University School of Medicine, using data from the
largest epidemiological study to date (almost two million Norwegians—practically the whole population of Norway over age fifteen) makes graphically clear in the following table the relative
mortality risks for women of various weights at a given age and
height. He calculated the probability, per thousand women, of sur-
viving to a given age in four theoretical groups of thirty-five-year-
old, five-feet-seven-inch women, the same height as a *Playboy*
centerfold who weighed 110 pounds.

Woman	*Weight*	*No. per 1,000 Live to Age 45*	*No. per 1,000 Live to Age 55*	*No. per 1,000 Live to Age 65*
Playboy model	110	976	890	730
Insurance ideal	122	986	937	824
Large-size model	224	982	942	844
Fattest 0.2% of population	287+	982	912	757

As you can see, the *Playboy* model is a third more likely to die
before her forty-fifth birthday than are her peers weighing three
times what she does. And Ms. June is not particularly thin for a

Playboy centerfold; and is, in fact, heavy for a clothes model. Moreover, Ernsberger points out, each pound Ms. June loses increases her risk of premature death by 1 percent. By contrast, each pound gained by the large-size model increases her risk by only 0.1 percent. So the gained weight of the large-size model carries one-tenth the risk of Ms. June's weight loss.

Perhaps particularly indicative of the fact that being moderately overweight is not unhealthy is that in the last thirty years as Americans have gotten fatter, life expectancy has increased, and cardiovascular mortality (the health problem most blamed on fatness) has decreased. Furthermore, women are twice as likely as men to be overweight, yet we live longer.

Fable: *Losing weight is healthy for you.*

Fact: *Dieting may shorten your life.*

Not only hasn't a single long-term epidemiological study ever proven that losing weight extends life, but several recent studies provide evidence that dieting may shorten it. Notably, Elsi Pamuk of the Centers for Disease Control, using data on 5,000 men and women between the ages of forty-five and seventy-four when they entered the study in the early 1970s, headed a team that examined who died and of what causes. They found that maintaining a stable adult weight and avoiding severe overweight is the best possible course, and that those who maintained a stable, moderately heavy weight had death rates as low as those who had stable average weights. Most telling, the study found that women who lost any amount of weight had a higher death rate than those who didn't; and the more weight they lost, the higher their risk.

Fable: *If you are fat and have hypertension (high blood pressure), elevated cholesterol, or diabetes, dieting and weight loss are vital.*

Fact: *While permanent weight loss may be advisable for these medical conditions, dieting can aggravate them.*

Obesity is associated with diabetes, hypertension, and elevated cholesterol, all of which are associated with heart disease, which does shorten life span. In fact, it is precisely because of the association of fatness with diabetes and the two risk factors for heart disease that weight has been portrayed as unhealthy. Therefore, the lack of a relationship between weight and mortality repeatedly verified in epidemiological studies is surprising. Nevertheless, the fact stands. A group from the Rand Corporation reviewed extensively the literature on the relationship of overweight to overall premature mortality, heart disease, diabetes, hypertension, and cholesterol, and it found no added risk from being moderately overweight. One explanation for this apparent incongruity, put forth by Dr. Reubin Andres, is that unknown benefits of mild or moderate obesity counteract all of the known associations between weight and these conditions.

Still, if you are overweight and have diabetes, high blood pressure or elevated cholesterol, weight loss may be advisable if you could keep it off. However, this is a big "if," especially as diabetics and hypertensives have even more trouble losing weight and keeping it off than most people. Otherwise, weight loss and regain in relation to all three of these conditions can leave you more at risk than you were before dieting. Let's examine each of these conditions individually.

Diabetes: While diabetes is associated with being overweight, there is no evidence that being overweight causes diabetes; rather, diabetes may well cause weight gain. Insulin has two functions: It breaks down blood sugar and promotes fat storage. In diabetics, the ability of the body to either produce or use insulin to break down blood sugar is impaired, while the ability of insulin to promote fat storage is not. Thus diabetics are often caught in a vicious cycle in which they need to receive or produce extra insulin to metabolize glucose; in turn this extra insulin promotes fatness, and in turn again fatness makes diabetics more insulin-resistant. Losing weight has been thought to be helpful to diabetics because it reduces insulin resistance, but Ernsberger questions if this is so. He points out that of course eating less lowers blood sugar, so that many of the studies supposedly showing the benefits of weight loss are really just showing that starvation lowers blood sugar. After the diet, in the short run the body's fat stores eagerly absorb glucose which makes it look like your glucose tolerance is great. However, as soon as your fat stores are partially restored, your glucose tolerance deteriorates to worse than it was before. Dieting may also not be helpful both because dieters tend to store regained fat in the abdomen, a weight pattern associated with increased insulin resistance, and because the stress of dieting can cause the release of the stress hormone adrenaline, which actually opposes the action of insulin. Moreover, fat diabetics tend to be less insulin dependent, and to have fewer complications and decreased mortality than leaner diabetics. This doesn't mean, however, that if you are diabetic you should try to gain weight, but you should be cautious about dieting. A better idea is to eat appropriately and to embark on a program of sensible aerobic exercise, which raises sensitivity to insulin and can help reduce abdominal fat even without weight loss.

If you are basically sedentary, almost any amount of exercise is beneficial to both your health and well-being, and if you have diabetes or heart disease, may well prolong your life. In addition, a recent study found that two to four hours of aerobic exercise a week reduces the risk of premenopause breast cancer by as much as 60 percent. A brisk half-hour or so walk most days is sufficient. Or, if you prefer, you can break up your exercise. A recent study found that the fitness of healthy, sedentary, middle-aged men who exercised for ten minutes, three times a day, five days a week improved as much after eight weeks as that of a similar group that trained for thirty minutes at a time, five days a week.

High Blood Pressure: With high blood pressure, too, dieting may worsen the very health problem it is prescribed for. Biomedical researcher Paul Ernsberger suggests that the reason fat people tend to have high blood pressure and that people with high blood pressure tend to be fat (though many fat people have perfectly normal blood pressure and many thin people have high blood pressure), and that this relationship is found only in humans, may well be because only humans go on diets.

Ernsberger experimented with putting laboratory rats on a crash diet, and their blood pressure fell almost immediately, before they had lost much weight, indicating that it was dieting itself, not weight loss, that produced this change. This conclusion was further supported by the return of the rats' blood pressure to their previous levels only two days after the end of the diet. These findings were repeated in a study of dieting humans, in which the fall in blood pressure from three weeks of stringent dieting was obliterated after only three days of moderately low-calorie eating.

Ernsberger also investigated the effects of yo-yo dieting by putting his rats through four cycles of feast and famine, which brought their blood pressure down and up until the rats developed permanent high blood pressure, indicating that chronic dieting may be the cause, and not the cure, of high blood pressure. If you're concerned about your weight because you have high blood pressure, rather than dieting, Ernsberger advises that you can lower your blood pressure through exercise, cutting down on salt, and through the use of blood pressure–lowering medications, which are quite effective without weight loss.

Cholesterol: We all know of the strong association of elevated bad cholesterol (LDL) with coronary heart disease, and death. However, much of the research on which these findings are based was done on men. Thomas Moore, a fellow at the Center for Health Policy Research at George Washington University, explains in his very informative book *Lifespan* that the epidemiological evidence showing an association between elevated cholesterol and heart disease holds primarily for young and middle-aged men with cholesterol levels around 280 or higher. Women are another story. Moore points out that the noted Framingham study found that cholesterol level was not a risk factor at all for women under fifty, and not a strong risk factor after that.

This is not to say that if your cholesterol is elevated, you should just ignore it. On the contrary, if your LDL or triglycerides are elevated, it may be helpful to cut down on the amount of fat, especially saturated fat, in your diet, and to stop smoking (which is a good idea in any case). But be aware that unless you cut your fat intake to 10 percent of your daily calories (which is not easy), studies show that dietary changes may have little or no effect on your cholesterol level. Moderate aerobic exercise can also help lower bad cholesterol and raise healthy cholesterol. What you should avoid, though, is losing and then regaining weight because weight regained after dieting tends to settle in the abdomen, and just as with diabetes, this is the very distribution of body fat that carries greater risk to your heart. Also, if you're fat, you may find it of interest to note that fat people have a slightly higher base cholesterol level than the nonfat.

Of further comfort to women who are concerned about weight and heart disease is the fact that cardiovascular disease is most strongly associated with overweight "apples," or people who carry most of their weight around the middle, and apples are primarily male. By contrast "pears," or people who carry their weight more in the lower body—most notably in the hips, thighs, and buttocks, as most women do (though there is some tendency among black women to store fat in the upper body)—have significantly less risk.

With regard to weight and health, it is also notable that women who live in cultures in which fat is considered beautiful—and therefore in which women do not diet—do not seem to have the health problems normally associated with fatness. Medical anthropologist Margaret MacKenzie studied women in Western Samoa, where women normally are quite fat by middle age. Yet not one of them had high blood pressure, heart disease, or arthritis. Five percent of them did have diabetes.

Fable: Your doctor knows best, realizes that being large is generally perfectly healthy, and understands that the body makes it difficult to maintain weight loss.

Fact: Many doctors are poorly informed about weight and health and are prejudiced against the fat.

Unfortunately, often the very doctors to whom large women turn for help are prejudiced against them. A survey of the attitudes of more than three hundred family-practice doctors, evenly divided between men and women, found that a sizable number of doctors hold negative or stereotypical attitudes toward fat patients. Two-thirds believe that fat patients lack self-control, almost 40 percent see their fat patients as lazy, a third report that their fat patients are sad, and 23 percent that their fat patients are happy (obviously, fat people can't be categorized as either especially happy or sad). Anecdotal evidence, too, tells tale after tale of doctors being unknowledgeable, insensitive, humiliating, or abusive. If you wish information about how to screen doctors for weight-positive attitudes, you can contact NAAFA, which has a helpful pamphlet on this and many other topics affecting fat people. (See Resources.)

Fable: Height/weight charts are a good indication of what you should weigh.

Fact: Height/weight charts have been responsible for a lot of dangerous misinformation.

The height/weight charts familiar to many of us from childhood doctor visits were developed by the Metropolitan Life Insurance Company in the 1940s, spearheaded by its chief statistician, Louis Dublin, a fataphobe who held sway at MetLife for over forty years. He based the charts on insurance company mortality rates; however, almost all the insured were upper-middle-class white males of northern European stock who lived in cities in the Northeast, a totally unrepresentative group and one substantially thinner than the general population. In addition, as fat policyholders had to pay an extra premium, it is likely that it was precisely those fat people who knew they had a fatal illness who were more likely to buy life insurance, thus further skewing the data. Besides using unreliable data, Dublin further arbitrarily decided, without any evidence whatsoever, that there was no reason to gain weight with age, although just about everyone does and that what was ideal was to be about 10 percent below the average weight of what insurees weighed at age twenty-five.

Suddenly people of perfectly normal and average weights were now labeled as overweight. Dublin then persuasively preached to the country's physicians and to the public that statistics show that fat causes premature death. Largely under the impetus of these insurance company findings, the country was urged to go to war against fat. Belatedly in 1983, MetLife, bowing to evidence that being underweight is associated with increased mortality, changed its charts to reflect genuine average weights. The U. S. Department of Agriculture also now has charts that reflect average weights as people age.

Fable: There are no specific health advantages to being fat.

Fact: Being moderately fat has a number of specific health advantages.

Not only doesn't being moderately overweight shorten life, but moderately fat people have a lower incidence of death from various kinds of cancer and are less likely to get lung diseases such as emphysema than are thin people. Also, moderately overweight women tend to have fewer menopausal symptoms, such as hot flashes, because estrogen is stored in fat cells. For the same reason, older fat women also often have fewer wrinkles and more youthful skin. Large women, moreover, are less likely to develop osteoporosis because carrying weight around strengthens bones. (On the other hand, the extra estrogen that heavier women have means that they are also more likely to have irregular periods, hormone imbalance, and up to six times the likelihood of developing uterine cancer.) The relationship between overweight and breast cancer is uncertain. While fatness has been consistently shown to be a protective factor against breast cancer in premenopausal women, a number of studies have found an association between postmenopausal breast cancer and fatness. This association is usually found in older postmenopausal women, particularly in elderly women who were lean as young adults.

I hope that by now you have an increased understanding of the powerful biological and genetic forces you are up against, and the health risks you may be running, when you try to force your body into a narrower mold than is right for it. Some of you may be eager to learn how to like the way you look at the weight that's right for you, if only you could. Others of you may still be willing to combat those forces and run those risks because you just can't imagine liking the way that you look and feeling good about yourself if you're anything but fashionably thin. If so, that's okay. It's important to listen to yourself and do what feels best to you. But first, experience how you feel after doing the exercises in the following chapter that are designed to teach you how to accept and appreciate your size and yourself at whatever weight you are.

Note: As this book was going to press the media was full of the latest volley from the advocates of "thin is healthy"—a Harvard study, published in the *New England Journal of Medicine,* of 115,000 white women nurses (ages 30–55 when the sixteen-year study started) which supposedly shows that what is healthiest for women is to be underweight and to not gain more than twenty-two pounds after age eighteen, and that being even of normal weight increases a woman's chances of dying in mid-life. What the study actually shows is that for all women—smokers and former smokers—there is a slight increased risk for women who are both underweight and fat, while for women who never smoked it is safe to be underweight. However, the mortality risk for any of these relatively young women was small. The nurses overall had only 0.25 percent chance of dying in any given year, while the heaviest women had a 0.33 percent chance—not much of an increased risk, and women who maintained stable weights were at even less risk. As an editorial in the same issue of the *New England Journal of Medicine* points out, the study shows that except for the heaviest women "there is very little relationship between body weight and mortality." What increased risk the study shows is really more a function of age (the women who were middle-aged when the study began were naturally more likely to die during the research period than those who were young, and they were also likely to be somewhat heavier, as people tend to put on weight as they age). As for a weight gain of twenty-two or more pouinds in adulthood increasing mortality, it is likely that many of these women were at one time dieters, and perhaps even took diet pills or had weight-loss surgery (which is exceedingly dangerous) and it is these measures, not the weight gain, that contributed to whatever increased risk they may have. Most important, in no way does the study indicate that it is gaining weight that is responsible for even the very small reported increased risk, or that losing weight would decrease the risk. In fact, women who lost weight did not live longer.

CHAPTER 8

WEIGHT — LOVING ALL OF YOU

However thin you may be, as we saw earlier, you may still think you are too fat and see yourself as much larger than you really are. If you are truly fat, you may well have an even more distorted view of your body and see it as monstrous, because large women, even more than other women, tend to overestimate their size and view their bodies as grotesque and loathsome.

It's vital to start to view your body with more realistic, loving, and approving eyes, but before we look specifically at how to do this, let's talk about the word "fat." Some of you may be offended by it, and would prefer that I use euphemisms like "overweight," "plump," "chubby," or even the medical term "obese," which even though it connotes grossness and disease may sound nicer to you than "fat." Many women think of "fat" as a bad name because it is so often said with cruelty, contempt, derision, and hostility. However, "fat," like "black," is merely a descriptive term. In reality, it's not having a lot of adipose tissue that's bad, but the tremendous prejudice against fat people. In the 1960s and 1970s, African-Americans vocally and accurately rejected the notion that dark skin is ugly or diminishes one's value, and proudly proclaimed that "black is beautiful." Similarly, large women and men in the size-acceptance movement choose to call themselves "fat" as the most accurate way to describe their size, thereby refusing to regard their weight as a shameful thing that has to be hidden and denied. As Karen Gavanda, writing in *Radiance,* a size-acceptance magazine, says, "*Fat* is honest, descriptive, non-judgmental and powerful."

If we women could lose our fear of fat, just think of all the power we would gain. All that time and energy spent on trying to get or stay thin, or thinner, could then be ours to use as we wish, as we enjoy our looks and ourselves. Instead of shrinking and constricting ourselves, we could expand our horizons, enlarge our expectations, amplify our power, and widen our impact. We could also eat according to our appetites and with pleasure, knowing that what's most beautiful and healthy is to be the size we are meant to be.

The first step in learning to like your size—whether you are a size six or a supersize—is to own and make friends with your body and start to view and treat it with love. Perhaps you, like many women, view your body as your enemy, something that betrays you despite your best attempts to control and mold it. Or maybe, in line with what you've been taught by our culture, you view your body as a commodity, something you can use to get preferential treatment of one kind or another. Unfortunately, not only does this usually either not work or leave you in someone else's power, but it also alienates you from yourself. An object is, by definition, other—it's not part of you. Men, on the other hand, tend to see their body as an *instrument,* a part of them they can use to ride a bicycle, lift their children, make love with, and do whatever else they wish or need to do. We women, of course, do these same things, but we are usually so focused on how we look that we often largely ignore the ways in which our bodies serve us—the ways in which our bodies are us. The next several exercises will help you to increase your awareness of your body as an instrument, but first a word about the most helpful attitude with which to approach the exercises in this and the following chapters.

As you explore your relationship with your body and work on

improving it, keep in mind that your goal is to own and love your body *unconditionally*. Unconditionally, as we discussed in Chapter 1, means just what it sounds like: no "when I's," no "if only's," no standards. Many women object at first that they can't do this because, they maintain, their disgusting bodies don't deserve unconditional love. What they are really saying is that they are disgusting and don't deserve unconditional love. Not true! Every child deserves unconditional love from her parents—just for being herself—and every adult deserves to have her inner child unconditionally loved by her inner caretaker. Learning to love your body and your looks is not about fooling yourself into believing that you meet some arbitrary criteria of beauty. Rather, body love is about throwing these standards away (they're artificial anyway), opening your heart to yourself, and giving yourself acceptance, support, approval, appreciation, tenderness, and caring. When you treat yourself in this way you will feel and become more attractive. As you do the following exercises, approach them in this spirit and with this goal in mind.

Physical/Sensual Exercises

LOOK WHAT MY BODY CAN DO

Choose a day to pay special attention to all they ways you use your body. Notice how your legs and thighs, arms, and hands help you get out of bed. Watch your feet, legs, and hips taking you into the bathroom; your behind sitting on the toilet; your feet and legs holding you up while your arms and hands brush your teeth. Notice how all of you participates in taking a shower. Be aware of which parts of your body you use when you dress; how your stomach accepts and processes whatever you eat for breakfast; how your thighs and stomach make a lap (perhaps for children to sit on); the way your elbows and arms lean on a table or desk and support you; the comfort your rear gives you when you sit; the way your hips and thighs direct your walk, making sure you can and will go where you want to go. As you continue through your day, be aware of the multiplicity of ways in which your body makes all things possible. Think about what it would be like if you didn't have a stomach, or thighs, or hips, or a rear, or legs, or arms, or a face. Pay particular attention to the things your body does that bring you joy, such as giving and getting a hug, pursuing a hobby, lying in the sun or bath, walking to the video store, or stretching out on the couch. From now on make it a point to think of your body as an instrument, not as an object, and appreciate it for being there for you.

EXERCISE

One great way to make friends with your body and to increase your experience of your body as an effective and pleasure-giving instrument is to purposefully *use* it. Particularly beneficial is aerobic exercise: the steady, sustained exercise that utilizes oxygen. Walking, running, swimming, and dancing are all aerobic exercises and have many advantages. Exercise of this kind, besides being beneficial to your health, helps forge a positive connection between you and your body by making you feel more alive and invigorated, increasing your overall energy level, allaying anxiety, improving your mood, and raising your sense of well-being and self-esteem.

When exercising, though, it's important to focus on enjoying what your body can do, and the sense of accomplishment that comes with increasing your ability, rather than on how you look. If your main reason for exercising is for weight loss or control, or to try to shape your body into the mold of the beauty ideal, it may well be counterproductive, as you're likely to fall short of your goal and be dissatisfied with your physique and yourself. Such a goal also keeps you focused on your body as an object. On the other hand, when you exercise to have fun and increase your strength, flexibility, and stamina, you will develop new pride in your body and yourself. See how much better you feel when you measure your progress not on the scale but by your sense of ability, competence, power, and well-being.

Choose to move in ways that are comfortable and enjoyable for you (for example, dancing for ten to fifteen minutes once or twice a day to your favorite music, taking enjoyable walks, or swimming at your local Y), and make it a regular part of your life. Remember, your goal is not to alter your appearance but to increase your appreciation for your body as an instrument that can bend, lift, and move. Remember, too, that movement is for life. So if for periods you can't manage, or don't want to exercise, don't worry about it. Don't make moving into a chore. Enjoy it, and you'll find yourself wanting to return to it.

However, if you don't wish to exercise, that's fine. You don't have to become more physically active to learn to see your body as an instrument and to love it at its present size. Do, however, make it a point to notice the various ways your body helps you to accomplish what you want to do and enriches your life.

If what keeps you from wanting to exercise, though, is the dread of being seen in shorts or anything spandex, or the fear that as an uncoordinated or large woman you aren't capable of the skill or exertion necessary, I highly recommend *Great Shape* by Pat Lyons and Debbie Burgard. This warm, informative, encouraging exercise and fitness guide for large women, which is also helpful for any beginning exerciser, tells you everything you need to know, including warm-up procedures, specific exercises, and even where to get attractive and comfortable workout clothes that fit. Evidence shows that fat people who exercise can achieve impressive levels of cardiorespiratory endurance, muscular strength, muscular endurance, and flexibility.

But enough about exercise. I hope you'll at least give it a try, so you can experience firsthand that strengthening your body builds pride and confidence in it and in yourself. However, whether or not you exercise, you can learn to love your body at any weight, connect with it sensually and viscerally, and learn to value it as a source of both pleasure and efficacy.

MY BODY GIVES ME PLEASURE

Take a bath or shower, and then slowly massage your dry naked body with warm lotion (you can warm up baby, massage, or mineral oil or any other lotion by leaving the bottle in warm water for a few minutes), concentrating on your physical sensations. During the massage turn the lights low and play nice music. Go slowly, really taking your time, and absorbing all those good feelings. Pay special attention to the part of your fat that bothers you the most. It may be your stomach, hips, thighs, another part, or all of you. Imagine that you are sending healing energy to your fatness. Concentrate on pleasurable feelings. Let yourself know that this warmth and softness is your warmth and softness, this roundedness and fullness is your roundedness and fullness, this sensuality is your sensuality, this sexuality your sexuality, this cuddliness your cuddliness. Know, too, that this largeness of experience, this expansiveness, this full-hearted openness to pleasure and to joy, to taking and giving, is also yours. Be aware that the greater the expanse of your flesh, the more room you have to experience loving pleasure. As you gently caress yourself, pay attention to all the nuances of enjoyment that your body gives you, going slowly as you would with a loved one and fully taking in the enormous enjoyment of giving and getting love and pleasure from your body, your size, and yourself. End by making conscious note of the pleasure your body gave you, and thank it. Repeat this exercise as needed.

I AM MY BODY AND IT IS ME

In privacy, dressed in comfortable clothes, either barefoot or in sneakers, stand on the floor, feet comfortably apart, with your knees slightly bent. Keep your feet planted, and rotate your hips, gently moving each one forward in turn and swaying side to side and front and back. Then come back to the middle, and feel the ground under your feet. As you stand there, be aware of your feet and legs holding you up, grounding you and giving you a sense of centeredness, at the same time as they offer you mobility. Try moving your arms in different directions—swing them forward and back, up and down, in small, then large circles. Move your head back and forth, side to side. Now put on some music you like and move in different ways, at different speeds and rhythms.

Try swaying your hips, moving your arms, sashaying, sliding, turning, skipping, jumping, dancing—whatever comfortably comes to you. Pay close attention to how you and your body feel. Your aim is to experience what it feels like to use your body, your *whole* body. Do some movements feel good while others are bothersome? Stop doing the bothersome ones and do more of the ones that feel good. Focus on getting a sense of the interconnection between you and your body. You decide how to move, and it moves; that movement feels good and it carries you to another movement; you can then decide to move in another way, or just follow your body's lead. As you get into the music, after a while perhaps you can't tell if you are leading your body or it is leading you. Your body is part of you, and you are part of it. You can go nowhere without it, achieve nothing without it—and it cannot survive without you.

Continue moving to the music. Perhaps you are dancing by now, or are in some other movement groove that feels pleasurable. Keep going. Know that together with your body you can go wherever you want. When you're ready, stop. End by thanking your body for giving you the joy of movement. Promise yourself that you will move in this pleasurable way at least five minutes a day, most days—and do so.

THIS BODY IS MADE FOR GOING WHERE I WANT TO GO

Take a walk for fifteen or twenty minutes (less if this is too much for you, or more if you feel like it) toward a destination. As you walk, think about the fact that your body can take you wherever you want to go. Remind yourself as you are walking that these are *your* two feet holding you up, this is *your* body that is carrying you along, that you need your body and it needs you, and together you can go wherever you want to in life. Be aware of how good it is to stand and move on your own two feet. When you reach your destination, thank your body for carrying you through the world and being your friend. Thank it again when you return home.

Emotional Exercises

MY WEIGHT IS ON MY SIDE

Identify positives about your weight. In our weight-phobic society we are trained to ignore the advantages that weight my bring. These include: looking more womanly, feeling more substantial and powerful, freeing yourself from societal dictates that are inimical to your well-being, being at the weight that is healthiest for you, and feeling more sexual. (Studies have repeatedly found that fat women are at least as sexual as those of normal weight, and researchers at a Chicago hospital found that plumper women desired sex more than thinner woman. On scales of erotic excitability and readiness, they outscored thin women by a factor of almost two to one.)

To identify positives, take a few slow deep breaths with your eyes closed to relax, then with your eyes still closed ask yourself, My fat, what advantages does it bring? Then see what comes to you. Whatever comes up, don't judge or stifle it. Just experience it. When you're done, restate these positives as affirmations, such as:

My weight is healthy for me.
My weight enhances my sexuality.
My weight makes me look more womanly.
My weight makes me a force to be reckoned with.

Recite these affirmations to yourself whenever you start to feel bad about your weight. If you have trouble identifying positives about your weight, have a dialogue with your fat.

TALKING WITH YOUR FAT

This dialogue can be done either in writing or out loud. Writing has the advantage of letting you easily look back, weeks or months from now, at what you have discovered. However, some of you will prefer the speed and immediacy of doing this exercise out loud. Either way is fine. If you do it out loud, you may want to jot down a few notes afterwards about what you learned.

Ask your fat what it does to help you (you already know how it gets in your way), and what positive images it projects. Whatever it says, listen to it nonjudgmentally and empathically, so you can really learn more about its role in your life. If you are doing this in writing, first write out your question, then your fat's answer, your response, its response, and so on, the way a script for a play is written out. But don't decide what to write. Just write as fast as you comfortably can, and let whatever comes out come out, even if it doesn't make sense to you or if you don't agree with it. If you're doing this dialogue out loud, place two seats facing each other. Start by sitting in one of them, be you, and ask your question. Then shift seats and be your fat and answer. Again, don't decide what to say, just let it flow, as if you're an actress in character feeling the part. When you're done, thank your fat for talking with you. Here's a sample dialogue:

> *Freda:* Fat, what do you do for me?
> *Fat:* I protect you.
> *Freda:* How do you do that and from what?
> *Fat:* I protect you from being sexually harassed by projecting an image that says "I'm big and you'd better not mess with me."
> *Freda:* But why do you do that? I'm not so afraid of being harassed.
> *Fat:* Sure you are; think about it.
> *Freda:* (Thinks about it.) . . . You're right. I *do* really hate and dread the comments, leers, and touching or grabbing that some men do. I've always known that I can't stand it, but I never realized the extent to which it intimidates me. Thanks for helping me.
> *Fat:* No problem.

Gloria's fat said that it helped her by being a protective shield that fended off her mother's competitive distancing and anger that occurred when Gloria was thin, and projected an image that said,

"You can't get at me, because the most valuable parts of me are inside, where you can't reach them." Harriet discovered that her fat was helping her by asserting itself against her very controlling father, because no matter how much he complained about her weight, he could not control her body, and projected an image that said, "I'm my own person, and I can live my life as I wish, and as life comes to me." After discussing it, all these women came to realize that the functions their fat carried really belonged to them, and they found other ways to protect and assert themselves and own their own power. But they also felt good knowing that their weight (which actually ranged from average to quite heavy) could project positive and protective images and messages.

Serena's fat told her that it wasn't doing anything special for her—it just was, and was there in just the amount it should be—and projected the message that it's great to love and accept yourself. Serena is a self-accepting fat woman in the size-acceptance movement, so she wasn't at all surprised at this answer. After a lifetime of hating her weight and herself and blaming herself for her genetic heritage, she had learned to truly accept her fat, to love her body, and appreciate her looks at the size she is.

DISSOLVING GUILT

Almost any woman who considers herself overweight feels guilty. How could she not when society tells her that fat is not only ugly but bad, and that she is a weak-willed sinner. Listen to the voices of some of these women:

Wyonna (24, 5'6", 132 pounds): I feel like a tub of lard. I've been dieting for years, but I always break down, and then I eat stuff I shouldn't eat, like sweets. As soon as I finish eating, I start feeling guilty and angry at myself. I hate the way I look, and I know it's my own fault. I should be able to stick to my diet, and I try very hard, but I must not be trying hard enough.

Phyllis (45, 5'2", 126 pounds): I used to weigh 114. Now I've grown so fat. I get sick every time I look in the mirror. I don't know why I keep gaining weight. I'm very careful about what I eat, and I work out all the time, but I still can't get back down. Sometimes I get so discouraged that I don't work out one day, or eat something I shouldn't, and then I feel even worse. I know all this is my fault, and that I must be eating too much.

Janice (38, 5'7", 250 pounds): I've been fat all my life. I was a fat child, a fatter teenager, and a fat adult. I started dieting when I was nine, and I'm still at it. I've tried every diet known to woman and have lost weight countless times, but it always creeps back. I guess I just don't have the willpower to deprive myself, though it doesn't feel as if I'm eating very much. I feel like such a failure. Sometimes when I see myself in the mirror, I feel so bad I just wish I'd die.

Elaine (57, 5'3", 160 pounds): When I was younger I was thin, but with each of my three pregnancies I put on more and more weight that I just couldn't seem to lose. Now I can't stand looking at myself. My best friend has three children, too, and has always been thin. I just wish I could be thin like her.

Do you feel upset as you read these women's stories? I do. They all have a distorted view of themselves and are blaming themselves for what is not their fault. Wyonna really has a great figure, but wishes she were as thin as fashion models, who are 23 percent leaner than the average woman. Phyllis, too, is of average weight. While she has put on a few pounds with the years, she looks fat only to herself. Janice is a striking woman, with large luminous eyes, beautiful skin, and a sexy voluptuousness, but when she looks at herself she sees only a hated mound. Her attempts to ward off her natural size by perpetual dieting have only served to make her fatter and hate herself more. Elaine has a warmth, vitality, and sense of humor that draws people to her, and she has never lacked for closeness or connections in her life, yet when it comes to her true attractiveness she can't see beyond her waistline.

In our weight-phobic culture, it is hard enough to have a body size that is considered overweight; it is even harder when you blame yourself and feel guilty. It's time we, whatever our size, let go of our guilt and proudly proclaim our right to our natural bodies in all their diversity.

Let go of your guilt now by accepting and believing that your fat is not your fault, any more than your bones are—it's just a natural part of your body. If you're still not convinced, read some of the academic articles cited in the end notes. Keep reading until you know once and for all that being fat is not your fault, nor is it under your control. The multinational corporations involved in the diet industry want you to blame yourself for being your weight, so they can grow rich off your doomed attempts to get thin or thinner. Sales of diet books, and weight-loss cassettes and videos have reached $203 to $215 million and are climbing. Don't let yourself be manipulated by an industry that promotes standards that require you to blame and hate yourself. Instead, combat guilt through the following affirmations.

Goodbye Guilt

Write out several times, in big letters, on a piece of oaktag or other thick paper:

I'M THE SIZE THAT MOTHER NATURE (or GOD) MADE
  ME.
I'M JUST THE SIZE THAT I'M SUPPOSED TO BE.
I AM A UNIQUELY BEAUTIFUL WOMAN.
I VALUE MY LOOKS AND MYSELF.

Leave these signs around your house where you can see them, in your pocketbook, and in a private spot at work. Put one where you will see it when you are dressing in the morning and undressing at night, and on your refrigerator. Start each day by reading these affirmations out loud, SLOWLY, with meaning, and pausing to take each in. Repeat them before and after each meal, before bedtime, and whenever else you start to feel bad about your weight.

Some of you may not want to leave these signs out in your home for fear of being made fun of. If the people with whom you live are critical of your weight, have a serious talk with them. Explain how your size is right for you, and ask for their support. Most people who truly care about you will be able to give it, though it may take several discussions (it's not easy to let go of prejudices).

Others of you may be living with a partner, parent, or other who is generally very critical not only of your weight but of you in general, and who cannot or refuses to be supportive. If so, it is important to realize that this censor comes from some problem this person has, and is not a true reflection of either what you truly look like or what your worth is. When living with this kind of hypercriticalness, it is especially important for you to support, encourage, and love yourself, and to refuse to accept these put-downs and cruelties as gospel. Protect yourself in whatever way feels best to you. For instance, you may wish to leave your signs where only you can see them, but be sure to read them several times a day, and to really take them to heart.

If you are noticeably fat and someone in public is rude enough (and too many people are) to criticize your size, the amount of food in your shopping cart, or what you are eating, think of these affirmations, and then respond with a comeback of your own choosing that you have prepared for just such an occasion. You may want to say simply, "This is my body and I like it." Or you can put the person on the defensive, by asking something along the lines of, "Are you always this rude and intrusive?" or (asked in a compassionate tone, which gives it more impact), "Do you have some sort of weight complex?" This comeback has the added advantage of reminding you that indeed the critic is the one with the problem. (There's a great T-shirt that says: "I don't have a weight problem. If my weight bothers you, you're the one with a weight problem.")

CARESSing Yourself

When you hate yourself for being fat, what's happening is that your inner critic is belittling your inner child, making her feel inadequate, deficient, ugly, depressed, unworthy, defeated—thus undermining your self-esteem and producing a negative self-image. To like yourself and the way you look, you need to get rid of this inner critical voice and amplify the voice of your inner caretaker. Your inner child needs to know—from *you*—that she isn't deficient if she is larger than the beauty ideal, and that you love all of her at just the size she is. Remember our discussion of unconditional love? Give your inner child the love and acceptance that she needs and deserves for just being her.

Using either the written or oral dialogue methods explained earlier in this chapter, have a nurturing dialogue between your inner caretaker and your inner child. Start by having your inner child say how she feels about her looks, and then have your inner caretaker respond by CARESSing her, by giving her compassion, acceptance, respect, encouragement, support, and stroking. Compassion for the pain she feels for being considered fat and therefore unattractive and unworthy. Acceptance of her as attractive and worthy. Respect for her as a person. Encouragement to face the world with pride. Support for the efforts you and she are making to appreciate yourself and your looks, and for her as a person. And Stroking. Physical stroking of your body as a way of affirming self-love and bodily pleasure, and emotional stroking—giving her and yourself much-deserved credit for your efforts to appreciate your looks and yourself, for all the pleasing aspects of your appearance, and for being the wonderful person you are. When you do this, you will be raising your self-esteem as well as learning to like the way that you look.

Wyonna, the twenty-two-year-old woman we met earlier in this chapter who at five six and 132 pounds felt like a tub of lard, normally had an inner dialogue that went like this:

> *Inner Critic:* You're too fat and you look disgusting.
> *Inner Child:* You're right. [Feels awful and ugly, and tries to disappear into the woodwork.]

Now Wyonna was determined to learn to accept and like her size, and love and support her inner child. Her new dialogue went like this:

> *Inner Child:* I feel fat and ugly.
>
> *Inner Caretaker:* I can understand your feeling that way [Compassion]. I know that after being called fat as much as you have by me, and after seeing all those pictures, magazines, movies, and ads that show and tell you that it is vital that you be very thin, you can't help feeling that way [Acceptance]. However, I'm starting to think that it's better to be whatever size is natural for us; and we are a nice size [Respect, Support], and I really like the way you look [Stroking].
>
> *Inner Child:* You do? That's a shock. You never told me that before.
>
> *Inner Caretaker:* I know. I was wrong. I was so caught up in what society was telling me was beautiful that I never really looked at you with open loving eyes. Now that I am, I see we really have a sexy, voluptuous body, and I like the softness and roundness of our body [Acceptance, Respect, Support, Stroking].
>
> *Inner Child:* You do? But you always told me you hated my body for being so fat.
>
> *Inner Caretaker:* I know, and I'm sorry. But things are different now. I love you, and I'm learning to love our body. Can you work with me on this?
>
> *Inner Child:* Sure. What do you want me to do?
>
> *Inner Caretaker:* Just tell me whenever you're feeling too fat, and I'll remind you you're not, and cheer you up by telling you how nice you look.
>
> *Inner Child:* Okay. But do you really think that I'm not too fat and look nice?
>
> *Inner Caretaker:* Uhmmmm, I'm learning to love our body, and I definitely love you and think you're great.
>
> *Inner Child:* (Smiles to herself and feels great.)

Remember, when you hate your body, you hate yourself. When you learn to unconditionally love your body, you are learning to love yourself, feel attractive, and build your self-esteem. Like Wyonna, you too can learn to accept and like your body and feel attractive when you CARESS your inner child. It works equally well at any size. Remember Janice, the thirty-eight-year-old woman who had been fat all her life and who at five seven and 250 pounds was so disgusted with herself that she even sometimes felt like dying? Here's her new dialogue.

Inner Child: I'm a whale and a freak. I know I look disgusting. People on the street are always staring at me when they think I'm not looking. When they do, I wish I could just drop through the sidewalk and disappear. Sometimes when I look at myself in the mirror, I feel so bad, I wish I were dead.

Inner Caretaker: You're really hurting. Some people have been very cruel to you. I really feel for your suffering [Compassion].

Inner Child: You do? You feel bad for me? But you've always told me that I disgust you.

Inner Caretaker: I know, and I'm sorry. I didn't understand before, but I do now. It's so hard to go through life blamed for something that is not in your control [Acceptance].

Inner Child: Not in my control?

Inner Caretaker: Of course not. You know you don't eat that much. And when you do binge, it's only because you diet so much, you constantly feel hungry and deprived.

Inner Child: I know, but everyone says I should be able to lose weight and keep it off, and that I just lack willpower and discipline.

Inner Caretaker: I think you have a lot of willpower and discipline. Look at how when things are tough at work or at home, you stick with it and don't give up till you've found a solution. And you saved money for a solid year, so much every week even though money is tight, so that you could go on that special vacation. And in general you're really organized and efficient [Respect, Support, Stroking].

Inner Child: Well, you're right about that, but what about my weight?

Inner Caretaker: As I said, that's biology and genetics. Some people are meant to be big. Anyway, I love your big body. It's so comfortable, and round, and soft, and womanly. It's also sexy [Acceptance, Stroking].

Inner Child: You can't mean that. You've always told me you hated my body.

Inner Caretaker: Not anymore. I realize I always looked at our body through society's eyes. It's like looking in a fun house mirror. Everything gets distorted. Who says thin is prettier than fat? In plenty of eras and societies women would love to be as fat as we are. We would be considered royalty, or maybe we would even have to put on some more weight before qualifying. Anyway, I like you, and I like the way you look [Acceptance, Support, Stroking].

Inner Child: I can't believe it! But it does feel very good to hear you say it.

Inner Caretaker: That's good because I am going to keep on saying it until you really do believe it [Encouragement]. And I'm going to keep on saying it after that, too, because I really am coming to see that beauty comes in all sizes, and I like the way you look [Acceptance, Support, Stroking].

Inner Child: Well, I don't know. I'm starting to feel a little better about how I look. Are you sure I don't disgust you?

Inner Caretaker: Yes. You're a great person and a fine size, and I love you and our body just the way we are.

As you can see from these dialogues, the more you give yourself unconditional love and approve of the way you look and CARESS yourself, the better you will feel about your size, your looks, and yourself. Also, you will come to feel like a "we" that is united in approval of how you look and who you are rather than remain caught in conflict and self-castigation. But remember, Rome wasn't built in a day. If you've hated your size and looks for some time, it is going to take time to build a more positive image, and in this process it is natural to take two or three steps forward and one step back. That's how change takes place. So don't get discouraged if your old habits of self-disparagement act up. Just do your best to nip them in the bud, recite your affirmations, and CARESS your inner child, giving her and your body unconditional love. When you do so, imagine that you are talking to the hurt, wounded part of you. In the beginning, the positive things you say to your inner child may feel forced, unnatural or ungenuine. That's okay. The more you keep it up and remain focused on giving yourself unconditional love and acceptance, the more natural and genuine they will become, and as they do, you will experience increased respect and liking for yourself and your looks.

AFFIRMING YOUR BEAUTY

Foster the growth of your inner caretaker by noticing whenever you start to have negative thoughts or feelings about your weight. (These are especially likely to emerge when viewing yourself in the mirror. Shortly, we will see how to improve your mirror image.) When such negative judgments arise, cut them off immediately. Remind yourself of the advantages to your size that you identified in "My Weight Is on My Side," and replace critical thoughts with positive messages, such as:

I am a good-looking woman.
I am just the size the Mother Nature (or God) made me, and
    I'm beautiful.
My body is attractive.
I like how I look.
I like my body and the pleasure it gives me (hugs, massages,
    sun bathing, hot baths, dancing, sports, exercise, sex,
    etc.).

I am a sexy and sensual woman.
I radiate attractiveness.
I am a uniquely beautiful woman.

BIG AND BEAUTIFUL (This exercise, while appropriate for any woman, is especially for decidedly fat women.)

Over 80 percent of traditional societies worldwide view fatness, and especially large hips and legs, as an ideal of feminine beauty. The Chinese associate fatness with prosperity and longevity, and their gods are always portrayed as fat. For a Punjabi Indian to greet you with "You look fat and fresh today" is a compliment. In the Arabic culture, thinness is regarded as socially undesirable while plumpness is symbolic of fertility and womanhood. In these cultures fatness symbolizes beauty. Now we are going to take a fantasy trip to one of these societies.

(See the Appendix for full visualization instructions.)

Get comfortable. Then close your eyes, and put your thumb and index finger together on each hand. Take a deep breath, deep into your diaphragm and abdomen, and hold it for five seconds, then gradually let it out to a slow count of five. Now, take five comfortable SLOW deep breaths, and when you finish, let your fingers open and continue breathing normally and comfortably. As you are breathing, in any way that is natural, let yourself become perhaps a little more peaceful, maybe a little more relaxed, letting go of tensions in any way that you know how, and going inside yourself to a lovely place of comfort and peace, or any other place that feels right to you.

As you are continuing to relax, imagine that you are visiting a lovely South Seas island. You walk down the street, and all around you are fat people. These fat people are walking, talking, laughing, flirting, just like people everywhere. The many very fat women you see carry themselves with grace and confidence, aware of their charm and desirability. You strike up a conversation with a group of people. If you're under 200 pounds, one of the men (or a woman, if you're a lesbian) tells you you are pretty, and could be really beautiful if only you put on some weight. If you're 200 pounds or more, he (or she) compliments you on your great body. In either case, he (or she) asks you to go with him (or her) to see some of the women dance in a secret ritual that tourists never see. You accept, and go.

The women dancers are all quite fat, and many are middle-aged or older. Your date explains that women are not allowed to do this very sexy and lascivious dance until they have reached this size because women have to be quite fat to be really sexy. The dance is truly amazing. It's the sexiest thing you have ever seen. As you watch these women express their sensuality and sexuality, they invite you, as a welcoming gesture to a visitor, to join them and you do, dancing along with them, glorying in the movement and the feel of your body and in your size.

The beat gets more frenetic, and you are carried along by the music, faster and faster, then slow, languid, sinuous, suggestive. You feel at one with your body, not knowing whether it is leading you or you are leading it, but it all feels fabulous, powerful, and beautiful. Then it is over and everyone is clapping, but you hardly hear. You are too busy listening to your inner voice which is telling you how attractive and sexy and beautiful, you are. Hear this voice now and take it in. Hear it telling you how sexy, sensuous, and beautiful you are. Listen to it praise your size, softness, roundness, and loveliness. Take it in and own the beauty that is you. Take your time. And while you're exalting in the sense of your own beauty, look around for a souvenir, something to take back with you as a reminder of your beauty. It might be the pulsation of the music, an abundantly lovely feather, a smooth round rock, an intricate seashell, a colorful necklace, the ample smiles of the women who danced, or anything else that feels right to you and that you would like to have with you. Then, when you find it, prepare to return home, knowing that whenever you want to be reminded of your own beauty, all you need do is to think of your souvenir, and the sense of your own beauty will come flooding back to you. And know, too, that you can return to this island, in your mind's eye, whenever you desire. So now take another minute or two to enjoy this warm, beautiful, wel-

*coming island, and your own beauty, then, when you're ready, open
your eyes and return to the room.*

How do you feel? What was it like to be in a place where people really admire fatness? Are you starting to believe that there is no
one intrinsically attractive size? Are you ready to start viewing your
body through more loving eyes? Know that this is just the beginning, and that you can go back to that South Seas island whenever
you want and enjoy having your size admired.

Visual Exercises

Now that you have started to make friends with your body
and to experience it as an instrument that gives you mobility and
pleasure, and you are working on ending guilty, self-blaming, and
demeaning thoughts and feelings and replacing them instead with
positive affirmations, you're ready to tackle what is for many
women the most difficult area of all: transforming your image in the
mirror.

Looking at ourselves in the mirror is a very loaded experience
for most women. Often we have a love/hate relationship with the
mirror. We may avoid full-length mirrors, or feel compelled to
constantly, or occasionally, check ourselves out. Frequently as the
image from the mirror bounces back to our eyes, it becomes distorted. We see our bodies not as they really are but with our perceived faults magnified. This is especially true of weight. As we saw
in Chapter 1, most women think they are fatter than they really are,
and very fat women often consider themselves to be monstrous. In
our society, the fatter a woman thinks she is, the uglier she is likely
to consider herself. To accept and love all of yourself, this has to
change. Rather than having the sight of yourself in the mirror turn
on the voice of your inner critic, you need to be able to look in the
mirror and experience approving thoughts and feeling. The following exercises, together with reciting your BEAUTIFUL ME list
whenever you look in the mirror, will help you to do so.

YOU'RE IDEAL

(See the Appendix for full visualization instructions.)

Get comfortable. Then close your eyes, and put your thumb and index finger together on each hand. Take a deep breath, deep into your diaphragm and abdomen, and hold it for five seconds, then gradually let it out to a slow count of five. Now, take five comfortable SLOW deep breaths, and when you finish, let your fingers open and continue breathing normally and comfortably. As you are breathing, in any way that is natural, let yourself become perhaps a little more peaceful, maybe a little more relaxed, letting go of tensions in any way that you know how, and going inside yourself to a lovely place of comfort and peace, or any other place that feels right to you.

As you are continuing to relax, you may want to imagine yourself floating on a cloud on a beautiful warm day, drifting along, slowly, gently, peacefully. Enjoying the good feeling of calming, effortless floating. And after a while you may find your cloud starting to gently float down, until it lands at a very beautiful, safe, lovely, and peaceful spot. It might be an inviting beach, a charming meadow, a captivating mountain, an elegant luxury house, or any other place that you find beautiful and peaceful, with the weather just the way you like it. Take your time to look around and explore this spot, absorbing its unique beauty and specialness. Be aware of all the ways your senses are taking in and responding to its beauty; what you are seeing, feeling, hearing, smelling, maybe even tasting. You may want to find a comfortable place to sit as you take in all this beauty and peacefulness.

While you're there appreciating and absorbing the wonder of this very special, very beautiful place, imagine that your shape and size are the new model of feminine beauty, and that all women want a body just like yours. You're proud of your body and the way it looks. You're sexy, sensual, enticing, captivating, beautiful. Admire yourself. Look at and take in all the things you like about your appearance, all the ways in which you are truly attractive. Stay with this image, and take in the good feeling of appreciating your looks and yourself. Let yourself know that you can carry this pride in your body and your looks with you always, anchored in your attractiveness, filled with liking and appreciation of yourself. Really enjoy and anchor that good, approving feeling. Then, whenever you are ready, turn away from the mirror and focus once more on that special, beautiful place where your cloud landed. Take your time and enjoy the peace, safety, beauty, and contentment of this place, so attractive to the eye, and so pleasing to you. Stay there as long as you like: then, whenever you are ready, open your eyes and come back to the room.

Now immediately go to a full-length mirror, imagining still that your shape and size are the new model of feminine beauty. Admire yourself, reminding yourself that every part of you is attractive, and that your size is especially captivating. Keep looking at yourself while saying to yourself: "This is what I look like, and I like it." "This is what I look like, and I'm a uniquely attractive woman." If your inner critic starts to speak up, hush her and call forth your inner caretaker. Tell yourself that this is you, and that you accept and love your body and yourself and like the way that you look. To help yourself internalize these positive feelings about you and your looks, end by saying your affirmations slowly out loud.

I am good-looking.
I am the size that is right for me.
I like how I look.
I like my body and the pleasure it gives me.
I am a sexy and sensual woman.
I radiate attractiveness.
I am a uniquely beautiful woman.

BEHOLDING YOUR BEAUTY I

This is another mirror exercise. After slowly reading out loud your BEAUTIFUL ME list, look in the mirror with your clothes on, focusing on the things about your appearance that you find attractive while ignoring your size. Let the parts of your appearance that please you grow in importance until they rivet your attention and dominate your view of yourself. Really take them in and admire them. Keep looking in the mirror and focusing on these attractive aspects of your appearance. Spend a while just admiring yourself.

Then allow your size to drift into your awareness and say something positive to yourself about it (for instance, I look soft and cuddly, or round and welcoming). Let your size enter into your feelings of appreciation of your looks. Continue to admire yourself while reminding yourself that you are just the size you are meant to be at this moment, and that there is a true beauty to being this size. If critical or shameful thoughts and feelings keep popping up, that's only to be expected. It's going to take some practice to look at yourself through approving and loving eyes. Keep nipping those disparaging thoughts and feelings in the bud, and go back to focusing on what you like about your appearance, letting those parts become more compelling in your eyes. Your aim is to let your size become just one aspect of your appearance, knowing that it is the right size for you at this moment, and that it is part of your natural beauty. After you have spent a while looking at your body in this way, end by telling the you in the mirror:

> I am a good-looking woman.
> I am the size that is right for me.
> I like how I look.
> I like my body and the pleasure it gives me.
> I am a sexy and sensual woman.
> I radiate attractiveness.
> I am a uniquely beautiful woman.

Repeat these affirmations whenever you look at yourself in a mirror, and do the mirror exercise daily for at least two months, and then whenever you need it. When critical thoughts pop up, silence them and replace them with appreciative comments and affirmations. As you do it, remember that change takes place slowly, with ups and downs. Don't get discouraged if you find yourself hating your size—old habits take time to break. Give yourself credit for trying, and keep at it. Encourage yourself by reminding yourself that you can learn to love your body and view your size positively.

BEHOLDING YOUR BEAUTY II (OPTIONAL)

When you are able to look in the mirror and feel comfortable with your image, if you wish, start doing the same exercise naked. Don't be surprised, if, as you do so, that the old feelings of body hate surge up at first. With practice they will fade and new feelings of body acceptance and liking will take their place. Some women find that learning to like their naked bodies really increases their self-acceptance and self-approval. Others find that it is too difficult to silence the voice of their inner critics, so prefer to skip this one. Listen to your own inner sense and do what feels right to you.

BEING PROUD OF YOUR SIZE

Now that you are starting to feel better about your weight, it is time to set straight all the people in your life who have ever made you feel diminished or unworthy because of your fleshiness. If you are fat, you may have a list that goes back a lifetime and includes family, friends, mates, strangers, coworkers, and a host of others. Even if you really are of normal size or thinner, you might have had family members or others who either told you directly or conveyed the impression that you were too fat, implying that this was a major failing. For some of you, the only one who ever called you fat is your inner critic, that inner voice you carry around with you that continually criticizes you and tells you that you don't measure up, that you are fat, ugly, and unworthly. Take advantage of the following exercise to experience how much better and more attractive you feel when you stand up to this debilitating inner voice and your original critics and assert your value and attractiveness.

In Chapter 5 you identified who taught you to dislike your looks. Take out your ORIGINAL CRITICS list, and remind yourself who in your family taught you to feel bad about your size. Add to this list other adults or peers who have made you feel fat and unattractive. Then do the following exercise.

(See the Appendix for full visualization instructions.)

Get comfortable. Then close your eyes, and put your thumb and index finger together on each hand. Take a deep breath, deep into your diaphragm and abdomen, and hold it for five seconds, then gradually let it out to a slow count of five. Now, take five comfortable SLOW deep breaths, and when you finish, let your fingers open and continue breathing normally and comfortably. As you are breathing, in any way that is natural, let yourself become perhaps a little more peaceful, maybe a little more relaxed, letting go of tensions in any way that you know how, and going inside yourself to a lovely place of comfort and peace, or any other place that feels right to you.

As you continue to relax, imagine that you are standing at the podium onstage in a large auditorium—feeling calm, confident, at ease, and looking great at your present size. The hall is full, and scattered among the people in the first ten rows are your inner critic and all the people in your life who have berated your size (even if some of them are, in fact, now deceased). They, like the rest of the audience, have all paid money to hear you talk, as you are an expert in the hot new movement: size acceptance. Visualize yourself telling them the real facts of body size: that the amount and distribution of body fat is largely genetically determined; that fat people don't eat any more than thin people; that the fat, rather than being neurotic and dysfunctional, are at least as mentally healthy as everyone else; and that beauty comes in all sizes.

Tell them, too, how much some people in the audience have hurt you, and made you hate yourself, by blaming you for something that is not your fault and by leading you to believe that you are unattractive. Name names and express whatever feelings you may have: anger, resentment, sadness, or any other emotion. Let the audience know that you are glad these people are here today, and you certainly hope they are going to start to change their attitudes and realize that people naturally come in many different sizes, and that no one size is inherently superior or more attractive than another, but that, in any case, you have changed yours. You now realize that size has nothing to do with beauty, that women of all sizes can be beautiful in their own unique ways, and that you have learned to appreciate your own appearance, and to love your body, your looks, and yourself at your current size. Tell them that you know that your true value and attractiveness have nothing to do *with your weight, and that you no longer hang your self-image on, or measure your worth by, something as irrelevant as the amount of fat tissue your body requires. Tell them that you are proud of the way you look, proud of your body, and proud of yourself.*

When you are finished speaking, almost all of the audience cheers wildly. Others look dubious or upset. Many ask for your autograph, others quickly leave. You enjoy the appreciation of those who support you and may be distressed or saddened by those who don't, but most of all you feel glad that you appreciate yourself and are determined to continue doing so. Feel how good it is to have yourself in your corner accepting you, liking you, praising you, and loving you and the way you look. Stay with this good feeling for as long as you like. Then, when you're ready, open your eyes and come back to the room.

How do you feel? Isn't it great to set straight all the people who have criticized your weight or put you down? When you assert your value and attractiveness, independent of your weight, you are not only standing up to others, but you are also helping to transform your inner critic to an inner caretaker who approves of and nurtures you.

FITTING CLOTHES

Do you have clothes in various sizes in your closet that you're hanging on to because you hope one day to fit back into them? Do you put off shopping for more than the bare essentials, not wanting to buy clothes in a size you hope will soon be too large for you? Are you afraid that buying clothes in your proper size means that you will continue to gain weight? Do you feel that at your weight there is no point in even trying to look good, so you wear the same few outfits all the time? If you answered yes to any of these questions, you're treating yourself like a second-class citizen. This approach will not help you love your body or like the way you look.

When you wear clothes you consider pretty, you feel more attractive. It's like silently proclaiming to yourself and the world that you are a worthwhile and attractive person, that you have a worthwhile and attractive body, and that you are going to clothe it the way pretty bodies should be clothed. I don't mean that you have to go high fashion or spend big bucks. But don't shortchange yourself, either. Keep clothes in your closet for this body, not some other body, past or hoped for. You wouldn't adopt a child and then give her clothes that don't fit her. Don't do this to yourself either. Get rid of the clothes that don't fit you and, within comfortable limits of your finances, buy clothes that you feel comfortable and pretty in.

Sally, a middle-aged woman who has been fat all her life, dresses in a way that is inspirational to me. Whether she has on leisure or business clothes, she always looks great. She has great color sense and mixes and matches things with great flair. When I first gave up dieting and was struggling with liking my new size, whenever I felt too fat to look good, I always thought of Sally, who always looks fabulous. I told myself that if she could dress so well and look so good, even though I don't have her flair, there was no reason I couldn't also dress well and look good. And so can you.

GETTING OFF THE DIET TREADMILL

Last, to really love all of you, it is important to stop dieting. It is difficult to accept your size while dieting, because the very act of dieting says that the size you are now is not good enough. Now, I know that if you're a dieter, whether you're a size six or twenty-six, that the idea of giving up dieting can be a very scary thought. It was to me, too. Despite all the evidence that dieting doesn't work and only leads to weight gain, you may be petrified that if you stop dieting you will become fat or fatter. After having put so much energy into trying to be or stay thin, you may not want to risk gaining even five pounds. If so, that's fine. It's important that you listen to yourself and do what's right for you. For a small minority of you, restrained eating as a way of life may even enable you to keep your weight down without yo-yoing. If this is the case for you, fine. However, as we have seen, it is not the case for most women. For most of us dieting leads not only to regained weight and added fatness, but also to lower self-esteem and less success. When we inevitably regain lost weight, we feel defeated, dejected—a failure. Thus dieting, rather than bringing us the elusive power and success we imagine accompany thinness, really serves to undermine our belief in our own worth and diminishes the confidence we need to pursue and achieve the things we want in life.

While it is beyond the scope of this book to go into the process of eating naturally in detail, the approach is really quite simple. EAT WHAT YOU WANT WHEN YOU WANT IT. STOP WHEN YOU FEEL FULLY SATISFIED, BUT NOT STUFFED. When you do, after a while you will stop bingeing and be able to eat whatever you want while maintaining a stable weight.

This may sound incredible, even impossible, but it's not. When you start to live in a world of plenty instead of in a constant state of deprivation, what you want and what your body needs change. Eventually your appetite, your metabolism, and whatever exercise you may or may not do enter into a natural harmony and balance, and you stop desiring more than you really need so you no longer feel tempted to binge. (A lifelong ice-cream addict, I was incapable most of my life of keeping any amount of ice cream in my fridge without finishing it within a day or at maximum two. Now, to my amazement, ice cream can sit in my fridge for weeks.)

Remember all those times you said you would give anything to be able to eat whatever you wanted without gaining weight? Well, you can when you recognize that what's really beautiful is to be the size you are meant to be, which is probably not that much larger than you are now, may well be smaller, and certainly isn't as large as you are likely to become if you continue to diet. No, this balance won't be established immediately. Your metabolism needs time to revert to its normal levels. Your body needs to be convinced that the famine is permanently over before it stops wanting you to eat as much as you can, especially of rich foods as the conscientious objectors did. This may take a year or more depending on how strictly and chronically you've been dieting, but eventually it will happen. Then you will discover that your food desires exactly match your body's needs, so you can easily and effortlessly maintain the weight that is best for you. Many of you will find yourselves eventually losing weight when you stop bingeing and dieting. Others of you may stay the same or level off at a somewhat higher weight. In any case, you will discover how much better you feel when you listen to your body and eat with pleasure and without guilt. Equally important, when you accept your weight as a natural part of you, it is much easier to really love your looks and yourself.

It's true that when I gave up dieting I went up a dress size or two (I can't remember exactly where on the seesaw I was when I stopped dieting) before leveling off, but remember, I have significant indicators of a genetically somewhat high setpoint: I was fat as a kid; had two large and wonderful grandmothers as well as other assorted fat relatives; I undoubtedly raised my setpoint by yo-yo dieting for thirty-five years; and I gave up dieting just at the beginning of menopause, a time when women naturally put on weight. You probably don't have all these factors that contribute to weight gain. But even if you do, let me assure you that at my present size, I feel better about myself and my looks than I ever did in all those years when I stayed at or around a size ten by going on one crazy diet after another.

When you feed yourself well, you are treating yourself like a respected, deserving, and honored person, and you will start to feel like one. Your life will also become freer when it no longer revolves around food and dieting, and you will discover new time and energy for pursuing the things that really matter to you. (It's been amazing to me, as I've been writing this book, how little time I have frittered away snacking. It's not that I've stopped myself. Rather—incredibly for me whose almost every waking, and often dreaming, thought revolved around food for thirty-five years—I just haven't felt much like noshing.) I hope you'll consider giving up dieting and put your energies instead into accepting and loving your body and yourself and enlarging your life. (For more information on eating naturally, see Recommended Readings.)

LIFE'S PROMISE

Promise yourself to never again avoid anyone or anything because you think you are too fat. We saw earlier that being young and thin doesn't necessarily bring riches or happiness. Ironically, when you give up the search for the magic amount of thinness that will transform you into a beauty with the world at your feet and decide instead that how you look is just fine, then some of what you want in life becomes more accessible. That is because self-acceptance is empowering—it gives you the confidence to go after what you want and the self-assurance that other people find so attractive. *Give yourself this kind of acceptance now. Stop telling yourself that you'll go after your heart's desires after you've lost weight, and instead encourage yourself to pursue whatever you want at your current size.* Remember, to get what you want out of life, you need to pursue it. Promise yourself to never again avoid applying for a job or other opportunity, or to miss out on a reunion or other social event because you fear others' judgments of your weight. Remember, size oppression is about constricting and controlling women. Don't let society do this to you. Remind yourself that you're a worthy person and deserve respect and success. Take control of your life and go wherever and after whatever you want.

JOIN THE SIZE-ACCEPTANCE MOVEMENT

More and more women (and men) are banding together to fight size discrimination. When you join with them, whatever your size, you are standing up to demand that your worth and beauty no longer be judged by the circumference of your body. You dare to say that it is okay for women to be substantial and powerful, rather than frail and helpless, and that women (and men) should look the wide range of ways we were born to look, rather than trying to squeeze ourselves into a hampering, narrow mold.

NAAFA, the National Association to Advance Fat Acceptance, is a national organization that is spearheading size acceptance. It works to end size discrimination and to empower fat people. Whatever your size, I urge you to add your voice to those fighting to liberate women from fat oppression. (See Resources.)

BREASTS, THIGHS, HIPS, STOMACHS, LEGS, AND OTHER BODY PARTS

Grace is of average weight and height, with a sexy, curvaceous body, but she hates it. She can't stand her "pendulous" breasts, "big" hips, "fat" stomach, "wide" thighs, "refrigerator door" rear, and "unshapely" legs. Whenever she looks in the mirror, these "flaws" jump out at her, and she gets a sick feeling in her stomach. She would give anything for a different body, "just so I could feel better about myself. I'd like to look in the mirror and feel proud of my body and myself, instead of sick."

Samantha, with a straight, thin figure, looks very different than Grace, but similarly hates her body. She feels very self-conscious about having small breasts and feels that there is no way she can be attractive when she is so flat-chested. She is so unhappy with her bra size that before the dangers of breast implants became widely known she was seriously considering having the surgery. Now she feels consigned to a life of being unattractive. She also hates the size of her thighs and stomach, which she imagines to be too big, and, of course, feels fat.

Julie also hates her body. She is moderately fat and can't stand the fullness of her stomach, hips, thighs, legs, and arms, and views each of these parts as tremendous and ugly.

Almost every woman, like Grace, Samantha, and Julie, have spent years critically examining her body, focusing on what she considers to be her trouble spots. The more she longs for a certain part of her body to be different, the larger significance this part takes on for her. After a while she sees only her "too small" breasts, "large thighs," or the fullness of her behind. She may dress to obscure her self-perceived faults, but she still imagines that others view her body in the same distorted way she does.

Does this sound familiar to you? Are there parts of your body that really bother you, that you would love to trade in for improved models? Do you feel that there is no way you could ever like your body with its big butt, small or large breasts, full stomach, wide hips, or full thighs? When you look in the mirror or think about your body, do your "wide" thighs, for example, jump out at you, obliterating everything else? When you're feeling good about yourself, does just thinking about those thighs take some of the wind out of your sails? And when you're feeling down, does looking in the mirror really push you over the edge? If so, you're a normal woman, experiencing the effect of living in a culture where women are encouraged to look at their bodies through a critical magnifying glass. Unlike men, we're encouraged to view each area of our bodies as vital to the measure of our worth. What do you think it would be like if we looked at men through the same magnifying glass? Let's see.

THROUGH THE MAGNIFYING GLASS

Make a list of at least five men you know who you think are good-looking. (Don't use movie or TV stars or other public figures.)

Rate each man on your list on a scale from 1 to 10, with 10 being the most attractive, on the following body parts:

Stomach (flatness, firmness)
Chest (broadness, hairiness, muscularity)
Waist (definition)
Triangular upper body (How closely does he match this ideal?)
Shoulders (broadness and muscularity)
Neck (length, thickness)
Arms (large, clearly defined muscles)
Chin (squareness)
Fingers (shape and especially length—you know what they say!)
Neck (tautness, length, size of Adam's apple)
Thighs (firmness, defined muscles, narrowness)
Hips (slimness, straightness)
Butt (fullness, shapeliness)
Legs (length, strength, form, shape)
Overall muscularity and body tone (a hard, solid look)

As you appraise the men on your list, really focus in on each of these body parts, and be sure to notice any flaws. It's important to be accurate, so, if possible, don't fill this list out from memory, which is usually hazy. Observe each man as closely as you can without changing the nature of your relationship with him. Some of these areas may be hard to judge on men you see only in a suit, but do the best you can and make every effort to be accurate. When you're done, you will have a chart that looks like this:

Body Parts	Michael	Bob
Stomach	9	6
Chest	8	5
Waist	8	5
Triangle shape	8	5
Shoulders	8	6
Neck	4	7
Arms	7	5
Chin	8	4
Fingers	3	9
Thighs	3	6
Hips	7	8
Butt	6	9
Legs	3	7
Muscles/Body tone	8	5
Average Score	6.4	6.2

How did you like doing this exercise? Did you have fun? Did you find it a pleasure to be the one doing the evaluating and rating, rather than being constantly focused on how others are viewing or judging you? Did you learn something from it? Did you notice that all this focusing on body parts is really beside the point? Michael has a well-developed upper body, but his spindly legs, fat stubby fingers, and so-so butt brought his rating down below 7. Bob is just the opposite. His thin upper body is not muscular, but he has a graceful neck, long tapering fingers, slim hips, shapely legs, and a great butt. He, too, averaged out around 6. In reality, these body part ratings have little to do with either of these men's real attractiveness. Many women find both of them attractive and desirable. That's because attractiveness is much more than the sum of body parts, and beauty is indeed in the eye of the beholder. Personality and self-esteem help a lot, too. Bob, for instance, is charming, fun, and has a wonderful twinkle in his eye, while Michael is caring, sensitive, and sincere.

Well, you may be thinking, men's body parts may not matter that much, but straight women's do, because while women care about personality and character, men are much more into looks, and are much more influenced by them. Well, think again. Yale University psychologist Alan Feingold did a metaanalysis of studies exploring the connection between physical attractiveness and romantic popularity and discovered that while looks are more important to men than to women, the differences are slight.

While it's true that some men are supercritical of every aspect of a woman's body, these men are not the ones you want to be with. A man like this is either narcissistic and needs you to meet his criteria for "beautiful" in order to feed his ego, or else he's just a supercritical person in general. In either case, it's a no-win situation. He'll never be able to appreciate you for yourself. However, men like this are not the rule. In fact, many men are much more accepting and appreciative of various aspects of their wives' or girlfriends' bodies than the women are themselves. That's because women expect to be judged by the standard they see held up around them—the superthin, airbrushed, computer-altered model—so that's how they judge themselves. Men, too, are influenced by this ideal, but can and do recognize that there's a lot more to a woman than how she looks.

Sue Browder, writing in *New Woman*, reports that when she asked dozens of sweet, caring, largely successful men "What about a woman really, really turns you on?" they almost never mentioned "notions of physical perfection." What these men found sexually attractive was "the woman as a whole person . . . her individuality . . . a quiet confidence that makes her comfortable to be around . . . intelligence," and most of all a woman "with whom they could share 'easy conversation.'" As for women's body parts, some of the men's comments included: "There's no such thing as the wrong size breast," saddlebags [mounds of flesh on the side of a woman's thighs] are "cute," and nose jobs a waste ("Why would any woman want to look ordinary when she can look like Barbra Streisand?"). Moreover, they said that they didn't notice when a woman gained an extra ten pounds.

More often than we realize, it is not others but ourselves who view our bodies through a magnifying glass. Let's see how we can take ourselves out from under the microscope and view our bodies as good enough rather than demanding perfection.

Being Whole

Choose a part of your body that you dislike.
(See the Appendix for full relaxation instructions.]

Get comfortable. Then close your eyes, and put your thumb and index finger together on each hand. Take a deep breath, deep into your diaphragm and abdomen, and hold it for five seconds, then gradually let it out to a slow count of five. Now, take five comfortable SLOW deep breaths, and when you finish, let your fingers open, and continue breathing normally and comfortably. As you are breathing, in any way that is natural, let yourself become perhaps a little more peaceful, maybe a little more relaxed, letting go of tensions in any way that you know how, and going inside yourself to a lovely place of comfort and peace, or any other place that feels right to you.

As you are continuing to relax, focus on the part of your body that you chose. Imagine this part growing and growing until it becomes gigantic and encompasses all of you, leaving the rest of you squeezed into a small area. Stay with this image and fully see and feel what it is like to be this shape. What it is like for almost all your body to be only, say, your love handles, or your stomach, or your hips, or your thighs, or your breasts, or any other part of your body? How do you look in the mirror? What is it like to move? Imagine this part growing even larger, and larger, and larger. Then suddenly collapse it, like letting the air out of a balloon, and see it quickly return to its normal size. Regard your body now at your normal size, and take it in. See how little room this part really takes up in your body, how small a part it is of the whole that is you, how tiny a piece of your body it is. Let yourself realize that it is wholly wonderful to be you, and that what really matters is not this part or that, but the whole way you look in your entirety, which really is unique and attractive. Let yourself entirely embrace who you are and how you look. Keep looking at yourself and taking in your attractiveness. Then, when you're ready, open your eyes and return to the room.

How do you feel? What did you experience? Does this body part now take up less room in your self-image? Are you able to feel that it's only a small portion of you, and not all of you? The more you do this exercise, the easier it will become and the less significance you will place on each body part. Repeat this exercise for each part of your body that you don't like, and let yourself really enjoy what you look like when you return to your normal size. Come back to this exercise whenever you are bothered by a particular part of your body.

SAME PARTS/DIFFERENT LOOKS

Now that you've started to see your body as a whole, rather than just as, say, your big hips, it's time to get a more realistic view of those hips, or any other body part that you are troubled by. List the parts of your body you don't like. Then look around for as many women as you can find who have at least one body part that matches one of your disliked parts. For example, if you dislike your hips, breasts, and stomach, see how many women you can find with the same shape and size hips, breasts, or stomach as you. One woman doesn't have to have all three or even two. It's fine to match each part separately. Be careful, though. Very likely you see your part as larger than or shaped differently from its reality. To match yourself realistically, it's best to take a companion along. Look at women everywhere: on the street, in the supermarket, waiting in line, at work, on the beach, and anywhere else you go. When you find a woman with a body part that matches yours, look at the whole woman and make a point of noticing how she appears in her entirety.

It should be easy to find many women with similar-size or -shaped body parts. After a while it should become clear to you that though these women all have the same size hips, or thighs, or breasts, or stomach as you, they all look vastly different from one another. There is a wide variety of ways women with similar-size individual parts look. If it's true for them, it's true for you, too. Your beauty does not rest on any one, two, or three body parts.

Now You See it—Now You Don't

Here's another exercise that will help you to accept and enjoy your body parts. Get out your BEAUTIFUL ME list. Hopefully, you've been reading it at least a couple of times a day, so it's close at hand. Read it slowly out loud. Then single out one part of your body that you want to increase your appreciation of. Next:

(See the Appendix for full relaxation instructions.)

Get comfortable. Then close your eyes, and put your thumb and index finger together on each hand. Take a deep breath, deep into your diaphragm and abdomen, and hold it for five seconds, then gradually let it out to a slow count of five. Now, take five comfortable SLOW deep breaths, and when you finish, let your fingers open, and continue breathing normally and comfortably. As you are breathing, in any way that is natural, let yourself become perhaps a little more peaceful, maybe a little more relaxed, letting go of tensions in any way that you know how, and going inside yourself to a lovely place of comfort and peace, or any other place that feels right to you.

As you're continuing to relax, visualize the parts of your body you like the most, all the things on your BEAUTIFUL ME list, and take them in. Allow yourself to experience the good feeling of liking and appreciating how you look, letting these good feelings grow and spread out, like the sun extending its warmth over your body, warming you, making you happy, and bringing a smile to your face. And as you take in the sun's warmth, you may find yourself suffused with a liking for your body and yourself. Perhaps you may even feel a new sense of confidence in your attractiveness, or maybe you are finding your own special and unique way to acknowledge and feel your beauty, or perhaps you are anchoring yourself in the certainty of knowing that how you look is attractive and right for you. Whatever you feel, you know you can go deeper within yourself, in whatever way is right for you, to a place of safety, peace, and beauty. Stay there in this peaceful and beautiful place, then briefly flash on the part of your body you chose to single out, returning almost immediately to what you like about your looks. Now amplify that feeling of liking how you look. Focus even more deeply on each aspect of your

*appearance that you appreciate, and imagine yourself flaunting
each of these attributes a little. You may flip your hair, put your
hands on your waist, twinkle your eyes, smile more broadly, sway
your hips, or do whatever else makes you feel good about yourself.
Allow yourself to fully and deeply appreciate and enjoy your attractiveness, then flash again quickly on your chosen part and return almost immediately to the aspects of your looks that you like. Keep
repeating this exercise, switching back and forth, each time allowing your chosen part to fade more and more into the background, as
you experience how good you really can feel when you focus on the
many ways in which you are attractive and beautiful. Continue
switching back and forth in this manner, each time recognizing even
more how attractive you really are. Then, when you are ready, open
your eyes and return to the room.*

Repeat this exercise for each part of your body that you dislike, and do it at least twice a week for a few weeks or months. You
are training yourself to associate body parts you are presently troubled by with positive feelings about your body and your looks. You
are also learning how to counteract any negative thoughts and feelings you have about certain parts of your body, and how to immediately replace them with positive thoughts and feelings. Whenever
you look in the mirror, center on what you like about your body. If
you feel drawn to focus on trouble spots, tell yourself to put away
your magnifying glass. Then concentrate again on what you like
about your appearance. As you do this, over time, you will feel better and better about how you look.

Welcome to Our Family

In the previous exercise you learned how to associate disliked
parts of your body with good feelings about your looks. Now you
are going to go one step further and develop positive feelings toward the body parts themselves.

(See the Appendix for full relaxation instructions.)

*Get comfortable. Then close your eyes, and put your thumb
and index finger together on each hand. Take a deep breath, deep*

into your diaphragm and abdomen, and hold it for five seconds, then gradually let it out to a slow count of five. Now, take five comfortable SLOW deep breaths, and when you finish, let your fingers open, and continue breathing normally and comfortably. As you are breathing, in any way that is natural, let yourself become perhaps a little more peaceful, maybe a little more relaxed, letting go of tensions in any way that you know how, and going inside yourself to a lovely place of comfort and peace, or any other place that feels right to you.

As you are continuing to relax, imagine that your body is a loving family, and your disliked body parts, whether your hips, stomach, thighs, or other body part, have been rejected and abandoned by this family for not projecting the right image. This family has been getting healthier, warmer, and more loving, and now it wants to bring your hips, stomach, breasts, thighs, rear, legs, or other disliked and rejected body parts back into the warmth and acceptance of the family circle. Imagine your body welcoming these parts back with love and comfort. Imagine the family apologizing to the formerly rejected body parts for picking on them, disliking them, and forsaking them. Imagine your body asking for their forgiveness. Hear your body tell each body part that it will never again reject it, and that you have enough love in your heart for every part of you. See the glad smiles of each part as it individually accepts this comfort and love. Promise each body part that you will continue to love and accept it for the rest of your life, no matter what. Imagine embracing each of these body parts, in turn, as it snuggles happily in your arms. Promise yourself that you will always love all of you, enjoying the good feeling of loving and being loved. Stay with that good feeling of loving and being loved for as long as you like. Then, when you are ready, open your eyes and come back to the room.

How do you feel? Did you experience what a difference it makes to your well-being and self-esteem when you accept and love your body just as it is? When you do, you are making room in your heart for not only your body but also for yourself. The more you love your body unconditionally, the more you will like the way you look and yourself as a whole, whatever your size or shape.

P.S. I LOVE YOU:

Write a love letter (or poem if you like) to each body part you formerly disliked, telling it what you like and love about it. In doing so, force yourself to find positives. Think of this body part as your child that you are determined to love unconditionally, and express that love. Here are a few samples. The poems are not by workshop participants. The first is by my friend, poet Anne Sadowski-Cassidy. The second is by poet Lucille Clifton, and is reprinted from *two-headed woman*.

Space to Store

Moon round
and just as full.
Life-giving carrier of two
now as tall as me.

Maternal still,
and soft like a pillow.
My center,
their resting place,
comfortable in the role
and loose clothing.

We share snacks and secrets
Some
as old as the earth,
some that hurt.

Hungry too often,
scarred three times,
missing three parts.
Awkward uncovered,
yet loved
in its fullness—

This belly—
my center—

space to store
life's sweets and sadness.

homage to my hips

these hips are big hips
they need space to
move around in.
they don't fit into little
pretty places. these hips
are free hips.
they don't like to be held back.
these hips have never been enslaved,
they go where they want to go
they do what they want to do.
these hips are mighty hips.
these hips are magic hips.
i have known them
to put a spell on a man and
spin him like a top!

Dear Stomach,

I love you. You're so big and round and full: big with desire and ambition, round with knowledge and experience, full with satisfaction. Your fullness and roundness reminds me of the fullness of my experience and the roundness of my life. I'm proud of myself for being willing to try different things, being open to all kinds of experiences, being able to connect with many different kinds of people. I'm also soft and warm, as you are, and with inner strength. There are a lot of things and experiences that we have digested together— some to our taste, some not to our liking, some really painful and difficult. But through it all, we've persevered, growing and expanding, becoming the full person we are—willing and happy to take up more space in the world, to expand our desires, to take risks, to digest whatever life serves us, and then to go on for more. I'm sorry for all the times I hated you and turned away. I truly love you.

Dear Breasts,

I love you. Well, at least I'm learning to love you. It's not easy after having hated you since I was sixteen, when I realized that you were never going to grow and become a normal size, let alone big and sexy. But I really want to accept and like myself, and when I think of you as a person, or as a part of me, I realize how much you must be hurting from having been hated so much by me, and I want to hug you and make you feel better. I feel for all the pain you have gone through, being teased by those hateful boys in school, and admire how you and I have kept struggling to feel good about ourselves.

I love you for being you. Your nipples are pretty and sensitive, and the tiny bit of fullness you have projects a hint of my inner lushness and sensuality. You also remind me of my courageousness, how I don't let people or things keep me down. From now on whenever I think of you I'm going to think of how I'm both strong and sensuous. Much love.

Dear Stomach,

I love you. On my mostly spare, lean body, you're the womanly part of me. Your roundness and fullness proclaims to the world that I am a woman with all the sexuality and lushness and roundness that makes women women. In my frenetic, often overscheduled life, you represent the "ease," the letting go part of me. I'm no longer going to suck you in, try to make you disappear. I like being a woman, and I love you for being the most visibly womanly part of me.

Dear Thighs,

I love you. Your strength gives me power. I like to think of you down there on my legs holding me up, giving me energy, protecting my sexual parts when they need protecting, and opening them up when I wish. When I hate getting up in the morning, you're there to help give me a push, and when I'm afraid to go toward something I want in life, it helps to know that you're ready to stride along. Your wideness enlarges my life. Keep on trucking, and much love.

Do you get the idea? Don't worry too much about what to say. Just start with "I love you" and keep writing until you feel done. Then add your new positive feelings about these body parts to your BEAUTIFUL ME list. Keep your love letters and read them every few days for a month or two or longer, until your loving feelings toward these body parts become increasingly integrated, and continue reading your BEAUTIFUL ME list at least twice a day.

TENDER LOVING CARE:

Now that you are starting to love your body and your looks, remember that it is important to treat your body like someone you unconditionally love. Stop picking at and criticizing it, and instead speak kindly and lovingly to it. Give it positive attention and praise, and continually let your body, and every part of it, know that you love it just the way it is. And, from time to time, give it a gentle, loving massage.

Bathe or shower, then stroke your naked dry body with warm lotion, concentrating on your bodily sensations. As you stroke the parts of your body that you have only recently learned to love, think loving, accepting thoughts, such as Hips, you're so big and powerful, whenever I look at you I feel powerful and capable. I'm glad you're part of my body. Even if this seems a little syrupy or ungenuine, do it with conviction. Remember, you are learning to develop a loving attitude toward your body, and it takes practice. What starts off as an exercise will in time become integrated into new feelings about your body. As you gently massage yourself, go slowly, really taking your time and absorbing all those good feelings. End by taking conscious note of the pleasure your body gave you and thank it. Promise every part of your body that from now on you will be its admirer and protector, just as a loving parent would be.

 POSITIVE AGING

I used to hate my wrinkles. I thought they made me ugly. Now I see them as signs of my life experience and wisdom, and they're beautiful to me.

Jean, age 78

In our youth- and beauty-oriented culture, aging is greatly feared by some women not so much because of the threat of diminished stamina and agility, but because they dread losing their looks and the status that looks confer. Many women go to great lengths to appear as young as possible. Yet the signs of aging can be staved off for only so long. At eighty, you just can't look like you're twenty-five.

Women's fear of aging is fueled by the media's depiction (or lack thereof) of aging women. The sad fact is that in Hollywood and on TV there is little room, status, or respect for middle-aged and older women. Men, on the other hand, are often considered to be quite attractive as they age. Robert Redford, Sean Connery, and Paul Newman are a few examples of men we appreciate for their appearance and virility, regardless of the fact that they range in age from their fifties to their seventies. On TV news, too, the male anchor is often in his forties, fifties, or even sixties or seventies (remember Walter Cronkite?). Like Dan Rather, he may well have lots of wrinkles, which are amply evident in the close-ups. This is fine. They show that he's been around a long time and is knowledgeable and credible. Meanwhile, the coanchor is typically a woman who is appreciably younger, heavily made-up, thin, stylish, and wrinkle-free. As she ages, she is likely to be forced into repeated cosmetic surgery, and even so may very well be replaced.

TV programming is no better. As we saw in Chapter 1, television actresses, by and large, disappear after age thirty-five until they reach fifty, when they reappear as character actresses. Meanwhile, the screen value of men in the thirty-five to forty-nine age group increases, as is evidenced by their increased numbers. Furthermore, only about 2 percent of TV females have gray hair, while about 14 percent of TV men do.

Middle-aged or older women receive the same treatment, or worse, in the movies, in which there is a dearth of good parts for women who are no longer young. A recent study found that men who received the Academy Award for best actor averaged forty-five; best actresses winners were closer to thirty-five. Older men, such as Jack Nicholson, Richard Gere, and Nick Nolte, remain leading men, commanding higher and higher salaries, while women of the same or even younger age are consigned to the too few character parts. In 1988, Sally Field played Tom Hanks's lover in *Punchline*. In 1994 she played his mother in *Forrest Gump*. And Paul Newman has remained a box-office attraction well after his very talented and attractive wife, Joanne Woodward. Moreover, when older women are represented in the movies they are often presented in unflattering roles. A recent study documented that older women in the movies today are shown as hags, nags, witches, or worse.

Magazines are even more guilty of emphasizing and glorifying youth and beauty, and it is not unusual for their covers to feature a teenager, covered with tons of makeup and dressed up to look like a woman, while older women are rarely pictured unless they're famous and glamorous. One study found that in magazine ads, 77 percent of women portrayed appeared to be under thirty, and that while 57 percent of adult women were over forty, only 4 percent of women in ads were portrayed as being that old. Among males, 37 percent appeared to be under thirty and 27 percent in their forties.

Newspapers largely ignore women of all ages, or relegate them to the women's page. Even when they do cover an issue of interest to women, like the dangers of breast implants, most of the experts they quote are men.

The good news is that despite the media's treatment of older women as either nonexistent or as over the hill, sexless, lifeless—leftovers—real women know better. *New Woman* magazine surveyed over six thousand women about their attitudes on aging. They found that women in their fifties and sixties are significantly happier with their lives, and have greater self-confidence, than younger women. While younger women fear aging, viewing it as a process by which they will lose their vitality, options, and sexual desirability, older women experience middle and old age as a time of opportunity, when they can stop being so concerned about beauty and what others think of them and focus instead on what makes them happy. The survey reported that older respondents "are proud of their wrinkles and curious about what the future will bring." And despite notions about old age being a sexless stage of life, many older women reported that they were more interested in sex than ever before, and about half of them had taken a younger lover.

Indeed, it was encouraging to learn that fewer than 10 percent of the women surveyed thought that the worst part of aging was losing looks and sexual attractiveness, and that fully 12 percent felt that there wasn't any bad part about aging. Over 80 percent of the more than six thousand women polled said that how a woman looks is not the most important factor in making her seem old, but, rather, that women look old when they lack enthusiasm or are not in good health. In other words, as long as our health holds up (and contrary to popular belief, most old people rate their health as good or excellent), in many ways we look as old as we feel.

Interestingly, the survey also found that as women get older, we change our view of what is the most attractive age for a woman. Women in their twenties say it is in your thirties, women in their forties say at thirty-eight, and those in their sixties say at forty-five. In another study, middle-aged women were most likely to perceive "attractive" faces as younger than their actual age, but not older women. As Gail Sheehy points out in the second part of *New Woman*'s article, the survey shows that older women "become motivated to stretch their independence, learn new skills, return to school, plunge into new careers, rediscover the creativity and passions of their youth, and, at last, to listen to their own needs. They laugh at themselves for having feared that losing their youthful looks would mean losing power."

Similarly, Rosalind Barnett and Grace Baruch of the Wellesley Center for Research on Women compared women aged thirty-five to fifty-five in all sorts of combinations of roles and found that instead of the expected decline of mental health with age, most women experienced a sense of resurgence, or revitalization, a new sense of self and self-worth in midlife that gave then great confidence.

Noted gerontologist Dr. John Rowe, president of Mount Sinai Hospital and Mount Sinai School of Medicine in New York, echoes the experiences of these older women. After studying a whole range of biological and other factors, he concluded that what makes for healthy and happy aging are two social factors: a sense of mastery and of self-efficacy. In other words, if, as you age, you feel you are choosing to live your life as you wish, involved in what interests you, and find meaning in your endeavors you are likely both to be well physically and to be contented with yourself and your life.

It is also important to note that old age generally brings neither the mental nor the physical decline normally ascribed to it. As Betty Friedan points out in *The Fountain of Age,* only 5 percent of Americans today suffer from Alzheimer's disease (which used to be considered senility), only 5 percent of Americans over sixty-five are in nursing homes, and only 10 percent ever will be. In fact, in age most people remain vital and healthy until shortly before death and even, it seems, develop a new kind of intelligence that more than compensates for whatever rote memory losses may occur.

So if being older is so much better than it is cracked up to be, why haven't the media discovered its value, and why haven't younger women received the word? The answer is not hard to figure out. If we women get off the beauty treadmill, where as we age we have to run faster and faster (and spend an awful lot of money) in a vain attempt to stay in place, multinational corporations—the people who place those ads own newspapers and magazines and sponsor TV programs—would lose a lot of income.

Imagine what would happen if women suddenly put no more effort into looking good than men do—that is, if we continued to care about how we look, but put it more in proportion, and less on the front burner with the flame turned all the way up. We'd probably look almost as good as we do now, just as men do, for a fraction of the cost in time and money. This would be very liberating for women, but devastating to the industries whose huge profits rely on keeping women dissatisfied with their looks. Diet centers would have to close their doors (good riddance, as none of them work anyway), cosmetic surgeons would have to turn their talents to helping maimed or disfigured people rather than cutting up perfectly healthy ones, face-cream producers would have to go out of business or produce something effective and useful, cosmetic companies would have to down-price, trendy hairdressers would no longer be able to get away with charging exorbitant sums to cut and dye hair, and the fashion industry would be forced to make clothes for women, as they already do for men, that are durable and practical, in styles that are attractive and abiding.

Does all this sound radical and impossible to you? If so, think about it. Do you really believe that men are so much more inherently attractive than women that we have to hide, highlight, or help our faces and bodies, and stave off signs of aging, while men are pretty much fine the way they are? Or are we just being sold a bill of goods that allows corporations to make a great deal of money by convincing us that we have no real worth if we don't look like the beauty ideal?*

---

*True, there has been an increasing attempt by corporate America to get men to feel insecure about their appearances and to spend money on improving their looks, but so far it has met with limited success.

It is so common for some older men to be considered appealing that there is a special word to describe such a man—"distinguished"—while there is no such word to describe a woman. The best our language does is to borrow a male word and sometimes call an older woman "handsome."

Do you wonder why there are only male words to praise the looks of an older woman? Certainly it's not because men age better than women. We all know that women as a group age well and outlive men. Rather, it is because our male-controlled society is invested in believing (rightly) that older men can be vibrant, sexy, and desirable, and it portrays them as such. These portrayals train our eyes to see attractiveness in men over a wide range of ages. By contrast, when it comes to older women, our male-controlled media are equally invested in believing (wrongly) that older women are sexless, drab, shriveled leftovers, and when older women are portrayed at all, this is usually how they are shown. We don't have a word to describe an attractive older woman because big business doesn't want us to believe such a being actually exists. If it let out the secret, maybe then women would spend less money on trying to look young.

Beyond the profit motive, the discrimination against older women in our culture also bespeaks men's desire to be revered and considered wise. In *You Just Don't Understand,* linguist Deborah Tannen explains that men are socialized to want to be one-up, and their conversation reflects this jockeying for position and power, while women look to find commonalties and to make connections. And who is more likely to look up adoringly at a man than a younger woman? An older women, with greater experience and maturity, presents a threat. Having come more fully into her own and knowing her own worth, she is more likely to speak up to a man with knowledge and confidence. This is not something that our male-driven culture is comfortable with, so it denigrates the older woman to take her voice away. In doing so it utilizes its tried-and-true method—tell her that she's worthless because of how she looks, and if that doesn't work, treat her as if she doesn't exist. As we noted before, gray-haired women are almost never seen in the media. If you were an alien trying to understand our culture through the media, you would likely conclude that most women die off young, as there are so few visible older women.

To like the way you look at any age, it is important to reject society's depiction of beauty as only the domain of the young and learn how you can claim your own beauty at any age. Two sets of exercises follow. One is designed for women who are middle-aged or older, and the other is for younger women. Do whichever feels appropriate to you, or both if you wish.

I Am Wise and Beautiful (For Middle-Aged or Older Women)

(See the Appendix for full relaxation instructions.)

Get comfortable. Then close your eyes, and put your thumb and index finger together on each hand. Take a deep breath, deep into your diaphragm and abdomen, and hold it for five seconds, then gradually let it out to a slow count of five. Now, take five comfortable SLOW deep breaths, and when you finish, let your fingers open, and continue breathing normally and comfortably. As you are breathing, in any way that is natural, let yourself become perhaps a little more peaceful, maybe a little more relaxed, letting go of tensions in any way that you know how, and going inside yourself to a lovely place of comfort and peace, or any other place that feels right to you.

As you are continuing to relax, let yourself go deeper into yourself, into your own safe, comfortable, inner space, and as you do so, start to look back over your life, allowing yourself to recognize and acknowledge what you have learned about people, life, and yourself up to now. Think deeply about the extent of your experience, knowing that true profundity, and wisdom, comes as we delve into ourselves and our lives. Review the developments that have deeply shaped you and your life, focusing on the factors that have most determined who you are today. Think about all you now know about how to deal with people: family, spouses, lovers, children, bosses, coworkers. And review all you have learned about yourself: what your needs are, what makes you happy, what you now know about sex and your sexual feelings and needs that you didn't know when you were younger, what place your spirituality plays in your life, what fulfills you. What skills have you acquired? What interests have you pursued? What kind of work have you done? What paths have you followed? Take as much time as you need to recognize all that you have acquired on your journey through life, all the places you have traveled, lessons you have learned, experience you have gained, wisdom you have acquired. Take as much time as you need to recognize the reality of all you have brought to realization, so you really realize what wisdom you have acquired from all you have encountered and reconnoitered in life. Then, whenever you are ready, open your eyes and come back to the room.

WISDOM

Now write down the things you have learned on your life's journey, considering each of the following categories:

People
Relationships
Feelings
Family
Sex
Work
Hobbies
Skills
Spirituality
Yourself
Life itself

Call this list WISDOM and make it as long as possible. Keep adding to it until it feels really complete. Then read it out loud slowly, starting each item with "I now know," "I now know how to," or "I now realize" before each item. For example:

I now know that it is really important to me to have time to
myself, and that there's no reason to feel guilty about it.

I now know that what really matters in life is not how I look
to other people, but how they treat me, and how I treat
myself.

I now know how to play the piano. I'm not great, but I love it.
And I'm getting better every day.

I now realize that I love learning new things.

I now realize that I am a good person.

After you finish your WISDOM list, immediately take it with
you, go look in the mirror, and closely examine your face and body.
Realize that your lines, wrinkles, gray hairs, age spots, sagging skin,
flabbiness, expanding waistline, or whatever are tokens of the incredible journey you've been on. Reread your WISDOM list
SLOWLY, out loud, in the same manner as before. Congratulate
yourself, as in traditional Chinese society, on your happy age. Allow
yourself to feel the strength of your experience and the power it has
brought you. And look forward to becoming even older, wiser, and
more your own person. Allow yourself to realize that age has a
beauty all its own, if you only look for it. Wrinkles are beautiful, as
the women in the *New Woman* survey found, when associated with
being wise, knowing, and experienced. Start to see yourself through
different eyes. Then immediately do the following exercise:

Sharing Your Wisdom

(See the Appendix for full relaxation instructions.)

*Get comfortable. Then close your eyes, and put your thumb
and index finger together on each hand. Take a deep breath, deep
into your diaphragm and abdomen, and hold it for five seconds,
then gradually let it out to a slow count of five. Now, take five comfortable SLOW deep breaths, and when you finish, let your fingers
open, and continue breathing normally and comfortably. As you are
breathing, in any way that is natural, let yourself become perhaps a
little more peaceful, maybe a little more relaxed, letting go of ten-*

sions in any way that you know how, and going inside yourself to a lovely place of comfort and peace, or any other place that feels right to you.

As you are continuing to relax, imagine that you are talking to the young woman you were at eighteen, who's wondering what life will hold in store for her. You can't change what she will experience, as you don't have that power, and even the memory of this encounter can't stay with her. But you can leave her with a changed feeling about her values and priorities. What advice can you give that younger you about what's really important to her and in her life? What can you teach her about the place of appearance and what true beauty is? Share with her the important lessons you have learned, and bestow on her the wisdom you have acquired. Then imagine her looking up at you with gratitude and admiration, being glad to know that she will one day be wise and acquire a beauty that shines forth from within. Accept this admiration and hug it close to you. Whenever you look in the mirror or think about your looks, think about all the wisdom you have gained, and this admiration that you truly merit. Stay there, as long as you like, taking in the good feeling of being admired for your looks that reflect the inner you. Then, whenever you are ready, open your eyes and return to the room.

YOUNGER WOMEN

If you're in your twenties or younger, the effects aging will have on your looks are probably the last thing on your mind. It's likely too far off to be of real concern. If you're in your thirties and have started to have an occasional gray hair, or more, and those laugh wrinkles around your face and eyes are starting to develop or deepen, fears about aging may be creeping or rushing in. If you've already turned forty, you're confronting the prospect of having to leave youth behind and being seen as middle-aged, no matter how young you may feel or look. Perhaps you're doing whatever you can to remain young-looking, and you dread the prospect of being called "ma'am" by the flirts who used to try to catch your eye. Or maybe they're still trying to catch your eye, but you wonder for how long. If so, you may view each additional line on your face as a traitor, pulling you into middle age when you long to stay young and attractive.

When you read the exercise for older women, you may have had trouble relating to it. You may not be far enough along on your life's journey to have experienced the sense of freedom that comes when you minimize beauty concerns and beauty work, stop being overfocused on pleasing others and being found pleasing, and instead focus your energies on your true interests, abilities, and values. The idea that wrinkles, gray hair, crow's-feet, and liver spots have a beauty of their own may seem Pollyannaish to you. If so, see how you feel after the following exercises.

OLDER WOMAN
(for younger women)

On the top of a piece of paper, write down OLDER WOMAN, and then list on this paper every adjective that comes to your mind. Don't censor yourself or try to be politically correct. Just let whatever comes to you flow, and write down whatever descriptions come to mind. Take as much time as you need. When you're done, divide your list into two columns, with positive descriptions in one column and negative descriptions in the other.

Is one side of your list much longer than the other? Some of you may have more positive descriptions. Perhaps you know some wonderful, loving, vibrant, wise older women, or have seen a woman close to you come into her own later in life. For many of you, I suspect, the negative side of your list will be a lot longer. Most younger women have been led to believe that old age is a horrible time, especially for women, and that there isn't much good about getting on in age. Well, check it out.

Talk to as many older women whom you know and like as you can. Try to talk to at least ten, more if you can. If you don't know this many, ask your friends if you could talk to some of their older relatives or acquaintances. When you speak with these older women, ask them how they feel about being older and what changes it has made in them and their lives. Ask them if they like themselves more and have more self-confidence now or when they were younger, and at what age they have felt most powerful and free. Ask, too, how the changes in their appearance have affected them, and how they feel about these changes. You may be amazed at their answers. Here's what some of the older women I talked with had to say:

Mary, 63: When I was young I was considered a real beauty. I thought it would be awful growing older and losing that special attention. And for a while it was. Then I discovered that people started taking me a lot more seriously than they ever had before. At sixty, after my children were out of the house, I went back to school. It's been wonderful. I never realized before how much I love learning, and how smart I am. I feel better about myself now than I ever have.

Ethel, 72: I always thought I was a "plain Jane" when I was young and hated the way I looked. I can't tell you how miserable it made me. When I hit middle age, it was a relief to leave all that worrying about looks behind—after all, most of my contemporaries were no longer considered great beauties, so what did it matter? I started to feel more equal. I also started to do things that really matter to me. I began doing volunteer work with the homeless, and I discovered I have a real talent not only for getting people to open up to me, but also for administration. Now I'm sorry I wasted so much time and energy worrying about my looks, instead of seeing and using all the abilities I have. In many ways, this is the happiest time of my life.

Ceil, 83: I look into the mirror sometimes, and I wonder if this wrinkled, gray-haired woman I see is really me. I don't feel old. My mind is as active as ever, and I'm in good health, though I don't have the stamina I used to. Still, I'm involved in a lot of activities and organizations. When I was in my forties, I wished I could turn back the clock and stay young forever. I felt it was so sad to be losing my looks. Not that I was a great beauty, but I wasn't bad-looking either. I think it was when I was no longer so concerned with my looks that a different part of me started to blossom. I was born in 1912, so when I turned sixty it was 1972. The whole world was changing—long hair, hippies, free love, women's liberation. At first it all shocked me, but then I was glad for some of the changes, especially for women. I used to think that men were almost gods, and I was always deferential and trying to please and impress, and men always did like me. When I got older, I started to think differently. I thought, what about them pleasing me?! I feel like Sophia on The Golden Girls: "At my age, what do I have to lose?" My husband died seven years ago, and that was very hard on me. But in the years since then I've also developed a new confidence. There used to be so many things I relied on him for that I've since learned to do for myself. I'm freer and more self-confident now than I have ever been. And when I look in the mirror, I still think I'm nice-looking, in a different kind of way, and I'm proud of my wrinkles.

Geri, 77: I'm a lesbian, and when I was young, there wasn't much acceptance and support as there is now for being gay. I was in the closet at work and with my family for many years, and always dressed very femme, so no one would suspect. I also liked looking attractive, and even though I wasn't interested in men, I enjoyed the fact that men would flirt with me. It was like getting the seal of approval. In midlife I came out at work and with my family, and went through a very butch period—cut my hair short and only wore pants and no makeup. It was a thrill not only not to hide, but to flaunt it. Now I've set-

*tled, sort of, in the middle. If I feel like wearing a pretty
dress, I do. If I want to go around in overalls, I do that,
too. I no longer feel defined by what I wear or how I
look. I've become much more interested in spirituality
and people's inner selves. I've also become very political.
I know that some younger people look at me and assume
that because I'm older, I'm uninteresting. I think that's
their loss. They'll never know what a dynamite, interesting woman they missed getting to know.*

After you have talked with older women whom you know and
like, write down what you have learned. Did they say things that
surprised you? Are you starting to have a different view of middle
and older age? Go back to your OLDER WOMAN list and see if
there are any changes you want to make, things you want to add or
delete. Remember, when you describe an older woman you are de-
scribing yourself in the future.

Admiring Older Women

Train yourself to look at older women differently. It takes
practice, but with time and effort you can do it. When you look at
older women, practice seeing lines, wrinkles, age spots, and gray
hairs as signs of experience that demand respect and admiration.
When you see an older women on the street or elsewhere, practice
thinking, There goes a woman with wisdom, or There goes a
woman who has lived her life, or What a distinctive, attractive-
looking woman she is, or She's beautiful. Your aim is to train yourself to see the signs of aging as signposts along life's journey,
recording where you have gone and preparing you for where you
are going. The following visualization will help.

The Road to Beauty and Wisdom

(See the Appendix for full relaxation instructions.)

Get comfortable. Then close your eyes, and put your thumb and index finger together on each hand. Take a deep breath, deep into your diaphragm and abdomen, and hold it for five seconds, then gradually let it out to a slow count of five. Now, take five comfortable SLOW deep breaths, and when you finish, let your fingers open, and continue breathing normally and comfortably. As you are breathing, in any way that is natural, let yourself become perhaps a little more peaceful, maybe a little more relaxed, letting go of tensions in any way that you know how, and going inside yourself to a lovely place of comfort and peace, or any other place that feels right to you.

As you are continuing to relax, imagine that you are looking in a mirror. Gently notice whatever signs of aging you may have. Be aware that they are signals that you are getting ready to leave on a very important journey that will take you places that will enrich your life. Who knows what will attract you, please you, bewitch you, charm you—what lovely, fascinating, and alluring ways of being will enter your life? It will be interesting to see what ways you will find to discover your true self, hear your own inner voice, find your own special path, enjoy life's scents, follow your music, dance to your own tune, taste the variety in life, in your own unique way, and to see in what ways you will expand and enlarge the beauty of your life—giving you a deeper, wiser understanding of what is truly important, and all of the different ways of being beautiful in the world. And it will be interesting in the future to look back on this day, knowing what you know then, and now, to see in what ways you will come to appreciate the wisdom that you already have, and will further acquire, as you proceed on your life's journey, discovering your own special way to enjoy yourself, your beauty, and the beauty of life. For the moment, enjoy the peacefulness of having the wisdom that you have already acquired. Then, when you're ready, open your eyes and return to the room.

How do you feel? Can you experience the power, self-satisfaction, and self-esteem that come with choosing to define beauty in a whole-person womanly way, rather than in the narrow, superficial beauty-ideal way? The more you practice admiring the looks of other women, of all ages, the better you will feel about your looks and yourself. In the next chapter we will look in detail at how to do so, but first let yourself, whatever your age, experience the healing energy of the following visualization.

Appreciating Your Life's Journey (For Women of Every Age)

(See the Appendix for full relaxation instructions.)

Get comfortable. Then close your eyes, and put your thumb and index finger together on each hand. Take a deep breath, deep into your diaphragm and abdomen, and hold it for five seconds, then gradually let it out to a slow count of five. Now, take five comfortable SLOW deep breaths, and when you finish, let your fingers open, and continue breathing normally and comfortably. As you are breathing, in any way that is natural, let yourself become perhaps a little more peaceful, maybe a little more relaxed, letting go of tensions in any way that you know how, and going inside yourself to a lovely place of comfort and peace, or any other place that feels right to you.

As you are continuing to relax, remind yourself that aging is part of life's journey, and each sign of aging is a signpost, recording where you have been, what you have dealt with, and how you have survived, overcome, and triumphed. Gray hair, wrinkles, age spots, and other signs of aging are symbols of accomplishment, as are Girl Scout badges, hugs from children and grandchildren, promotions and raises at work, and other awards. And it really is good to be rewarded, and to know how much you have learned and accomplished in your life, where you started from, and where you are now. And you know, just as lakes, with their clearness and openness, have one kind of beauty, and trees, with their many leaves and branches, another, and mountains, with their mixture of foliage and barrenness, crests and valleys, yet another, so do different ages. And the mountaintop, while perhaps scarcer in foliage, or snow-

covered, also has the best view. And it really is quite an accomplishment to climb that mountain and see that view. And as we're going up, it's interesting to experience all the different ways we can sense ourselves, and all the vistas that life offers on the way, and the beautiful view from the top. It can be nice to share that view with someone else, and it can also be nice to view it by yourself, knowing that you are the one who is making this journey, overcoming obstacles, and heading toward the top in all its magnificence. And you may notice how interesting and different things look as you go along. Things that loom large at the bottom stages of your journey appear to be mere specks when viewed from the top. And there really are many different ways to view the landscape and enjoy its beauty in all its diversity: ponds and rivers, trees and meadows, hills and flatlands, and above it all, the sun, bringing life, and warmth, comfort, and peace, and an inner sense of serenity, and beauty. Stay there now, in whatever place you're in, enjoying the beauty and diversity of the view. Then, whenever you are ready, open your eyes and return to the room.

CHAPTER 11

"SHE LOOKS SO GOOD, I JUST HATE HER": DEALING WITH OTHER WOMEN

At a party Marcy, who is short, of average weight, and nice-looking, with dark curly hair, sees Lauren, who is tall, lithe, blue-eyed, with classical features and straight blonde hair that falls over her shoulders. Marcy instantly thinks, She looks so good, I just hate her.

Have you ever felt envious in this way? If so, you have lots of company. Most women feel competitive about looks. When we enter a room, usually the first thing we do is to check out the other women—what they're wearing and, most importantly, how attractive they are compared to us. If we spy a woman who we think is much better-looking than we are, we typically feel envious, resentful, and upset with our own looks. What do we do with these feelings? You know what we do: We try to prop up our faltering self-image by mentally tearing the beauty down.

Marcy, clutching at straws, thinks, Look, she's starting to have lines near her eyes, and that's a tacky shade of red she's wearing. Besides, I bet she's really stuck up.

This sour grapes approach offers scant comfort and doesn't really make Marcy feel any better. In fact, it has the opposite effect. Belittling an attractive woman's looks is like pushing an alarm button in our deeper selves. The alarm warns us that we're in danger of being devalued and dismissed in comparison to her. Ostensibly, we're worried about being devalued by others; in reality, often we are the ones who see ourselves as diminished. When you disparage an attractive woman's looks, it's as if you're saying to yourself, She's beautiful, and I'm not; and it's awful that I'm not because my worth lies in my looks, and next to her, I don't measure up.

But, you may want to argue, it's not me who thinks that my worth lies in my looks; it's others who judge me by my appearance. And you're right, of course. Society does put much too high a premium on how a woman looks. But we are also part of society, and we have internalized its values and judgments, so we treat ourselves accordingly.

One way to understand this concept more clearly is to see yourself as having an inner child and an inner parent. Your inner child expresses your feelings, while your inner parent expresses your values and judgments. As we saw in Chapter 8, some of us have an inner parent that acts as an inner caretaker, supporting and nurturing us, pointing us in the right direction and being by our side when we falter. Others of us have an inner parent who is really an inner critic, always telling us how we're not good enough. In *Recovery of Your Self-Esteem,* I examined this process in detail, explaining how you can build your self-esteem by turning your inner critic into an inner caretaker. Now let's see how to do this with regard to our feelings about our appearance.

If your inner parent is nurturing, she tells you how good you look, and that she thinks you're attractive. If you carry around this inner message, you can't help feeling that you look good. On the other hand, many of us carry the voice of our inner critic, who continually tells us that our hair is out of place, that we're not standing straight enough, that we're too fat, and that we're just not pretty enough. If you carry a voice like this, you know how hard it is to like your looks and yourself when part of you is constantly tearing you down.

We respond to our inner critic, as we would to a real parent, by trying to show her that we're not as bad-looking as she thinks, that our sister and rival whom she admires isn't really that beautiful, and that we are better-looking than some of our other sisters. Marcy's inner dialogue sounds like this:

> *Inner Critic:* My God. Look at Lauren. She's gorgeous! And you, you . . . you don't look like anything next to her. Why can't you look like her?!
>
> *Inner Child* [thinks to herself, while feeling rejected, envious, angry, resentful, and sad, I hate her! I want you to admire me the way you do her. God, I must really look awful if even you, my own inner parent, don't think I look like anything. I hate the way I look. What can I do to get your approval, and to get you to believe that she's not all that much better than I?]: You know, she's not all that gorgeous. You can see that she's starting to have lines around her eyes, and that's a tacky shade of red, and I bet she's really stuck up.
>
> *Inner Critic* [dripping disgust]: You're pathetic! Lines around her eyes?! A tacky shade of red?! Yeah, tell me another one. On your worst day you should look as good as she!
>
> *Inner Child:* [in silent acknowledgment]: You're right. [Feels awful and ugly.]

This type of inner dialogue, which uses the beauty ideal to measure our worth, usually occurs so quickly that we're not even aware of it. All we are aware of are its results: We feel inferior and bad about our looks and ourselves, and experience a loss of confidence. If this is so for you, it is important to stop and identify the voice of your inner critic so that you can learn to stop undermining yourself.

The undermining voice of your inner critic is also at work

when you criticize another woman's looks from a superior position. Then the inner dialogue goes like this:

> *Inner Critic:* You're good-looking, but not good-looking enough. There are so many other women prettier than you. I wish you looked like a model or a movie star.
>
> *Inner Child:* Yeah, me too. I wish I could be beautiful like them, instead of just good-looking. Then everyone would love and admire me.
>
> *Inner Critic:* I want that too, but forget it. You're just not that attractive.
>
> *Inner Child* [feeling rejected, unappreciated, and bad about her looks]: Well, wait a minute. I'm kind of attractive. Look at Fran over there, she has a big nose and I don't; Latisha is disgustingly fat, and I'm thin; and Aliya has thick legs, while mine are shapely.
>
> *Inner Critic:* Yes, that's true. You're not so bad, I realize that, but you're still not good-looking enough. I wish you were gorgeous; then everything would be wonderful. But you're not.
>
> *Inner Child* [goes from feeling slightly better to feeling even more rejected and hurt]: You're right. [Feels awful about her looks and herself.]

These inner dialogues show how these women, like many of us, have internalized society's values, so that it is now we who are measuring our self-worth by our appearance and using the hierarchical beauty ideal as the measure of that worth. The more we do this, the worse we feel about our looks and ourselves, no matter how attractive we really are.

When you really feel good about yourself, you don't have to tear others down or feel superior to them in order to build yourself up. This defensive reaction, in fact, is the prototypical mechanism that fuels prejudices such as racism.* If racists really felt good about

*Racism, of course, is also fundamentally fueled by one group wanting to benefit economically and politically by disenfranchising another.

themselves, they wouldn't have to arbitrarily define themselves as superior to another group. And neither do you. You don't have to belittle another woman's looks in order to feel pretty. True self-esteem cannot be built on scapegoating.

So why do we do it? Because we've been taught to, because society encourages us to, and because we often really don't know what else to do to shore up our flagging body- and self-esteem except to give in, feel lousy, and slink away.

The Beauty Imperative teaches us that beauty is a scarce commodity and that other women are our competition, not only for potential mates, but also for the prize of being considered good-looking and therefore valuable. Big business touts the beauty ideal and pushes the Beauty Imperative in its advertising and media messages because it knows that this ideology keeps women spending. No matter how good-looking you may be, even if you're a model, you're bound to find some woman who you think is even prettier. So how do you deal with the competition? That's easy: Get a new hairstyle, spruce up your wardrobe, go for a makeover, try a new cream, buy an exercise machine, join a diet program—in short, buy beauty. Corporate America knows that the more competitive you feel, the more desperate you'll be to look good, and the more you'll be willing to spend on beauty products.

Ads and commercials preach at you that you can lose weight like Jill, or have hair that looks like Cindy's, or skin that looks like Christine's. What they're really telling you is that you should look like Jill, Cindy, and Christine, and that if you don't, you just don't measure up. With a message like that, how can you help hating these women and anyone who looks like them? It's like being consigned to be the less-loved, less-favored younger sister. Corporate America casts us in this role and, like an unloving parent, urges us to compete with one another, according to their rules, for the dubious prize of being found better-looking. When we do so, we play right into their hands. If we try to change the rules, tremendous pressure is brought to bear on us. The last thing in the world corporate America wants is for women to join together in liking the way they and other women look.

It's time that we women recognize that competing over looks

is not in our best interests, and instead we need to band together to insist that:

1. We look great just the way we are.

2. Our worth lies in our personhood, not our appearance. Our looks are lovely in all their multiplicity, but only incidental to our value.

Most of us, of course, want to achieve this for ourselves. While we may want to be found pretty, we also want people to see below our surfaces and appreciate our talents, intelligence, skills, achievements, and human qualities. To receive this kind of acknowledgment for ourselves, we also have to give it to other women!

When we competitively put down another woman's looks or size, whether out of feelings of inferiority or superiority, we strengthen the Beauty Imperative and uphold the beauty ideal. We are, in effect, saying that we believe that women should look only one way, and that if they don't they (and we) are inferior and merit scorn because women's worth lies not in who we are and what we do, but in how closely we match the beauty ideal.

On the other hand, celebrating other women's looks in all their diversity helps us appreciate our own beauty. In doing so, we transform our view of beauty from an elusive goal that belongs to only the very few at the top—a male pyramidal perspective that makes for few winners and many losers—to a vision that is inclusive and available to all.

Let's talk about that pyramid for a moment. It really is very male. Boys and many men like to play "king of the mountain," pushing others off so they can reign alone on the top. Women operate very differently. We prefer forging connections and find that life is most enjoyed when lived in a spirit of cooperation, with an emphasis on mutual empathy, support, and caring.

Noted feminist psychiatrist Jean Baker Miller argues that mainstream psychology's view of mental health is based on male values that define maturity as being able to separate and be independent and autonomous. Women, however, she continues, have a different view and experience, which is that health and happiness are found in interdependence, connection, and mutually empowering relationships in which each person "uses their intellectual and emotional abilities . . . to build [the other's] strength, resources, effectiveness, and well-being." In addition, Miller argues, for "men as well as women, individual development proceeds only by means of connection."

Let's look at this concept of "mutually empowering relationships" as it applies to how we deal with other women. It is often the hallmark of women's friendships. If you have a good friend, you know how you always try to understand and support each other, and how you can count on each other. Sure, jealousies, misunderstandings, hurt feelings, and anger sometimes arise. After all, you're both human. At the same time, you both really love and care about each other, accept each other as you are, and want the best for each other. Whenever one of you experiences difficulties, is wrestling with a life change, is considering taking a risk, is exploring an interest, needs a hand with something, or just wants someone to share with, the other is there with ready empathy, support, and help. Supporting each other's growth and development in this way is what mutual empowerment is all about.

Of course, not all friendships between women are like this, but many are. Wouldn't it be great to give and get this kind of mutual support and mutual empowerment from many other women, not just your close friends? You can begin now in the area of looks. Decide to stop building yourself up at other women's expense, which not only isn't mutually empowering, but, as we saw earlier, lowers your own self-esteem and self-confidence. Promise yourself that from now on you are going to strive to appreciate and admire other women's looks.

Start by making a point of becoming aware of when you are about to belittle another woman's appearance, either out loud or in your own thoughts. Immediately stop yourself and examine what you are feeling about your own looks at this moment. What is happening that you feel the need to put down another woman? Take the time to experience what you are really feeling about yourself and your looks.

Perhaps you want to put down a fat woman because you also feel fat (whatever size you are), so you're trying to make yourself feel better by seeing her as "gross" and therefore yourself, in comparison, as thin. Or maybe because you feel bad about having pimples, you mentally criticize another woman's complexion so you won't feel too bad about your own. Or perhaps you have very mixed feelings about your looks—feeling simultaneously confident and insecure, as is typical of many women—so you try to reassure yourself by constantly telling yourself how plain this woman looks, while you have a pretty face, or that woman is dumpy while you have a nice shape, or a third woman has thick legs while yours are slender.

Marcy, for example, the woman at the party who was envious of Lauren, came to recognize that she felt pretty, but not outstanding, and that while sometimes this felt fine to her, other times she felt ordinary and undesirable, especially when she was around women she considered gorgeous. These women made her fear that they would be the stars and she would be seen as inferior. She tried to cover and compensate for her feelings of inferiority by belittling her "rivals'" looks, hoping to boost her sagging ego.

After some exploration Marcy came to realize that her reaction was both irrational and ineffective. It was irrational because most of the time she wasn't in competition for anything real. For instance, at the friend's party where she had met Lauren there was no real prize to compete for. Marcy had come with a date and wasn't there to meet any one (in fact, she was becoming pretty serious about her date), wasn't looking to make business contacts, and had no secret hopes of being "discovered" and finding herself on TV or in the movies. So what were her envious and competitive feelings about, if there wasn't anything she was competing for?

Marcy realized that what she was "competing" for was the prize of being found attractive, and therefore worthy and valuable, and that the real judge was her own inner critic. Belittling Lauren, as we saw, only amplified her self-criticism. It also made Marcy feel bitter and catty, which didn't help her to feel better about herself either.

I suggested that Marcy make a conscious effort to react to women she finds especially beautiful by praising them in her mind and then praising herself in turn. Marcy practiced this out loud in my office, pretending she was first seeing Lauren at the party:

She really is great-looking. Look at that body and hair and eyes. She looks so good, I just hate her. Oops. [Stops herself.] Let go of the envy. I promised myself. I don't have to hate her. I can enjoy looking at her. She is great-looking. [Takes time and admires Lauren.] And I also know that there are many different kinds of beauty in the world—her kind and my kind. I don't have to compete. I really like my dark curly hair, and I have a nice face and shape, and I'm happy to have them.

Can you feel the difference in this approach? When Marcy stops comparing, adopts a cooperative view, and allows herself to admire Lauren's beauty without envy, she makes room to affirm herself and enjoy her own beauty. Her inner dialogue is now like this:

Inner Critic: My God. Look at her. She's gorgeous! And you, you . . . you don't look like anything next to her. Oops. [Stops herself.] I promised you and myself that I wasn't going to do that anymore. Okay. Let's just enjoy her looks. She really is beautiful—tall and lanky with that great straight blonde hair.

Inner Child: Yes she is.

Inner Caretaker: And you're pretty, too. You really have a pretty face and a nice body, and I love your dark curly hair. I think we look pretty good.

Inner Child: You really think I'm pretty, even after looking at Lauren? You really think it's okay that I look like me and not like Lauren?

Inner Caretaker: Yes. I'm through comparing you to other women. I really love you, and I think the way you look is just fine.

Inner Child: I love you, too. (Smiles broadly.) Maybe I'll go say hello to Lauren. She might be a nice person.

Did you notice the change in Marcy's inner parent? When she stopped trying to make Marcy into something she isn't, and appreciated her for what she is and how she looks? She stopped being an inner critic and became an inner caretaker. You can learn to do this, too.

Envy is based on the pyramidal approach that says there are few winners and many losers, and that there's not enough love and approval to go around. Letting go of envy makes room to appreciate many different ways of being attractive, and to feel pretty and lovable just as you are. It's like going to a museum. Who cares whether Rubens paints better than Rembrandt or Picasso, or O'Keeffe, or someone you never heard of? True enjoyment comes when you let each artist's work resonate uniquely, and you allow yourself to relate to the beauty in each of them.

But, you may be thinking, maybe that works for someone who's pretty like Marcy, but what about someone who's really fat, or plain? Actually, ceasing to compare yourself to other women works equally well whatever your size, shape, or features.

Ellen is twenty-eight, five four, and weighs 142 pounds. She has been full-bodied since puberty, and has spent her whole life comparing herself to other women, wondering if she looks larger or smaller than they. If she thinks she looks smaller, she fleetingly feels a little better about her looks. If she thinks she's fatter, her self-image sinks. Her inner dialogues go like this:

Inner Critic: Look at Dana. She's so thin and pretty. You look so fat next to her. I can't stand the way you look. Why can't you stick to a diet?! If you were thin you would be really great-looking.
Inner Child: You're right. [Thinks, Dana looks so good I just hate her, and feels fat and ugly.]

Or

Inner Critic: Look at Sue over there. She's your size and she's fat. That's what you look like—fat and ugly.
Inner Child: Yes, I am. [Feels fat and ugly.]

Or

Inner Critic: Look at Lee over there. She must be at least 250 pounds. How ugly! Thank God you're not as fat as that. Next to her you almost look slender.

Inner Child: That's good. I'm glad I don't look like her. [Feels momentarily relieved.] I mean, I know I'm too fat, but at least I don't look as fat and bad as she does.

Inner Critic: That's right. You're too fat and look bad, but not as bad as she.

Inner Child: Yeah. [Feels fat and ugly.]

Now let's see how Ellen feels when she stops competing with other women and instead looks for the beauty in all women, including herself.

Inner Critic: Look at Dana. She's so thin and pretty. You look like an elephant next to her. No. Wait. I want to stop comparing you to other women. Let's just admire Dana. [Pauses and does so.] She's very pretty.

Inner Child: Yes, she is.

Inner Caretaker: And you're pretty, too, in a different kind of way. You have a very womanly roundness, and I love your sexy hips, the light in your eyes, and those big, sensuous lips.

Inner Child: Really? You never said that to me before.

Inner Caretaker: I know and I'm sorry about that. Now that I'm learning to appreciate how you look and to love you unconditionally, I'm starting to see how attractive you really are.

Inner Child: [Smiles to herself and feels better.]

Or

Inner Critic: Look at Sue over there. She's fat and looks terrible, and you're as big as she is. No. Wait. I don't want to be critical or compare, I want to look at what I do like about her looks. Let me see. [Pauses and looks.] You know, she has great eyes, fabulous hair, and I love her smile. And here's Lee coming in. Let me see what I like about the way she looks. [Pauses and considers.] She has a really sexy walk, the way she sashays her hips, and she has such a voluptuous body—very round and full and ripe.

Inner Child: You know, you're right. I never noticed those things before. Lee's and Sue's bodies also look soft and comforting.

Inner Caretaker: So does yours. You have a very womanly roundness, and I love your sexy hips, the light in your eyes, and those big, sensuous lips. I think you're really attractive.

Inner Child: Really? [Pauses to take this in and enjoy it.] If Lee and Sue are attractive, maybe I am, too.

As we just saw with Ellen, it is just as important to stop comparing yourself to women who you think are less attractive than yourself as it is to stop comparing yourself to those who you think are more attractive. When, rather than focusing on another woman's big nose, small breasts, or large size, you focus instead on her sexy walk, striking eyes, or full-figured sensuality, you are actively expanding your vision of beauty and setting up guidelines to appreciate your own looks. Let's review how to regard other women and ourselves in a mutually empowering way.

Liking Your Looks by Being Mutually Empowering

1. Promise yourself that from now on you're going to strive to appreciate and admire other women's looks.

2. Stop comparing your appearance to that of other women.

3. Cease criticizing and belittling other women's looks, and instead praise both them and yourself.

4. If you find yourself about to belittle another woman's appearance (either out loud or in your head), immediately stop your-

self and examine what you are feeling about your own looks that is making you want to do this. Help yourself with these feelings by CARESSing yourself and praising your looks. Then find at least three things to praise about the other woman's looks.

5. Make a special point of reacting to women you think are knockouts by praising them without comparing yourself to them. Then praise yourself. Use your BEAUTIFUL ME list to remind yourself of everything you like about your looks.

6. Practice finding at least three things you like about the looks of every woman you see. You won't have time to do this all the time, but do it as much as you can. It is a great way to expand your concept of beauty, can entertain you on the bus or subway, during boring meetings, or while waiting in line at the supermarket, and it really works. You'll be surprised how much wider your appreciation for your own looks becomes, as well as for other women's, when you train yourself to look for the beauty in every woman.

7. Turn your inner critic into an inner caretaker. The job of your inner caretaker is to CARESS you—to give you the Compassion, Acceptance, Respect, Encouragement, Support, and Stroking that builds self-esteem and enables you to like your looks and yourself. This means having compassion for whatever you are feeling about your looks, and accepting these feelings nonjudgmentally. Respect yourself just as you look now. Encourage yourself to expand your concept of beauty by looking at all the ways in which you are attractive, and support yourself in this effort by continually reminding yourself of what you like about your looks. Lastly, and importantly, stroke yourself by giving yourself credit for all the steps you have been taking to like the way you look, for all that you are doing to value yourself as a whole person, for learning to praise yourself and your appearance, and most importantly of all, for being the beautiful, valuable person that you are.

8. Affirm your own attractiveness through at least daily reading of your BEAUTIFUL ME list.

As you strive to change how you view other women's appearance, remember that this is a goal. You won't be able to do it all the time, and you may have to catch yourself frequently. That's okay.

You're learning, and a lifetime of socialization doesn't go away overnight. Don't expect perfection from yourself. Just be clear about the direction in which you want to move. And remember:

THE MORE YOU PRAISE, RATHER THAN CRITICIZE, OTHER WOMEN'S LOOKS AND YOUR OWN, THE MORE YOU WILL LIKE YOUR LOOKS AND YOURSELF.

*L*ETTING THE GLINT IN YOUR EYES CAPTURE THE GLINT IN HIS (OR HERS): FINDING AND KEEPING A MATE

*I*hope you're excited about the prospect of embracing the notion of cooperative beauty, in which women appreciate one another's diverse looks. But if you're straight you might be worrying about how accepting and priding yourself on your natural appearance will affect you with men. Having been told all your life that women's appearance is very important to men and that men want women who look like models, you may fear that in order to get or keep a man you have to lose weight, work out, and maybe even get a nose job or a face-lift. Similarly, if you're a lesbian, you may fear that you need to alter your face or body in order to find a satisfying and lasting relationship.*

Well, stop worrying. The truth is that there are plenty of coupled or married women (some even several times married) who were

---

*All the exercises in this chapter apply equally to finding and keeping a partner of either sex. However, because men are generally considered to be more judgmental of women's appearance than are women, I will focus more in this chapter on attracting men. If you are a lesbian, please substitute gender where needed.

never thin, don't have a face that could launch a thousand ships, and have never seen the inside of a health club. Remember the sensitive, successful men quoted in Chapter 9 who, when asked what in a woman most turned them on, talked about personality, confidence, and compatibility rather than physical perfection? Sure, it's true that men are socialized to place great emphasis on a woman's physical appearance (as are women) and to view a beautiful partner as a status symbol, but it's also true that men are often not nearly as judgmental of a woman's appearance as the woman herself is.

It's common for a man to really like the way his wife or girlfriend looks, while she doubts her own attractiveness. We all know how those conversations go. You say, "How does my hair look?" Or, "I don't know if this color looks good on me." Or, "I think this outfit makes me look really fat." He examines you carefully, then tells you that your hair looks fine, he likes that color on you, and that you don't look fat. You know he's always truthful when he gives his opinion. Are you now reassured and satisfied? Don't be silly. You remain in front of the mirror fussing, asking again if he's sure about your hair, the color, and the outfit. You may even change it all. How you look is not good enough for you.

Others of you are on a perpetual diet. Your husband or lover assures you that you look fine, that he likes you at whatever size, and he doesn't understand why you're dieting. You explain that if you're not very careful you'll really get fat, or fatter. He says that's okay with him, he likes a woman with flesh on her, and that he wishes you would stop dieting because dieting makes you irritable. Do you breathe a sigh of relief, throw away your diet books, stock up on snacks, and let your belt out a notch? Fat chance. You get upset with him. You tell him how hard you're trying to keep your weight down, what a battle it is for you, and that you'd appreciate a little support.

In reality, it's often not men or lovers we're really trying to please. We want to look good because society says we must to be respected and valued, even though women who look like models are more likely to be put down as bimbos than respected. In our quest for society's approval, we believe the propaganda that says that men are most attracted to women who achieve the beauty ideal, but this is frequently not the case. When April Fallon and Paul Rozin asked women college students to choose the size body (from a series of body shapes along a continuum) that men would consider most attractive, they indicated a thin body much like that of the beauty ideal. But when these researchers asked college men to indicate which size body they found most attractive, they chose a size significantly larger.

Rozin and Fallon found that mature women, too, are just as mistaken about what body size men prefer. In a study of both parents and their college-age sons and daughters, they found that both generations of women believe that men of their own generation prefer much thinner women than those men actually indicated they prefer. (The men, on the other hand, believed that women liked heavier men than the women actually did.) Lesbians, too, as David B. Herzog and his colleagues at Massachusetts General Hospital found, think potential partners prefer slimmer women than they themselves find ideal.

Okay, you may want to argue, maybe a lot of men, as well as lesbians, like more roundness and fleshiness than the models have, but there are limits to how fat you can be, and how you can look, if you want to get a mate. We all know which woman is sought out for dates, who's chosen as prom queen, and whom everyone wants to get next to, and it's not the woman with glasses who can quote Shakespeare and Emily Dickinson. Well, true, and false.

Yes, boys do want to date the prettiest girls, or at least the most popular. But why? Because it's a feather in their caps. It boosts their egos, increases their status, makes them somebody. Adolescents want more than anything to fit in and be accepted and admired by their peers, and they can be very cruel to those who are different. Men, however, are not boys.

By the time a man, or at least a man you would want to be with, is ready to settle down and marry, he has usually learned that there is a lot more to a woman than her wrapping. He wants a woman who has the personal qualities he values, a personality that meshes well with his, and someone who shares his outlook, goals, and values. If she is also great-looking, all the better, but no man worth marrying would choose a wife based primarily on how she looks.

The reality is that if you like yourself and the way you look, chances are he will, too. You think that's crazy? Remember the girls who were cheerleaders and prom queens when you were in high school? Were they all raving beauties? I doubt it. They probably had something else—a certain vibrancy, an enthusiasm, a self-confidence that radiated attractiveness. I know that was true of the cheerleaders and prom queens in my high school, and I see the same pattern now in my daughter's school.

The reverse is true, too. Do you remember girls from your high school who were really very conventionally pretty but not popular? (If not, look at your yearbook.) Have you read of women movie or TV stars who were not popular as teenagers? Neither is uncommon because conventional good looks without self-confidence often fall flat, while self-esteem and self-confidence radiate beauty.

Well, you may be thinking, it's true that the most popular girls in high school or college weren't gorgeous and pretty girls weren't always popular, but none of the popular girls were really fat. What chance does a really fat woman have to get a man, given the great fat prejudice that presently exists in our society? Well, yes. The sad truth is that many men will automatically reject a very fat woman based on her size alone. Sadder still, this rejection is not always based on the man's personal dislike of her size, but on society's scorn for this size and his consequent unwillingness to be seen as a loser for being with such a woman. On the other hand, many fat women are in stable relationships, and many thin women are not. Undoubtedly, some very large women got fat after they married, but many were always fat (because a woman who is genetically destined to be quite fat often has struggled with her weight since childhood).

Whether you are a size 8, 14, or XXXLarge, you may think you are too fat to attract Mr. (or Ms.) Right. Some of you may be young and single, others not so young and still single, or single again after a breakup, divorce, or being widowed. Whatever your age or size, if you think you are too fat to attract a partner, this feeling may in all likelihood be self-fulfilling.

We all tend to step up to, or down to, levels of expectation. If you tell yourself you're too ignorant to be able to understand the stock market, or too bad at spatial relations to put together your child's toy, or too old to learn how to program your VCR, you probably won't succeed at any of these things, even if you try. On the other hand, if you tell yourself that people with less intelligence than you have learned to understand the stock market, and that it just takes time and persistence, or if you tell yourself that whatever your spatial relationship abilities, if you go step by step, even if you make mistakes and have to redo parts, you'll eventually get the complicated toy together, or if you tell yourself that if a six-year-old can program a VCR, then so can you, then it's very likely that you will succeed. Expectations have a powerful influence on outcome. For instance, teachers told (falsely) that average and below-average pupils have been predicted by a test as being about to academically bloom produce great leaps in learning.

When you feel that you are too fat to get a mate, you are responding to society's expectation: Society expects fat women to be scorned and rejected. When you buy into this expectation, what's happening within is that your inner critic is telling your inner child that you are fat and ugly and don't stand a chance. When you give yourself this message, it is very difficult to project a positive image.

Don't internalize society's expectations. Expect more of yourself. Stop telling yourself that you are too fat to attract someone. If you want to find a mate, whether or not you're fat, start giving yourself positive messages, such as:

> I am a uniquely beautiful woman.
> I like my body and my looks.
> I am a sexy and sensual woman.
> I'm a wonderful person, and the right man (or woman) will be
> lucky to get me.
> I radiate attractiveness.
> Someone has to be a quality person to interest me.
> I'm sure that sooner or later I will enter into a relationship
> with someone who's right for me.

Add to this list your own affirmations that tell you what you most need to hear. The more you give yourself these messages and internalize them, the more likely you are to connect with the person of your dreams. Experience tells us that the more attractive a woman (or a man, either, for that matter) feels, the more attractive she is perceived by those around her. When you like the way you look, you get that self-confident glint in your eyes that others find so attractive. You know that glint when you see it in a man's eyes. It makes any man sexy and desirable. It works the same for you. That glint is like a sign that declares to all comers that here's an attractive woman of worth, who knows her value. It makes people want to get to know you and discover your value, too. It's like silently proclaiming that you like yourself and your looks, and you expect others to do so, too.

The power of positive expectations is formidable, but it's not magic. It doesn't mean that the first time you go out with your new attitude you'll be besieged by suitors. Many very attractive, thin, confident wonderful women go to social events and don't meet anyone. But over time the more you like the way you look and feel good about your looks and yourself, the more men, and women, will see you as attractive and desirable.

I don't mean to suggest that there aren't any men, or some lesbians as well, who are very hung up with how a woman looks and make appearance their number-one priority. But these people will not be able to make you happy, whether or not you meet their requirements. How happy can you be in a relationship in which your role is to be a status symbol? A satisfying and lasting relationship needs to be based on a lot more than beauty standards.

There is also no evidence that women who meet society's definition of ideal beauty have better, longer-lasting, or happier relationships. Just look at people you know or the divorce rate in Hollywood. What counts most in a successful relationship are commitment, sharing, caring, and mutual empowerment.

Whether you're looking to meet someone, dating, or in a permanent relationship, the more attractive you feel, the more attractive you will appear. And the better you feel about yourself and your looks, the more your partner will continue to prize you. The exercises in the previous chapters taught you how to learn to see your own beauty. Now, let's see how to hold onto these positive feelings about your looks when you're under the pressure of looking for a partner and fear being rejected on the basis of your appearance.

One of the most pressured situations any woman can find herself in is a blind date. Your date's never seen you, and you worry that once he or she gets a look at you maybe he or she won't ever want to see you again. On any other first date, at least you have the comfort of knowing that your date knows what you look like. But with a blind date it's easy to create self-defeating fantasies: Maybe he'll think I'm too fat or not pretty enough or be repelled by the slight gap in my front teeth or by this pimple I just got, etc., etc. By the time you actually meet your date, you may be such a wreck that he or she sees you at your least self-confident.

As difficult as or worse than a blind date is attending a singles event. It doesn't help any woman to feel attractive if she goes to a singles event and no one tries to make her acquaintance or wants to dance with her. At an event like this, it's really important to like the way you look and to hold onto these feelings. For one thing, you're more likely to meet someone. A confident woman holds her body differently, projecting a different body language, and has a more alluring look in her eye than that of a woman who expects rejection. For another, the more you like the way you look, the easier it is to use a singles event as an opportunity to scope the field out and approach those that catch your eye.

Well, you may be thinking, of course I want to feel confident, but it's one thing to say, "Like the way you look" and "Be confident," and it's another thing to feel it.

Much as you may want to feel centered and in control, and be the chooser, you may find this hard to do. The very thought of a blind date, or the pressure of attending a singles event or other social occasion at which you're hoping to meet someone, may drive all positive thoughts and feelings about your looks and yourself from your mind, and you may find yourself a nervous bundle of insecurities. If so, make it a point to do the following exercise several times before going out. If you have time, it's best to do it daily for four or five days before the event. Otherwise, do it at least once or twice on the day of the event. The more you practice it, the more ingrained its message will become, but even a little practice can go a long way.

Centering Yourself in Feelings of Attractiveness

Take out your BEAUTIFUL ME list and read it SLOWLY out loud. Then:

[See the Appendix for full relaxation instructions.]

Get comfortable. Then close your eyes, and put your thumb and index finger together on each hand. Take a deep breath, deep into your diaphragm and abdomen, and hold it for five seconds, then gradually let it out to a slow count of five. Now, take five comfortable SLOW deep breaths, and when you finish, let your fingers open, and continue breathing normally and comfortably. As you are breathing, in any way that is natural, let yourself become perhaps a little more peaceful, maybe a little more relaxed, letting go of tensions in any way that you know how, and going inside yourself to a lovely place of comfort and peace, or any other place that feels right to you.

As you continue breathing comfortably, let yourself become even more relaxed in any way that you know how, knowing that it is relaxing to let go, and that letting go is relaxing, and that sometimes even as you tense up you are able to become more relaxed—perhaps just by feeling where the tension is in your body, and then letting it go—and that relaxation has its own way of releasing tension, and it really doesn't matter whether you use tension to relax yourself, or relaxation as a way of letting go of tension, because you really do know how to relax in the way that is best for you.

And as you continue to relax, let all the things you like about your face, your body, and your appearance in general float into your awareness. Let yourself really absorb these assets and take them in. Allow your good feelings about the way you look, the many ways in which you are attractive, and desirable, to spread through your body, bringing with them a sense of comfort, and confidence, filling you with good feelings about yourself and the way that you look. Just as the sun on a cool day can shine down and warm your body, spreading warmth and good feelings throughout, in the same way, good feelings about your looks and yourself can suffuse your body with a calm, warm confident feeling, filling you with the knowledge that you are an attractive, worthwhile, desirable woman who has a lot to offer any partner, knowing that the partner you end up with will be very lucky to have found you, because you really are an attractive, desirable, and wonderful woman. And it really is lovely to recognize how your inner value shines through. And I wonder what ways you will find to remind yourself of all the ways you are attractive and desirable. Perhaps you will think of the sun and be immediately suffused with confident feelings of being attractive, and desirable, or maybe you will find your own special way of recognizing and feeling your desirability, knowing that whatever way you find will be right for you. And each time you use the method that is right for you to recognize and experience your real attractiveness, you may find it easier and easier to get in touch with, and anchored in, feeling attractive and desirable. So, stay now, and let the good feeling of appreciating your looks continue to spread its warmth and confidence throughout your body, reminding you of how attractive you really are. Stay with that good feeling for as long as you like. Then, when you're ready, open your eyes and return to the room, feeling relaxed, refreshed, and more confident.

Before going on that blind date, or to the singles event or other social occasion, read your WHAT I LIKE ABOUT MYSELF and BEAUTIFUL ME lists to remind yourself of all the things you like about yourself and your looks. Once there, dismiss whatever negative feelings about yourself and your looks that may pop up, and instead focus on all the positive assets you have identified. Use the image of the sun, or whatever other cue you chose, to remind you of your attractiveness and desirability. Continue to give yourself positive messages such as:

I am a wonderful and uniquely beautiful woman.

My worth or attractiveness has nothing to do with whether or not someone approaches me. I will not give this power to someone I don't even know.

I really have a wonderful face, soft, bouncy hair, warm and inviting body, etc. (Go through all the things you like about your appearance.)

I am a sexy and sensual woman.

Mr. (or Ms.) Right will be lucky to find me.
I radiate attractiveness.
I am a wonderful and uniquely beautiful woman.

Being the Active Chooser, Rather Than a Passive Object

Often we women are so focused on whether we will be found attractive and desirable that we have little energy left to focus on being the chooser. Instead, we feel like a flower hoping to be picked. This is a very vulnerable and dangerous position to put yourself into—vulnerable because you're putting all the power into the hands of another, who can then decide whether you're worthy or not merely by whether or not he or she deigns to talk to you. It's dangerous because in this vulnerable state you can be easily hurt, your self-esteem undermined, and your judgment clouded. You may be so anxious to be chosen that you make little or no effort to really evaluate whether a given person is someone who would be good for you and to you.

When looking for a mate, it is very important to remember that he or she has to be able to meet your needs. I'm not talking about being so picky that no one is ever good enough for you, but I am talking about recognizing what is important to you in a partner and checking a potential mate out to see if he or she has the qualities you want. Remember, this is your opportunity to look at and evaluate him or her. If you tend to freeze up or feel unconscious, it can help to have a mental list of questions prepared beforehand. As you focus on getting the answers to your questions, it adds to your sense of feeling powerful, desirable, and in control. Some questions you may want to consider are:

1. Does he/she ask questions about you, or does he/she just go on and on about himself and his interests?

2. Is he/she interested in getting to know you, or is he/she just trying to see what you can offer him?

3. Do you have enough in common?

4. Does he/she seem to be a good person?

5. Does he/she share outlooks and interests that are vital to you? Does he/she have any special talents or interests that especially appeal to you?

6. Would you like him/her as a friend?

7. What's his/her track record with past relationships?

Using these questions, or others that are pertinent to you, to appraise a possible partner, rather than being all focused on hoping he or she likes you and worrying about how you look, has several advantages: You get important information; you put yourself in the confident, power position of being the evaluator and the chooser; and you'll be too busy interviewing him or her to worry about how you look. He or she may be interviewing you, too. That's fine. You can both be powerful. What you don't want to do, though, is abdicate your own power and hand it over to the other person, then desperately hope you can meet his or her expectations. When you're overfocused on pleasing, and trying to look good for him or her, rather than trying to figure out if he or she can please you, you're presenting yourself as a person of little value and power, thus making it less likely that your date will see you as desirable, attractive, and worthwhile. Why should he or she see you as a prize if you don't?

UNHYPE YOURSELF

When you want to form a relationship, part of what you're up against, as we saw earlier, is your own negative expectations which come from society's hype that you have to look like the beauty ideal to get a mate and find happiness. The more you accept this hype, the harder time you're going to have being successful in your search for that right somebody because of the power of expectations. Let's demystify this hype.

1. Think of every married or permanently coupled woman you know, especially those of your age, and write her name down on a list until you have at least twenty-five to thirty. How many of them look like models? Unless all your friends are models, at best, maybe 5 percent. The rest undoubtedly distribute themselves over a

diverse range of shapes, features, and sizes. Realize that there's only one way you have to look to get married—the way nature made you.

2. Look at couples wherever you go: the street, supermarkets, meetings, parks, restaurants, the movies. Again, how many of the women look like models? How many look very different from models? Recognize again that this is how you have to look to get a mate—the way nature made you.

3. Think of every woman you know who is single or divorced, especially those your own age, and write her name down. Make the list as long as possible. How many of these women approach the beauty ideal or are attractive? Likely there are as many as or more on this list than the coupled or married women on your previous list. Is it starting to sink in? Beauty doesn't bring marriage or happiness, and despite the media hype you don't have to look like a movie star to attract a mate.

4. Make a list of couples you know who have been together many years. Are the women in these relationships particularly good-looking, or have they aged particularly well? Are these women more conventionally pretty than their divorced or single peers? Likely not. Again, there's only one way you have to look to stay happily mated—the way nature made you.

Of course, some men do leave their wives for younger, presumably prettier women. But the story may be more complicated than that. Perhaps the first marriage was troubled, or real issues were ignored and glossed over. In other cases, the man was simply attracted to a younger woman who would enhance his ego with her youthful looks and admiration for him.

If you were married to such a man, as painful and perhaps as economically difficult as his leaving may have been for you, it is also possible that his leaving opened new possibilities. Perhaps you are freer now to listen to your own sense of what is important to you, what interests you, what fulfills you. Perhaps you can now stop being overfocused on pleasing him and others, and consider what pleases you. Most of all, perhaps you can come to know what your real value is, and that it does not lie in how you look, no matter how attractive you may be, but who you are.

Letting the Glint in Your Eyes Capture the Glint in His (or Hers)

In short, the more you like the way you look, proudly hold your head high, and feel worthwhile and valuable—a catch—the more present and potential partners will appreciate you, too. No, this attitude won't erase fat prejudice and beauty-ideal elitism—we women as a group need to band together, along with like-thinking men, to do that. Nonetheless, even without these changes, and whatever your size or features, when you accept and like the way you look, you put that all-important scintillating glint in your eye that beckons others to you and announces that you are a woman worth knowing and having. Appreciate yourself and your looks, and others will, too.

CHAPTER 13

SEX AND BODY IMAGE

Janice met Michael when they worked together as volunteers in the last City Council election. She really liked him, more than any man she had known before, and was thrilled when he asked her out. When, after several dates, they first made love, she was very excited but she couldn't relax and enjoy. She kept thinking about her body and how Michael must be thinking that her thighs were too flabby and her stomach too big. She felt so self-conscious that her excitement soon faded, and she couldn't wait to get it over with. This pattern continued whenever they made love. At first, Michael reacted to Janice's lack of responsiveness by trying harder to arouse and satisfy her. This added attention to her body made Janice feel even more self-conscious and uncomfortable. Soon, Michael began to feel inadequate and rejected, and he responded by distancing and withdrawing. Within a few months the relationship had soured because of what had become a sexual problem.

Janice is not typical of the women who consult me because of a sexual difficulty. While many women are self-conscious about their bodies when making love, it usually doesn't interfere with their enjoyment to the degree that Janice experienced. But I'm sharing Janice's story because her difficulty clearly illustrates a common phenomenon: Worrying about being seen as sexy interferes with being sexy.

Good sex requires two people meeting each other with desire and pleasure, full of positive feelings and thoughts. The body is the medium of pleasure and needs to be embraced and accepted. But commonly women have difficulty viewing their bodies in the positive way. With new lovers, many women, like Janice, are often afraid that their bodies will be found wanting. In long-term relationships, women may be less afraid of rejection, but often women reject their own bodies. It is hard to abandon yourself to the joys of sex if you're preoccupied with how your breasts are sagging, the flab on your body, the wrinkles on your face, or your stretch marks. In addition, if you only feel comfortable making love in the dark, you are robbing yourself of the opportunity to enjoy the visual stimulation of viewing your partner's body and face, the excitement that comes from seeing as well as feeling your partner respond to you and your touch, and the deep connection that's established when you look into each other's eyes with caring, excitement, and pleasure. Many women's very real and even powerful sexuality is interfered with by their worry about looking sexy.

Lucy: When I was first married, I loved to make love in the morning with the light streaming in the windows. I really enjoyed looking at Rick's body and into his eyes, and seeing him admiring my body. Now, after fifteen years and three children, I'm just not comfortable like that. I've put on some weight, and everything seems to be falling, and I have these stretch marks, and crow's feet around my eyes. Rick says he thinks I look great, but I just don't feel comfortable in all that light anymore. Now we only make love at night with the lights off.

Leslie: *I've been dating Tom for about six months. I have this big stomach, so when we make love I like to stay on my back so it looks flatter. Sometimes Tom would like me to be on top, but I don't dare let him see me like that, with my stomach hanging down.*

Erica: *I've always been self-conscious about having small breasts. They're so small that I haven't ever needed a bra. And my lover, Betsy, has really large full breasts. Betsy says she loves my small breasts, but I think she's just trying to make me feel better. When we make love, I don't like her to touch them because when she does, I can't help thinking about how small they are and I get a little upset and distracted.*

Lucy, Leslie, and Erica are all sensual women whose true sexuality is being dampened by worrying about how they look. Lucy has given up a part of lovemaking that she used to enjoy—making love at her favorite time of day under the warm rays of the sun with lots of visual stimulation and pleasure. Leslie is limiting her sexual adventuresomeness not out of true timidity (she really is adventurous), but because she's afraid of how her body will be judged. And Erica is depriving herself of a type of stimulation that many women find at least pleasant, if not extremely exciting, because of her own negative judgments about having small breasts. All three needed to learn to focus on their bodies as instruments—something they use to get and give pleasure—not objects, while making love. When they did, they all experienced a surge in sexual pleasure.

Do you, like Lucy, Leslie, and Erica, have difficulty embracing your body as a source of pleasure because you're so busy worrying about how your partner is viewing it? Imagine the following scenario. You're making love and really getting into it when you suddenly realize that in your present position your partner has a full view of your wide fleshy thighs. If you like your thighs, this thought can be a real turn-on, making you feel even sexier—as you picture how enticing, alluring, and exciting you must look and be to your partner—so that you turn to your partner with added enthusiasm.

On the other hand, if you hate your thighs and think they're revolting, realizing that they're on display may well have the opposite effect—lessening your enjoyment as you imagine your partner being turned off or disgusted by the sight of them. Perhaps you can shrug this image off, but it may well stay there, diminishing your pleasure just a little bit or a lot. The more your mind dwells on how "revolting" your thighs are, the more it turns away from pleasurable experiencing, and so, generally, does your body along with it. Maybe you tense up just a little bit, or your breathing tightens slightly, or you feel impelled to change your position. Any or all of these reactions will diminish your pleasure as you move from being wholly involved in making love to being in the position of a spectator, in which you are standing outside yourself watching yourself. The more you spectate, instead of being in the moment, the less pleasure you will experience.

Men, too, experience diminished pleasure when they spectate, and sometimes it causes anxiety that seriously interferes with sexual functioning. However, they generally worry not about how their bodies will be seen, but about how their penises will function.

Women, as opposed to men, rarely worry about their actual physical performance. Unless we have a sexual difficulty, we take it for granted that if we're excited and enjoying ourselves, we will lubricate (unless we're postmenopausal, and then may need to use some additional lubricant) and experience pleasure and perhaps orgasm. We also know that there is a lot more to enjoying sex than the typical male linear drive to orgasm. Good sex, for women, generally requires a whole person–whole body experience in which what is in your heart, head, body, and soul comes together with another person whom you at the very least trust, or, even better, love. Most women also deeply enjoy nongenital touching, and for some women it's the best part about sex, even if they are easily orgasmic. While women typically enjoy coming to orgasm we don't necessarily experience it as the be-all and end-all of sex, but rather as just one pleasurable part of the giving, getting, caressing, and sharing that sex entails. Many women can enjoy making love whether or not they reach orgasm, because there are so many other ways in which they experience deep pleasure.

Men, by comparison, tend to be genital- and orgasm-focused. It is rare for a man to really enjoy a sexual experience that doesn't entail ejaculation, while seduction, romance, and foreplay may not be as important. For example, hardly a man would complain if his woman came home, wordlessly unzipped him, and engaged in oral sex. On the other hand, if the situation were reversed, many women would be a lot less than thrilled.

Because good sex is such an encompassing experience, anything that distracts a woman from her inner eroticism and pleasurable experiencing and giving is a turnoff. Of course, many things besides being worried about how her body looks can provide this turnoff. Past sexual trauma, depression, distrust or fear of her partner or of sex itself, anger, anxiety, everyday worries, and even the thought of things that need doing or of upcoming events can intrude, acting to lessen enjoyment and, in some cases, to mute it entirely. Other sources of distraction can also be intensified by negative emphasis on appearance.

Some women have sustained sexual difficulties. They may be unable to have an orgasm, allow for intercourse, or experience sexual desire or pleasure. If this is true for you, give yourself the chance to reclaim your sexuality and sexual pleasure. Consult a sex therapist. If you are a survivor of sexual abuse, be sure to ask any therapists you are considering working with about their experience in working with survivors. For referrals, see Resources.

Even if you don't have a sexual problem, that doesn't mean you won't occasionally freeze up, turn off, or, more commonly, experience diminished pleasure. This may happen because you're upset about or distracted by something, or because you're spectating; perhaps because you're worrying about how your body looks to your partner. If so, you need to stop focusing on your body as an object, especially as a disliked object, and increase your focus on it as an instrument of your pleasure.

Sex is the time, par excellence, when you need your body to be you, and you to be it, so that you are a whole: body, mind, feelings, and spirit coming together to experience pleasure and exchange it with your partner. Even if you don't generally spectate (everyone does some of the time), increasing your focus on your body as an instrument will heighten your sexual pleasure. Let's see how we do this.

MY BODY IS FOR SEXY ME

List each section of your body (feet, legs, thighs, hips, genitals, stomach, chest, breasts, back, shoulders, butt, neck, arms, hands, head, eyes, ears, nose, and mouth). Next to each section list at least two or three ways this part of your body gives you pleasure during sex, and label this list SEXY ME. For instance:

Stomach:

Feels wonderful when it's rubbed.
Gives me a warm, close feeling when it is pressing against my
    partner.
One finger very lightly dragged around it really excites me.
Thinking about its roundness makes me feel sexy.
Breathing deeply into it relaxes me and makes me feel re-
    ceptive.

Thighs:

Stroking the inside of my thighs, in a light teasing way, really
    turns me on.
My thighs are my guardians and protectors, refusing to open
    up until I'm ready for genital touching, so they give me a
    good feeling of safety, which lets me relax and get more
    turned on.
Pressing them against my partner is really erotic.
The power in them makes me feel powerful and sensual.

Butt:

I get very passionate when I feel hard pressure on it from my
    partner's hands.

When it's gently cupped, it sends little shivers up me.

Slow kneading of it creates a comfort and an excitement in me.

Grinding it against my partner is very sensual.

Playfully mooning my partner turns me on.

Hips:

Gentle stroking of them feels so good and caring and loving, it really gets me in the mood.

Moving them, and my pelvis along with them, sends all kinds of delicious feelings through my body.

In any position that we make love, rocking my hips increases my pleasure.

Their width and breadth make me feel as if I'm built for sex, which gives me a lot of confidence in myself sexually and makes it easy for me to let go and follow my own instincts.

These examples are not a list of how you should feel—just of how you might feel. On the other hand, you might experience pleasure from these body parts in entirely different ways. That's fine. Each of us has our own individual ways of experiencing our body, our partner's body, and our own pleasure. Listen to yourself and your own body, and see how the different parts of your unique body contribute to the good feelings you experience when making love. In doing so, concentrate especially on the body parts that you are most self-conscious about, and be sure to come up with at least two or three ways in which these parts of your body add to your sexual enjoyment. If you have trouble identifying ways in which different parts of your body give you sexual pleasure, this may be because you've been so focused on your body as an object that some of your sensual feelings have gone unnoticed. The next several times you make love, in the back of your mind pay attention to the ways these parts of your body are adding to your excitement and pleasure, and add them to your list. When you have listed at least two or three ways these body parts give you pleasure, read your SEXY ME list over slowly out loud several times to yourself, and really take it in. Then do the following visualization.

I've Got a Secret

(See the Appendix for full relaxation instructions.)

Get comfortable. Then close your eyes, and put your thumb and index finger together on each hand. Take a deep breath, deep into your diaphragm and abdomen, and hold it for five seconds, then gradually let it out to a slow count of five. Now, take five comfortable SLOW deep breaths, and when you finish, let your fingers open, and continue breathing normally and comfortably. As you are breathing, in any way that is natural, let yourself become perhaps a little more peaceful, maybe a little more relaxed, letting go of tensions in any way that you know how, and going inside yourself to a lovely place of comfort and peace, or any other place that feels right to you.

As you're continuing to relax, breathing in any way that is comfortable for you, allow yourself to imagine that you live in a society where highly sexual women teach other women how to increase their enjoyment of sex. You are one of the teachers, and today you will be talking to your students, who are entering the room now, about how to focus on their bodies as instruments and not objects. You start by telling them of your own transformation, how you learned to focus on the ways in which your body gives you pleasure. Tell them about each of the ways you experience pleasure in every part of your body. And let them know how much fuller, and richer, your sex life has become since you began more completely realizing the pleasure available to you in every part of your body. Explain how all these parts come together to form a highly erotic whole, and how you no longer know if you are immersing yourself in your body, or if your body is immersing itself in you, but you really do know that you have come to experience ever-deepening levels of pleasure, excitement, and eroticism. Tell your students that you know that they, too, will come to experience what you have learned to experience, and to feel how good it is to be one with your body, and to have it be one with you. As the class ends, and as the grateful students leave, you know that you have done well, passing on important wisdom and knowledge to your students, a knowledge and wisdom that you yourself are continuing to experience and build on in new and different ways. And it will be interesting to see, in the days, weeks, and months to follow, all the different ways in which your wisdom and knowledge may heighten your sexual experience and enrich your life. Now, take another minute to savor the prospect of sexual growth and enrichment. Then, when you are ready, open your eyes and return to the room.

That Feels Good

The next step in focusing on your body as an instrument is to learn more about how each part of your body likes to be touched. Plan a touch session with your partner. If you don't have a partner, do this with yourself, touching all the parts you can reach easily. Tell your partner you want to hone your sensuality by discovering how each part of your body responds to different types of touch. Start by lying on your stomach, and ask your partner to touch each part of your back from the top of your head to the bottom of your toes. Have your partner try different types of touch on each part. Then switch sides and do the same thing on the front, excluding your genitals. Tell your partner to feel free to use oil, fabrics, and mouth. See what you discover. Maybe you find that your toes like to be gently sucked, your knees to be massaged with oil, your stomach to be brushed with velvet, your shoulders to be rubbed with silk, your nipples to be squeezed hard, your face to be stroked gently, your neck to be covered with small kisses, and the rest of your body to be caressed lightly. Some parts of your body may like lots of different types of touch. Other parts may be very choosy and like only a certain type of touch in a certain type of way. Sometimes a part of your body may like one type of touch before you are aroused, and another type of touch after. Take as much time as you need, as you slowly explore your body.

When you finish, if you wish, you may continue the same type of gentle exploration with your genitals, again trying different types of touch and movements to see which are most pleasurable for you. Make this a time of real exploration, rather than just falling into your regular pattern. Maybe after exploring you'll find that your usual pattern is perfect for you, or perhaps you'll discover new ways to augment your enjoyment. Whatever you learn, let it become incorporated into your lovemaking in the way that feels best for you, and add it to your store of knowledge of the ways in which various parts of your body give you pleasure.

When you are done, your partner may wish to have you explore his or her body in the same way. That's fine, but only after you've had ample time in which to stay focused on and savor your own sensations and experience.

Having a Mental Image of Yourself as Beautiful

Now that you have learned how to focus on your body as an instrument, it's time to combine the sensual pleasure your body gives with your overall body image, so that when you make love, all your positive feelings about your body, your looks, and yourself are working together to increase your pleasure.

Take out your BEAUTIFUL ME and WHAT I LIKE ABOUT MYSELF lists. Hopefully, by now you are increasingly integrating positive feelings about your looks and yourself. When you first mentally prepare to make love, review these lists to yourself, reminding yourself of everything you like about the way that you look, and of how attractive you really are. Then read your SEXY ME list. Use these positive images of yourself not to look at and judge your looks and yourself, but to enter into your lovemaking with a sense of yourself as a beautiful, sexy, sensuous, wonderful woman.

From now on, whenever you are making love, remind yourself beforehand that you want to experience maximum pleasure by using all of your senses and your whole body. If you find yourself reverting to anxiety about how a certain part of your body looks to your lover, quickly switch to focusing on what that part of your body is experiencing right now, and what you can do to increase its pleasure. You may find it helpful to take a slow deep breath or two, and as you do so, focus on pleasurable feelings in that part, and every part, of your body. You can also increase your pleasure by switching your focus away from your body and on to your partner, paying attention to what it feels like to be seeing, feeling, sensing, smelling, and touching him or her in whatever way you are.

Remember how sexy you are, and that how much you enjoy sex has nothing to do with how you look, and everything to do with fully connecting with and appreciating yourself, your body, and your partner. Any size or shape body that is swaying, moving, caressing, brushing, giving, getting, slowing, sweating, exuding, cuddling, teasing, pleasuring, enticing, connecting, engaging, joining, taking, exploding is irresistible and erotic. The more you embrace your body as an instrument of your pleasure, the sexier you'll feel and the more sexual and sensuous you will become.

A Final Word

I hope that by now you have at least started to enlarge your view of beauty and to increase your appreciation for yourself and your looks. If you haven't done any of the exercises, I encourage you to do so. Don't forget to tape (or send for) the full relaxation instructions and the visualizations, so that you can fully immerse yourself into these experiences. Real change takes place when we look within, struggle with our negative feelings, and find self-acceptance and self-approval. If you don't wish to do all the exercises, do whichever ones feel relevant to you. If you don't do any of the others, at the very least make up a BEAUTIFUL ME list and get in the habit of reciting it to yourself whenever you look in the mirror. Allow yourself to experience the power you acquire when you learn to accept and love your body unconditionally and to like the way you look.

Appendix

RELAXATION INSTRUCTIONS

Get comfortable.... Then close your eyes, and put your thumb and index finger together on each hand.... And take a deep breath, deep into your diaphragm and abdomen, and hold it for five seconds,... then gradually let it out to a slow count of five.... That's right.... Now, take five comfortable SLOW deep breaths, ...that's right, five comfortable, slow, deep breaths.... That's good,... breathing slowly, deeply, comfortably.... And when you finish, let your fingers open, and continue breathing in any way that is normal and comfortable for you.... And as you do so, let yourself become perhaps a little more relaxed,... with each breath releasing tension in any way that you know how,... letting go of the cares of the day,... and going inside yourself to a secure place of comfort... and peace,... finding a place that is comfortable for you.... Knowing that there are many different ways to become relaxed,... and it really doesn't matter what ways you find to perhaps let go a little bit more,... without even having to know that you're doing it.... And knowing too that if whatever is said, either now or later, isn't right for you, you can disregard it, or change it into whatever you need to hear to relax in the way that is best for you,... and to benefit in the ways you need to benefit.... Finding your own way to deepen your relaxation, and to feel an attractive sense of peace and comfort,... perhaps relaxing your muscles just a bit,... or going deeper into yourself,... or letting your breathing carry you into a lovely sense of calm and safety,... a beautiful peacefulness.

Resources and Suggested Readings

THE BEAUTY IMPERATIVE

Bordo, Susan. *Unbearable Weight: Feminism, Western Culture, and the Body* (Berkeley: University of California Press, 1993).
> An intelligent exploration of the interaction between cultural forces, feminism, and conceptions and pressures surrounding women's bodies.

Chapkis, Wendy. *Beauty Secrets: Women and the Politics of Appearance* (Boston: South End Press, 1986).
> A feminist analysis coupled with a refreshing look at the various faces of beauty.

Chernin, Kim. *The Obsession: Reflections of the Tyranny of Slenderness* (New York: Harper & Row, 1982).
> A recovered anorexic's moving analysis of society's increasing demand that women be thin, why men have encouraged this obsession, and why women have embraced it.

Douglas, Susan J. *Where the Girls Are: Growing Up Female with the Mass Media* (New York: Random House, 1994).
> An entertaining, irreverent, revealing look at the influence of the mass media on women's relationships with themselves and their appearance.

Faludi, Susan. *Backlash: The Undeclared War Against American Women* (New York: Anchor/Doubleday, 1991).
> A page-riveting account of the counterassault on women's progress.

Hirschmann, Jane R. and Munter, Carol H., *When Women Stop Hating Their Bodies: Freeing Yourself from Food and Weight Obsession* (New York: Fawcett, 1995).

This exciting new book from the authors of *Overcoming Overeating* discusses the symptoms, etiology, and cure for body-bashing and body-hatred.

Wolf, Naomi. *The Beauty Myth* (New York: Doubleday, 1991).
A must-read, ground-breaking exposé of the ways beauty is used to control women.

SIZE-ACCEPTANCE

Association for the Health Enrichment of Large People (AHELP)
Joe McVoy, Director
P.O. Drawer C
Radford, VA 24143
Phone and fax: (540) 731-1778
Group for health professionals who use the nondieting approach.

Council on Size and Weight Discrimination
P.O. Box 305
Mount Marion, NY 12456
(914) 679-1209
Fax: (914) 679-1206
Provides information on size discrimination, including bibliographies, court decisions, antidiscrimination laws, and pending legislation; makes referrals to attorneys for size-discrimination cases; and advocates for size-acceptance with decision-makers in such areas as health care, scientific research, news reporting, and media entertainment.

Largesse, the Network for Size Esteem
P.O. Box 9404
New Haven, CT 06534-0404
Phone and fax: (203) 787-1624
E-mail: 75773.717@compuserve.com
An international clearinghouse for size-diversity empowerment. Not a membership organization, it offers free research

and referral services and all kinds of information and re-sources related to size empowerment and special-interest and special-need products for people of size.

National Association to Advance Fat Acceptance (NAAFA)
P. O. Box 188620
Sacramento, CA 95818
(916) 558-6880; (800) 442-1214 for recorded message.
Fax: (916) 558-6881
E-mail: pmzg10c@prodigy.com

A national organization with many local chapters that does education about and activism against fat discrimination, runs conferences, and has a newsletter and a mail-order book ser-vice. Within NAAFA there is also a feminist caucus and a les-bian fat activist network. Some local chapters focus on both activism and socializing while others primarily offer size-pos-itive social events for fat people and their admirers. (The books marked with an asterisk are available from NAAFA.) I strongly recommend that whatever your size, you help fight the tyranny of the Beauty Imperative by joining NAAFA, which needs your money and your energy.

Radiance
P. O. Box 30246
Oakland, CA 94606

This is a great magazine for large women seeking to accept their size, increase their self-esteem, and like the way they look. Its articles profile fat women who are having adven-tures, doing important things, making a difference, or just en-joying life. It also features excellent articles on fatness and health, size-acceptance poetry, fashions for large women, and lists catalogs and stores where attractive large-size clothes can be obtained. Very empowering.

Brown, Laura S. and Esther D. Rothblum, *Overcoming Fear of Fat** (New York: Harrington Park Press, 1989).

A collection of articles on fat oppression in psychotherapy.

Hall, Lindsey, ed. *Full Lives: Women Who Have Freed Themselves from Food & Weight Obsessions* (Carlsbad, CA: Gurze Books, 1993).

Sixteen women, many of them authors of well-known eating disorders recovery books, speak about their own personal journeys in relation to food and their bodies.

Newman, Leslea. *Fat Chance* (New York: G. P. Putnam's Sons, 1994).

Written in the form of the diary of a five four, 127-pound, thirteen-year-old girl who becomes bulimarexic because she feels she is fat. Beautifully and movingly written. Recommended for preteens or teens struggling with body image or eating disorders.

Roberts, Nancy. *Breaking All the Rules* (New York: Signet, 1983).

A fat woman and actress, Roberts tells of her own journey toward self-acceptance and self-assertion. The second half of the book is devoted to concrete advice on how to dress with pizzazz when you're fat.

Schoenfielder, Lisa and Barb Wieser, ed. *Shadow on a Tightrope: Writings by Women on Fat Oppression** (San Francisco: Aunt Lute Books, 1983).

A moving and empowering collection of writings and first-person experiences with fat oppression.

WEIGHT, HEALTH, AND THE PHYSIOLOGY OF DIETING

Atrens, Dale M. *Don't Diet* (New York: Morrow, 1988).

Very readable and highly informative, it explains why diets don't work and how, for most people, there is nothing unhealthy about being fat.

Bennett, William, and Joel Gurin. *The Dieter's Dilemma** (New York: Basic Books, HarperCollins, 1992).

A wonderful, highly readable book full of information about setpoint, metabolism, myths about weight and health, and other aspects of the physiology of weight.

Berg, Frances M., ed. *The Health Risks of Weight Loss* (Hettinger, ND: Obesity and Health, 1993).
Telling facts from the publisher of *Obesity and Health*. Order by phoning (701) 567-2845. Fax: 701-567-2443.

Ernsberger, Paul, and Paul Haskew. *Rethinking Obesity: An Alternative View of Its Health Implications** (New York: Human Sciences Press, 1987).
Very informative book full of annotated research that examines the protective functions of fatness and explains in detail how many of the health risks usually blamed on fatness may result not from being overweight, but from dieting.

Moore, Thomas. *Lifespan* (New York: Simon & Schuster, 1993).
Revealing information about the myths surrounding cholesterol, high blood pressure, heart disease, and weight.

Seid, Roberta. *Never Too Thin: Why Women Are at War with Their Bodies** (New York: Prentice Hall, 1989).
An engrossing history and exposé of how women are made to believe that their body size is unacceptable and should, and can, be modified.

HOW TO STOP DIETING AND EAT NATURALLY

Garrison, Terry Nicholetti with David Levitsky. *Fed Up: A Woman's Guide to Freedom from the Diet/Weight Prison* (New York: Carroll & Graf, 1993).
A warm, down-to-earth, encouraging, very accepting guide written by a woman who lost and regained thirty-five to seventy pounds many times, starting at age seven, before giving up dieting and learning to maintain her weight by eating naturally.

Hirschmann, Jane R. and Carol H. Munter. *Overcoming Overeating* (New York: Fawcett Columbine, 1988).

A practical and understanding guide that answers lots of specific questions about how to break out of the diet/binge cycle and start eating naturally. Carol Munter pioneered the non-diet approach.

Kano, Susan. *Making Peace with Food: Freeing Yourself from the Diet/Weight Obsession* (New York: Harper & Row, 1989).

A helpful workbook, written by a vegetarian and recovered borderline anorexic who's health food conscious but doesn't overly push this kind of eating.

Roth, Geneen. *Breaking Free from Compulsive Eating* (New York: Plume, 1993).

A moving book and guide, full of compassion, acceptance, humanity, and her own experiences.

The National Center for Overcoming Overeating
315 West 86th Street, #17 B
New York, NY 10024
(212) 875-0442

This national center is directed by Carol Munter and Jane Hirschmann. There are also centers at:

Chicago Center for Overcoming Overeating
P.O. Box 48
Deerfield, IL 60016
(708) 853-1200

Houston Center for Overcoming Overeating
12609 Memorial Drive
Houston, TX 77024
(713) 464-6152

New England Center for Overcoming Overeating
(617) 341-4885 or (508) 686-4432.

The Women's Campaign to End Body Hatred and Dieting
(800) 299-0577
> This campaign, sponsored by the National Center to Overcome Overeating, provides literature. You can also subscribe to the *Overcome Overeating* newsletter at the Women's Campaign number.

EATING DISORDERS: INFORMATION AND REFERRALS

American Anorexia/Bulimia Association (AA/BA)
293 Central Park West, #1R
New York, NY 10024
(212) 501-8351
> National referrals for therapy and support groups and free information packets.

Anorexia Nervosa and Related Eating Disorders (ANRED)
P.O. Box 5102
Eugene, OR 97405
(503) 344-1144
> A national clearinghouse for information about eating and exercise disorders. Free information. (No referrals.) Staff leads workshops and self-help groups.

National Association of Anorexia Nervosa and Associated Disorders (NAANAD)
Box 7, Highland Park, IL 60035
(708) 831-3438
> NAANAD supplies national and international referrals, sponsors hundreds of free support groups, and sends out free information packets.

REFERRALS FOR SEX THERAPY

American Association of Sex Educators, Counselors, and Therapists (AASECT)
(319) 895-8407
E-mail: 102105,2075@compuserve.com
> This is the national professional association that certifies sex therapists.

HEALING FROM SEXUAL ABUSE

Bass, Ellen, and Laura Davis. *The Courage to Heal: A Guide for Women Survivors of Child Sexual Abuse* (New York: Harper & Row, 1988).
> A classic and the one to start with. Has an extensive bibliography and resources section.

Davis, Laura. *Allies in Healing* (New York: Harper Perennial, 1991).
> For partners of survivors.

Herman, Judith Lewis. *Trauma and Recovery* (New York: Basic Books, 1992).
> A very clear and helpful book about the aftermath of trauma and the process of healing.

Maltz, Wendy. *The Sexual Healing Journey* (New York: Harper-Collins, 1991).
> An excellent book with lots of practical advice and suggestions about the process of reclaiming your sexuality after abuse.

IMPROVING BODY IMAGE

Hutchinson, Marcia Germaine. *Transforming Body Image* (Trumansburg, NY: Crossing Press, 1985).
> Exercises developed by a psychologist who has helped many women come to accept and like their bodies.

Naidus, Beverly. *One Size Does Not Fit All** (Littleton Colorado: Aigis Publications, 1993).
> A wonderful art book that through drawings and collages shows the transformation from body loathing to body love.

Newman, Leslea. *Some Body to Love* (Chicago: Third Side Press, 1991).
> Exercises developed by a gifted writer who herself has overcome eating disorders.

OTHER BOOKS AND RESOURCES OF INTEREST

Friedan, Betty. *The Fountain of Age* (New York: Simon & Schuster, 1993).
> Lots of interesting information about aging and the vitality enjoyed by most older people.

Grealy, Lucy. *Autobiography of a Face* (Boston: Houghton Mifflin, 1994).
> An unflinchingly frank, powerful memoir written by a woman who was facially disfigured by childhood cancer surgery. It movingly describes her pain at feeling ugly and her ultimate triumph.

Lyons, Pat, and Debby Burgard. *Great Shape: The First Fitness Guide for Large Women** (Palo Alto, CA: Bull, 1990).
> What every large woman and beginning exerciser needs to know about exercise. Compassionate and encouraging.

Melpomene Institute. *The Bodywise Woman: Reliable Information on Physical Activity and Health* (Champagne, IL: Human Kinetics, 1990).

> Put out by the Institute (see below), it's full of helpful information.

Melpomene Institute
1010 University Avenue
St. Paul, MN 55104
(612) 642-1951; fax: (612) 642-1871

> Named in honor of the Greek woman who scandalized officials at the 1896 Olympics by running the marathon even after she was told that women could not enter the race. The institute is dedicated to research on exercise and women's well-being. It has a number of helpful information packages on such topics as body image, larger women, menopause, PMS, and pregnancy.

Notes

CHAPTER 1: THE BEAUTY IMPERATIVE

Page 20: **Research consistently shows:** Laurie Mintz and Nancy Betz, "Sex Differences in the Nature, Realism, and Correlates of Body Image," *Sex Roles* 15(3/4): 185–95 (1986); Sharlene Hesse-Biber, Alan Clayton-Matthews, and John A. Downey, "The Differential Importance of Weight and Body Image Among College Men and Women," *Genetic, Social, and General Psychology Monographs* 113(4): 509–28 (1987); Harriet Mable, William D.G. Balance, and Richard J. Galgan, "Body-Image Distortion and Dissatisfaction in University Students," *Perceptual and Motor Skills* 63 (1986): 907–11; Marci McCaulay, Laurie Mintz, and Audrey Glenn, "Body Image, Self-Esteem, and Depression Proneness: Closing the Gender Gap," *Sex Roles* 18 (7/8): 381–91 (1988); Patricia Pliner, Shelly Chaiken, and Gordon L. Flett, "Gender Differences in Concern with Body Weight and Physical Appearance over the Life Span," *Personality and Social Psychology Bulletin* 16 (2): 263–73 (1990); Ruth Striegel-Moore, Lisa Silberstein, and Judith Rodin, "Towards an Understanding of Risk Factors for Bulimia," *American Psychologist* 41 (1986): 246–63; J. Kevin Thompson and Colleen M. Thompson, "Body Size Distortion and Self-Esteem in Asymptomatic, Normal Weight Males, and Females," *International Journal of Eating Disorders* 5 (6): 1061–68 (1986); *Reflections of Risk: Growing Up Female in Minnesota* (Minneapolis: Minnesota Women's Fund, February 1990); J. Kevin Thompson, "Larger Than Life," *Psychology Today,* April 1986, pp. 38–39, 42, 44.

Page 20:   **beauty survey:** Carin Rubinstein, "Through the Looking Glass, the 1994 *New Woman* Beauty Survey," *New Woman,* October 1994, pp. 90–95.

Page 22:   *The Beauty Myth:* Naomi Wolf (New York: Doubleday, 1991), pp. 9–19.

Page 23:   **"A cultural fixation . . . and how fast":** Ibid., p. 187.

Page 23:   **"Researchers . . . in our bodies":** Ibid, pp. 187–88, 197.

Page 24:   *Playboy* **centerfold:** Melpomene Institute, *The Bodywise Woman* (Champaign, IL: Human Kinetics, 1990), p. 32. 23 percent below: Wolf, *Beauty Myth,* p. 11.

Page 24:   **Weight loss . . . $33 billion industry:** Marjorie Rosen et al., "Hollywood Takes It Off," *People,* January 1, 1992, pp. 72–82.

Page 25:   **large increase . . . purely decorative roles:** Gary L. Sullivan and P. J. O'Connor, "Women's Role Portrayals in Magazine Advertising: 1958–1983," *Sex Roles* 18 (3/4): 181–88 (1988).

Page 25:   *Ladies' Home Journal:* Judith Rodin, *Body Traps* (New York: Morrow, 1992), p. 166.

Page 25:   **The continual message:** Brett A. Silverstein et al., "The Role of Mass Media in Promoting a Thin Standard of Bodily Attractiveness for Women," *Sex Roles* 14 (9/10): 519–32 (1986).

Page 25:   *Seventeen* **magazine:** Kate Pierce, "A Feminist Theoretical Perspective on the Socialization of Teenage Girls Through *Seventeen* Magazine," *Sex Roles* 23 (9/10): 491–500 (1990).

Page 25:   satisfaction with ... physical attractiveness diminished:
           Marsha L. Richins, "Social Comparison and the Ideal-
           ized Images of Advertising," *Journal of Consumer Re-
           search* 18 (1991): 71–83.

Page 25:   four thousand network TV commercials: Chris A.
           Downs and Sheila K. Harrison, "Embarrassing Age
           Spots or Just Plain Ugly? Physical Attractiveness Stereo-
           typing as an Instrument of Sexism on American Televi-
           sion Commericals," *Sex Roles* 13 (1/2): 9–19 (1985).

Page 26:   near absence of women's voices: Lynn T. Lovdal, "Sex-
           Role Messages in TV Commercials: An Update," *Sex
           Roles* 21 (11/12): 715–24 (1989).

Page 26:   effects of beauty commercials: Alexis S. Tan, "TV
           Beauty Ads and Role Expectations of Adolescent Female
           Viewers," *Journalism Quarterly* 56 (1979): 283–88.

Page 26:   Donald Davis: Donald Davis, "Portrayals of Women
           in Prime Time Network Television: Some Demo-
           graphic Characteristics," *Sex Roles* 23 (5/6): 325–32
           (1990).

Page 27:   Christine Craft: Christine Craft, *Too Old, Too Ugly, and
           Not Deferential to Men* (Rocklin, CA: Prima, 1988).

Page 27:   actresses became thinner: Silverstein et al., "Role of
           Mass Media," pp. 519–32.

Page 28:   Carol Alt: "The Body Game," *People,* January 11, 1993,
           p. 84.

Page 28:   Kim Alexis: Ibid., p. 82.

Page 28:   Beverly Johnson: Ibid., pp. 83–84.

Page 29:   up to 85 percent ... diet: Carol Bloom et al., *Eating Problems* (New York: Basic Books, 1994), p. xi.

Page 30:   **Thomas Cash:** Thomas F. Cash, Barbara A. Winstead, and Louis H. Janda, "The Great American Shape-Up," *Psychology Today,* April 1986, pp. 30–37.

Page 30:   **beauty survey:** Rubinstein, "Through the Looking Glass," pp. 90–95.

Page 31:   *Glamour* survey: "Feeling Fat in a Thin Society," *Glamour,* February 1984, pp. 198–201, 251–52.

Page 31:   **studies have similar findings:** Sharon Desmond et al., "The Etiology of Adolescents' Perceptions of Their Weight," *Journal of Youth and Adolescence* 15 (6): 461–73 (1986); Adam Drewnowski and Doris K. Yee, "Men and Body Image: Are Males Satisfied with Their Body Weight?" *Psychosomatic Medicine,* 49 (11/12): 626–34 (1987); Robert W. Jeffery et al., "Prevalence of Overweight and Weight Loss Behavior in a Metropolitan Adult Population: The Minnesota Heart Survey Experience," *American Journal of Public Health* 4 (4): 349–52 (1984); Mable, Balance, and Galgan, "Body-Image Distortion," pp. 907–11; McCaulay, Mintz, and Glenn, "Body Image, Self-Esteem, and Depression," pp. 381–91; Susan J. Paxton et al., "Body Image Satisfaction, Dieting Beliefs, and Weight Loss Behaviors in Adolescent Girls and Boys," *Journal of Youth and Adolescence* 20 (3): 361–69 (1991); Anita Stewart and Robert Brook, "Effects of Being Overweight," *Journal of Public Health* 73 (2): 171–78 (1983); Thompson and Thompson, "Body Size Distortion," pp. 1061–68; Thompson, "Larger Than Life," pp. 38–39, 42, 44; Marika Tiggemann and Esther Rothblum, "Gender Differences in Social Consequences of Perceived Overweight in the United States and Australia," *Sex Roles* 18 (1/2): 75–86 (1988).

Page 31:   **Cash and colleagues:** Steven W. Noles, Thomas F. Cash, and Barbara A. Winstead, "Body Image, Physical Attractiveness, and Depression," *Journal of Consulting and Clinical Psychology* 53(1): 88–94 (1985).

Page 31:   **Mandy McCarthy:** Mandy McCarthy, "The Thin Ideal, Depression and Eating Disorders in Women," *Behavior Research and Therapy* 28 (3): 205–15 (1990).

Page 33:   **Nearer to our times, from around:** Allan Mazur, "U.S. Trends in Feminine Beauty and Over-Adaptation," *The Journal of Sex Research* 22 (3): 281–303 (1986).

Page 33:   **(Such corseting . . . : miscarriages)** Melpomene Institute, *"Bodywise Woman,"* p. 12.

Page 33:   **By midcentury . . . has reigned supreme:** Mazur, "U.S. Trends of Feminine Beauty," pp. 281–303.

Page 34:   **In over 80 percent of the developing societies:** Peter J. Brown and Melvin Konner, "An Anthropological Perspective on Obesity," *Annals of the New York Academy of Sciences* 499 (1987): 29–46.

Page 35:   **"fattening houses":** Claire Cassidy, "When the Big Body Is Better," *Medical Anthropology* 13 (1991): 181–213.

Page 35:   **more positive about their weight and body image:** William C. White, Jr., Lisa Hudson, and Stephen N. Campbell, "Bulimarexia and Black Women: A Brief Report," *Psychotherapy Theory, Research, Practice, Training* 22 (1985): 449–50.

Page 35:   **place less emphasis on food and weight control:** James J. Gary, Kathryn Ford, and Lily M. Kelly, "The Prevalence of Bulimia in a Black College Population," *International Journal of Eating Disorders* 6 (6): 733–40 (1987).

Page 35:   **and on slimness:** Veronica Thomas and Michelle James, "Body Image, Dieting Tendencies, and Sex Role Traits in Urban Black Women," *Sex Roles* 18 (9/10): 523–29 (1988).

Page 35:   **African-American men . . . sexier and more attractive:** Mary B. Harris, Laurie C. Walters, and Stefanie Waschull, "Gender and Ethnic Differences in Obesity-Related Behaviors and Attitudes in a College Sample," *Journal of Applied Social Psychology* 21 (16): 1545–65 (1991).

Page 35:   *Essence* **. . . survey:** Linda Villarosa, "Dangerous Eating," *Essence,* January 1994, pp. 19–21, 87.

Page 35:   **eating disorders . . . increased dramatically in the 1920s:** Deborah Perlick and Brett Silverstein, "Faces of Female Discontent: Depression, Disordered Eating, and Changing Gender Roles," in *Feminist Perspectives on Eating Disorders,* ed. Patricia Fallon, Melanie A. Katzman and Susan C. Wooley (New York: Guilford, 1994), p. 80.

Page 36:   **reports . . . 60 percent . . . survivors of sexual abuse:** Susan C. Wooley, "Sexual Abuse and Eating Disorders: The Concealed Debate," in *Feminist Perspectives on Eating Disorders,* ed. Fallon, Katzman, and Wooley, p. 177.

Page 36:   **bulimic women . . . high rates of sexual assault:** Ibid., p. 192.

Page 37:   **Three recent studies:** Ruth H. Striegel-Moore, Naomi Tucker, and Jeanette Hsu, "Body Image Dissatisfaction and Disordered Eating in Lesbian College Students," *International Journal of Eating Disorders* 9 (1990): 493–500; David B. Herzog et al., "Body Image Satisfaction in Homosexual and Heterosexual Women," *Inter-*

national Journal of Eating Disorders 11 (4): 391–96 (1992); Pamela A. Brand, Esther D. Rothblum, and Laura J. Solomon, "A Comparison of Lesbians, Gay Men, and Heterosexuals on Weight and Restrained Eating," *International Journal of Eating Disorders* 11 (3): 253–59 (1992).

Page 37: **Fallon and . . . Rozin:** April Fallon and Paul Rozin, "Sex Differences in Perceptions of Desirable Body Shape," *Journal of Abnormal Psychology* 94 (1): 102–5 (1985); Paul Rozin and April Fallon, "Body Image, Attitudes to Weight, and Misperceptions of Figure Preferences of the Opposite Sex: A Comparison of Men and Women in Two Generations," *Journal of Abnormal Psychology* 97 (3): 342–45 (1988).

CHAPTER 3: UGLY MYTHS, BEAUTIFUL YOU

Page 52: **Madeline Heilman:** Madeline Heilman and Lois Saruwatari, "When Beauty Is Beastly: The Effects of Appearance and Sex on Evaluations of Job Applicants for Managerial and Nonmanagerial Jobs," *Organizational Behavior and Human Performance* 23 (3): 360–72 (1979).

Page 52: **Liability when a woman tries to get ahead at a firm:** Madeline E. Heilman and Melanie H. Stopeck, "Being Attractive, Advantage or Disadvantage? Performance-Based Evaluations and Recommended Personnel Actions as a Function of Appearance, Sex, and Job Type," *Organizational Behavior and Human Decisions Processes* 35 (1985): 202–15.

Page 53: **Linda Jackson:** Linda Jackson, "Gender, Physical Attractiveness, and Sex Role in Occupational Treatment Discrimination: The Influence of Trait and Role Assumptions," *Journal of Applied Social Psychology* 13 (5): 443–58 (1983).

Page 53: **Heilman and Stopeck:** Madeline E. Heilman and Melanie H. Stopeck, "Attractiveness and Corporate Success: Different Causal Attributions for Males and Females," *Journal of Applied Psychology* 17(2) (1985): 379–88.

Page 54: **Spencer and . . . Taylor:** Barbara Spencer and G. Stephen Taylor, "Effects of Facial Attractiveness and Gender on Causal Attributions of Managerial Performance," *Sex Roles* 19 (5/6): 273–85 (1988).

Page 54: **David Gilmore:** David C. Gilmore, Terry A. Beehr, and Kevin G. Love, "Effects of Applicant Sex, Applicant Physical Attractiveness, Type of Rater, and Type of Job on Interview Decisions," *Journal of Occupational Psychology* 59 (1986): 103–9.

Page 54: **Paula Morrow:** Paula C. Morrow et al., "The Effects of Physical Attractiveness and Other Demographic Characteristics on Promotion Decisions," *Journal of Management* 16 (4): 723–36 (1990).

Page 54: **physical attractiveness. . . .:** Ibid., p. 725.

Page 56: **Dennis Krebs and Allen A. Adinolfi:** "Physical Attractiveness, Social Relations, and Personality Style," *Journal of Personality and Social Psychology,* 31 (2) 1975: 245–53.

Page 56: **more egocentric:** Nicholas T. Gallucci and Robert G. Meyer, "People Can Be Too Perfect: Effects of Subjects' and Targets' Attractiveness on Interpersonal Attraction," *Psychological Reports,* 1984, 55, pp. 351–60.

Page 56: **egotistical, snobbish, and materialistic:** Marshall Dermer and Derrel L. Thiel, "When Beauty May Fail," *Journal of Personality and Social Psychology* 31 (6), 1975: 1168–76.

Page 56: **stereotypes of very attractive people don't match reality:** Alan Feingold, "Good-Looking People Are Not What We Think," *Psychological Bulletin* 111 (2): 304–341 (1992).

Page 57: **81 percent of traditional cultures:** Peter J. Brown and Melvin Konner, "An Anthropological Perspective on Obesity," *Annals of the New York Academy of Sciences* 499 (1987): 29–46.

Page 58: **Bull and . . . Rumsey:** Ray Bull and Nichola Rumsey, *The Social Psychology of Facial Appearance* (New York: Springer-Verlag, 1988), p. 39.

Page 58: **"in each of the instances. . . .":** Ellen Berscheid and Elaine Walster, "Physical Attractiveness," *Advances in Experimental Social Psychology* 7 (1974): 201.

CHAPTER 4: FAMILIAL MESSAGES, INFLUENCE, AND MODELS

Page 66: **Eating-disordered women often report:** Judith Ruskay Rabinor, "Mothers, Daughters, and Eating Disorders: Honoring the Mother-Daughter Relationship," in *Feminist Perspectives on Eating Disorders,* ed. Patricia Fallon, Melanie A. Katzman, and Susan C. Wooley (New York: Guilford, 1994), p. 275.

Page 74: **lingering effects of abuse:** Judith Herman, *Trauma and Recovery* (New York: Basic Books, 1992), p. 121.

Page 75: 60 percent . . . survivors of sexual abuse: Susan C. Woo-
          ley, "Sexual Abuse and Eating Disorders: The Concealed
          Debate," in *Feminist Perspectives on Eating Disorders,*
          ed. Fallon, Katzman, and Wooley, p. 177.

Page 77: only 13 percent . . . thought . . . mother had liked their
          bodies: Susan C. Wooley and O. Wayne Wooley, "Inten-
          sive Outpatient and Residential Treatment for Bulimia,"
          in *Handbook of Psychotherapy for Anorexia Nervosa
          and Bulimia,* ed. David M. Garner and Paul E. Garfinkel
          (New York: Guilford 1985), p. 393.

Page 77: mothers who dislike their own bodies: "Feeling Fat in a
          Thin Society," *Glamour,* February 1984, p. 201.

Page 78: "a respondent's perception. . . .": Wooley and Wooley,
          "Intensive Outpatient and Residential Treatment for Bu-
          limia," p. 392.

Page 78: mothers . . . judging . . . daughters: Mark Nichter and
          Mimi Nichter, "Hype and Weight," *Medical Anthropol-
          ogy* 13 (1991): 249–84.

Page 78: cross-sectional study: Adam Drewnowski et al., "Early
          Puberty May be Linked with Extreme Dieting in Girls,"
          American Family Practitioner, October 1988, pp.
          269–70.

Page 78: Judith Rodin: Judith Rodin, *Body Traps* (New York:
          Morrow, 1992), pp. 34–35.

Page 78: survey of college women: Wooley and Wooley, "Inten-
          sive Outpatient and Residential Treatment for Bulimia,"
          p. 399.

Page 79: *Glamour* survey: "Feeling Fat in a Thin Society," pp.
          198–201, 251–52.

CHAPTER 6: "I JUST DON'T HAVE A PRETTY FACE"

Page 118: **what makes a face beautiful:** Judith Langlois and Lori Roggman, "Attractive Faces Are Only Average," *Psychological Science* 1 (2): 115–121 (1990).

Page 123: **Lucy Grealy:** Lucy Grealy, *Autobiography of a Face* (Boston: Houghton Mifflin, 1994).

CHAPTER 7: FAT: FEARS, FABLES, AND FACTS

Page 130: **over half ... size fourteen or larger:** Denise Cowie, "No Lack of Style Beyond a Size 6," *The* [Bergen County, New Jersey] *Record,* October 27, 1994, p. B2.

Page 130: **Slim women are seen as:** Marika Tiggemann and Esther Rothblum, "Gender Differences in Social Consequences of Perceived Overweight in the United States and Australia," *Sex Roles* 18 (1/2): 75–86 (1988).

Page 131: **fat young people had good self-esteem:** Steven L. Gortmaker et al., "Social and Economic Consequences of Overweight in Adolescence and Young Adulthood," *New England Journal of Medicine,* September 30, 1993, pp. 1008–12.

Page 131: **Investigating weight discrimination in employment:** Esther D. Rothblum et al., "The Relationship Between Obesity, Employment Discrimination, and Employment-Related Victimization," *Journal of Vocational Behavior* 37 (1990): 251–66.

Page 132: **William McReynolds:** William T. McReynolds, "Toward a Psychology of Obesity: Review of Research on the Role of Personality and Level of Adjustment," *International Journal of Eating Disorder* 2 (1): 37–57 (1982).

Page 132: **Rand Corporation:** Anita Stewart and Robert Brook, "Effects of Being Overweight," *Journal of Public Health* 73 (2): 171–78 (1983).

Page 133: **probably . . . only a small proportion of fat people:** William Bennett and Joel Gurin, *The Dieter's Dilemma* (New York: Basic Books, 1992), p. 25.

Page 133: **Janet Polivy and Peter Herman:** Janet Polivy and C. Peter Herman, "Clinical Depression and Weight Change," *Journal of Abnormal Psychology* 85 (1976): 338–40.

Page 133: **For the same reason, it is primarily dieters:** Bennett and Gurin, *The Dieter's Dilemma,* p. 46.

Page 133: **no relationship between food intake and body weight:** Jeffery Sobol and Albert Stunkard, "Socioeconomic Status and Obesity: A Review of the Literature," *Psychological Bulletin* 105 (2) (1989): 265.

Page 133: **"obese people do not, . . .":** Susan C. Wooley and Orland W. Wooley, "Obesity and Women—I: A Closer Look at the Facts," *Women's Studies International Quarterly* 2 (1979): 69–79.

Page 134: **many fat people eat less:** Susan C. Wooley, Orland W. Wooley, and Susan R. Dyrenforth, "Theoretical, Practical, and Social Issues in Behavioral Treatments of Obesity," *Journal of Applied Behavior Analysis* 12 (1979): 5.

Page 134: **study of almost 2,500 French children:** Marie-Françoise Rolland-Cachera and France Bellisle, "No

Correlation Between Adiposity and Food Intake: Why Are Working Class Children Fatter?" *American Journal of Clinical Nutrition* 44 (1986): 779–87.

Page 134:   **Michael Mahoney:** Michael Mahoney, "The Obese Eating Style," *Addictive Behaviors* 1 (1975): 52.

Page 134:   **Kissileff:** K. S. Kissileff, H. A. Jordan, and L. S. Levitz: "Eating Habits of Obese and Normal Weight Humans," *International Journal of Obesity* 2 (1978): 379.

Page 134:   **government health survey:** U.S. Department of Health and Human Services, Public Health Service, Centers of Disease Control and Prevention, National Center for Health Statistics, "Vital and Health Statistics: Health Promotion and Disease Prevention, Untied States, 1990, Series 10: Data from the National Health Survey, No. 185," pp. 26 and 28.

Page 135:   **Some people burn calories:** Wooley, Wooley, and Dyrenforth, "Theoretical, Practical, and Social Issues," pp. 8, 10.

Page 135:   **Differences in resting metabolic rate:** Ibid., p. 8.

Page 136:   **classic study:** Geoffrey A. Rose and R. T. Williams, "Metabolic Studies on Large and Small Eaters," *British Journal of Nutrition* 15 (1961): 1–9.

Page 136:   **amount and distribution of fat . . . genetically determined:** Bennett and Gurin, *The Dieter's Dilemma,* pp. 71, 260.

Page 136:   **Adopted children . . . more like their biological parents:** Albert J. Stunkard et al., "An Adoption Study of Human Obesity," *New England Journal of Medicine* 314 (4): 193–98 (1986); Jane E. Brody, "Fat in America: For Most Trying to Lose Weight, Dieting Only

Makes Things Worse," *New York Times,* November 23, 1992, p. A12.

Page 136:   identical twins: Judith Rodin, Lisa Silberstein, and Ruth Striegel-Moore, "Women and Weight: A Normative Discontent," in *Nebraska Symposium on Motivation, 1984,* ed. T. B. Sonderegger (Lincoln: University of Nebraska Press, 1984), pp. 267–307.

Page 137:   setpoint: Bennett and Gurin, *The Dieter's Dilemma,* pp. 6, 7, 62.

Page 137:   Setpoints . . . moderately lowered . . . and raised: William Ira Bennett, "Beyond Overeating," *New England Journal of Medicine* 332 (10): 674 (1995).

Page 138:   a protein has been discovered: Ylying Zhang et al., "Positional Cloning of the Mouse Obese Gene and Its Human Homologue," *Nature* 372 (December 1, 1994): 425–32.

Page 139:   classic study . . . done: Ancel Keys et al., *The Biology of Human Starvation* (Minneapolis: University of Minnesota Press, 1950), pp. 821–917.

Page 142:   failure of all weight-loss techniques: National Institutes of Health Technology Assessment Conference Panel, "Methods for Voluntary Weight Loss and Control," p. 947.

Page 143:   after only a few weeks on a low-calorie diet: Bennett and Gurin, *The Dieter's Dilemma,* p. 85.

Page 143:   When dieting: "Losing Weight: What Works. What Doesn't," *Consumer Reports,* June 1993, p. 348.

Page 143:   fatter people ... metabolisms slow down the most:
             Wooley, Wooley, and Dyrenforth, "Theoretical, Practi-
             cal, and Social Issues," p. 9.

Page 143:   use less energy to digest their food: Ibid., p. 10.

Page 143:   burn fewer calories during exercise: Wooley and Woo-
             ley, "Closer Look at Facts," p. 73.

Page 144:   longer to lose weight: Rodin, Silberstein, and Striegel-
             Moore, "Women and Weight," p. 285; Kelley D.
             Brownell et al., "The Effects of Repeated Cycles of
             Weight Loss and Regain in Rats," *Physiology and Be-
             havior* 38 [1986]: 459–64. Kelley Brownell of Yale Uni-
             versity found that the first time rats lost weight it took
             them 21 days to reduce and 46 days to gain it back,
             while in the next cycle it took them over twice as long
             (45 days) to lose the same amount of weight, on the
             same diet, and only 14 days to regain it. Moreover,
             after each period of weight loss, the animals chose to
             eat more fat and less protein, indicating that a craving,
             after dieting, for high-fat, high-calorie foods may be a
             sign not of weak will, but of the body's drive to restock
             your fat stores the quickest and easiest way possible—
             by eating lots of fat.

Page 145:   Americans are getting fatter: Robert J. Kuczmarski et
             al., "Increasing Prevalence of Overweight Among U.S.
             Adults: The National Health and Nutrition Examina-
             tion Surveys, 1960 to 1991," *Journal of the American
             Medical Association* 272 (3): 205 (1994).

Page 145:   consuming fewer calories ... fat: Rita Rubin, "1994
             Health Guide: Fat and Fit," *U.S. News & World Re-
             port,* May 16, 1994, pp. 64–71.

Page 145:   prevalence of fatness . . . a third . . . deemed to be over-
            weight: Kuczmarski et al., "Increasing Prevalence of
            Overweight Among U.S. Adults," p. 205.

Page 145:   Even before puberty: Rodin, Silberstein, and Striegel-
            Moore, "Women and Weight," p. 282.

Page 145:   At puberty . . . 15 to 100 percent greater: Deborah
            Dunlap Marino and Janet C. King, "Nutritional Con-
            cerns During Adolescence," *Pediatric Clinics of North
            America* 27 (1): 125–39 (1980).

Page 145:   In adulthood: Melpomene Institute, *The Bodywise
            Woman* (Champaign, IL: Human Kinetics, 1990), p.
            62.

Page 145:   "dieting at the time when. . . .": Judith Rodin, *Body
            Traps* (New York: Morrow, 1992), p. 177.

Page 146:   have been found to be more likely to diet: Adam
            Drewnowski et al., "Early Puberty May Be Linked with
            Extreme Dieting in Girls," *American Family Practi-
            tioner,* October 1988, pp. 269–70.

Page 146:   tend to be fatter than their peers: Ruth Striegel-Moore,
            Lisa Silberstein, and Judith Rodin, "Towards an Un-
            derstanding of Risk Factors for Bulimia," *American
            Psychologist* 41 (1986): 253.

Page 146:   two other times when hormones: Rodin, Silberstein,
            and Striegel-Moore, "Women and Weight," pp.
            282–84.

Page 146:   beneficial to gain weight during pregnancy: Bennett
            and Gurin, *The Dieter's Dilemma,* p. 140.

Page 146:   study of thousands of Americans: David F. Williamson
            et al., "The 10-Year Incidence of Overweight and

Major Weight Gain in U.S. Adults," *Archives of Internal Medicine* 150 (1990): 665–72.

Page 147:   **Women typically have lower metabolisms:** Barbara J. Rolls, Ingrid C. Fedoroff, and Joanne F. Guthrie, "Gender Differences in Eating Behavior and Body Weight Regulation," *Health Psychology* 10 (2):139 (1991).

Page 147:   **metabolisms slow down with age:** Paul Ernsberger, "Health, Weight and Aging," *Radiance,* Summer 1987, pp. 34–36.

Page 147:   **midlife women's metabolisms:** Ibid., p. 283.

Page 147:   **redistributed primarily around the stomach:** Brody, "Fat in America," p. c8.

Page 147:   **After sixty:** Paul Ernsberger, private communication, March 9, 1995.

Page 148:   **Studies of appetite:** Wooley and Wooley, "Obesity and Women," p. 73.

Page 149:   **"no indication of increasing death rate. . . .":** Ancel Keys et al., *Seven Countries: A Multivariate Analysis of Death and Coronary Heart Disease* (Cambridge, MA: Harvard University Press, 1980), pp. 328–29.

Page 149:   **"Both extreme under. . . .":** Ancel Keys, "Overweight, Obesity, Coronary Heart Disease and Mortality," *Nutrition Review* 38 (9): 306 (1980).

Page 149:   **Many other studies and experts:** Framingham, a highly respected longitudinal study of over 5,000 men and women in Framingham, Massachusetts, initiated in 1950 to explore the causes of heart disease and stroke—and still ongoing—found that for men the thinnest had the worst life expectancy (even when controlled for cigarette smoking) and the fattest men the best. Women had a slightly higher mortality rate only if they were in the lowest and highest 20 percent of the weight distribution, and even then they still had lower mortality rates than thin and average-weight men. (Paul Sorlie, Tavia Gordon, and William B. Kannel, "Body Build and Mortality? The Framingham Study," *Journal of the American Medical Association* 243 [1980]: 1828–31.) The world's largest epidemiological study to date—almost two million Norwegians (nearly the whole population of Norway over age fifteen)— found, similarly, increased risk of mortality only at the weight extremes, with the lowest mortality for people around 30 percent overweight, and with women who were morbidly obese having lower death rates than underweight women.

Page 149:   **Dr. Reubin Andres:** Reubin Andres, "Effect of Obesity on Total Mortality," *International Journal of Obesity* 4 (1980): 382.

Page 149:   **"As you might expect. . . .":** Bennett and Gurin, *The Dieter's Dilemma,* p. 120.

Page 150:   **precisely these women:** David M. Garner and Susan C. Wooley, "Confronting the Failure of Behavioral and Dietary Treatments for Obesity," *Clinical Psychology Review* 11 (1991): 756.

Page 150:   **Paul Ernsberger:** Paul Ernsberger, "Is It Unhealthy to Be Fat?," *Radiance,* Winter 1986, p. 13.

Page 151:   **women . . . live longer:** Dale M. Atrens, *Don't Diet* (New York: Morrow, 1988), p. 33.

Page 151:   **evidence that dieting may shorten it:** "Losing Weight," *Consumer Reports,* p. 348. The Framingham study, at thirty-two-year follow-up, also showed that compared with people whose weight either remained stable, at whatever weight, or steadily rose with age, those whose weight fluctuated frequently or by many pounds had higher mortality rates and also had a 50 percent higher risk of coronary heart disease. Moreover, it was for the youngest people in the study, ages thirty to forty-four, precisely the ages at which dieting is most common, that weight fluctuation was found to be the most risky. (Lauren Lissner et al., "Variability of Body Weight and Health Outcomes in the Framingham Population," *New England Journal of Medicine* 324 [1991]: 1839–44.) In addition, a 1988 study of nearly 12,000 middle-aged and elderly Harvard alumni found that the men whose weights changed the least between the 1960s and 1977 (years when their weights had been recorded) had the lowest death rates. Any significant weight change, whether up or down, increased the risk of dying from cardiovascular disease. This finding was not attributable to cigarette smoking, physical activity, or degree of fatness. (I-Min Lee and Ralph S. Paffenberger, "Change in Body Weight and Longevity," *Journal of the American Medical Association,* 268 (15): 2045–49. [October 21, 1992].)

Page 152: **Rand Corporation reviewed extensively:** Stewart and Brook, "Effects of Being Overweight," pp. 171–78.

Page 152: **unknown benefits of mild or moderate obesity:** Andres, "Effect of Obesity on Total Mortality," p. 385.

Page 152: **Ernsberger . . . points out . . . worse than . . . before:** Paul Ernsberger, Internet Posting, August 15, 1995.

Page 153: **a weight pattern . . . insulin resistance:** William B. Kannel and L. Adrienne Cupples, "Cardiovascular and Noncardiovascular Consequences of Obesity," in *Eating, Sleeping and Sex*, ed. Albert J. Stunkard and Andrew Baum (Hillsdale, NJ: Erlbaum, 1989), p. 118.

Page 153: Stress of dieting: Atrens, *Don't Diet,* p. 67.

Page 153: fat diabetics tend to be less insulin dependent: Paul Ernsberger and Paul Haskew, *Rethinking Obesity* (New York: Human Sciences Press, 1987), pp. 28–29.

Page 153: any amount of exercise is beneficial: A longitudinal study done at the Institute for Aerobics Research on the effects of fitness on mortality found that the greatest risk was run by thin women and men who were sedentary, and that major reduction in the death rate from all causes occurred for sedentary people who became just a little more fit. (Stephen N. Blair et al., "Physical Fitness and All-Cause Mortality: A Prospective Study of Healthy Men and Women," *Journal of the American Medical Association* 262 (17): 2395–401 [November 3, 1989].) In addition, a just-published study found that two to four hours of aerobic exercise a week reduced the risk of premenopausal breast cancer by as much as 60 percent. (Jane Brody, "Regimen of Moderate Exercise Tied to Drop in Breast Cancer," *New York Times,* September 21, 1994, p. C10.)

Page 153: A brisk . . . walk: S. N. Blair et al., "How Much Physical Activity Is Good for Health?," *Annual Review of Public Health* 13 (1992): 115.

Page 153: ten minutes, three times a day . . . improved as much:Robert F. DeBusk et al., "Training Effects of Long Versus Short Bouts of Exercise in Healthy Subjects," *American Journal of Cardiology* 65 (1990): 1010–13.

Page 153: Ernsberger experimented . . . crash diet: Paul Ernsberger, "Fat and Health: Biological Roots," *Radiance,* Summer/Fall 1986, pp. 26–27.

Page 154: Ernsberger . . . yo-yo dieting: Ibid., p. 28.

Page 154:   Thomas Moore ... 280 or higher: Thomas Moore,
             Lifespan (New York: Simon & Schuster, 1993), p. 192.

Page 154:   cholesterol level, not a risk factor: Ibid., pp. 191–92.

Page 154:   unless you cut your fat intake to 10 percent ...
             studies ... no effect: Center for Medical Consumers,
             "More Research Exposes the Great Cholesterol
             Myth," *Health Facts* 17 (16), September, 1992, p. 3.

Page 155:   fat people ... base cholesterol: Ernsberger, private
             communication, March 9, 1995.

Page 155:   "apples": Kannel and Cupples, "Cardiovascular and
             Noncardiovascular Consequences of Obesity," p. 118.

Page 155:   "pears"... have significantly less risk: "Losing
             Weight," *Consumer Reports*, p. 348; M. R. C. Green-
             wood, "Sexual Dimorphism and Obesity," in *Eating,
             Sleeping and Sex,* ed. Stunkard and Baum, p. 36.

Page 155:   tendency among black women to store fat in the upper
             body: Daryn Eller and Susanna Levin, "Finally the
             Truth About Fitness," *Essence,* June 1993, pp. 77–80.

Page 155:   Margaret MacKenzie: Margaret MacKenzie, "A Cul-
             tural Study of Weight: America vs. Western Samoa,"
             Radiance, Summer/Fall 1986, p. 24.

Page 155:   survey of the attitudes ... family-practice doctors: James
             H. Price et al., "Family Practice Physicians' Beliefs, At-
             titudes, and Practices Regarding Obesity," *American
             Journal of Preventive Medicine* 3 (1987): 339–45.

Page 156:   height/weight charts: Roberta Pollack Seid, *Never Too
             Thin* (New York: Prentice Hall, 1989), pp. 116–21.

Page 157: moderately fat people have a lower incidence . . . than are thin people: Ernsberger, "Fat and Health," p. 29.

Page 157: Large women . . . strengthens bones: Ernsberger, "Health, Weight and Aging," p. 34.

Page 157: On the other hand . . . uterine cancer: Ibid., p. 35.

Page 157: While fatness . . . between postmenopausal breast cancer and fatness: Ernsberger and Haskew, *Rethinking Obesity,* p. 14.

Page 157: This association is usually found: Ibid., p. 15.

Page 158: "there is very little . . . and mortality.": Tim Byers, "Body Weight and Mortality," *New England Journal of Medicine* 333 (11): 723.

CHAPTER 8: WEIGHT—LOVING ALL OF YOU

Page 161: Large women, even more . . . tend to overestimate their size: Kay Deen Miller, "Body Image Therapy," *Nursing Clinics of North America* 26 (1991): 729.

Page 162: "*Fat* is honest. . . .": Karen Gavanda, "Fat People Deserve Dessert," *Radiance,* Winter 1986, p. 22.

Page 165: fat people who exercise: NAAFA Newsletter, 24 (2): 2 (August/September 1993).

Page 168: Studies have repeatedly found: Henry A. Jordan and Leonard S. Levitz, "Sex and Obesity," *Medical Aspects of Human Sexuality,* 13: 104–17 (1979); Colleen S. W. Rand, "Obesity and Human Sexuality," *Medical Aspects of Human Sexualtiy,* 13: 140–52 (1979); Thomas N. Wise and Jacqueline Gordon, "Sexual Functioning in the Hyperobese," *Obesity/Bariatric Medicine,* 6 (3): 84–87 (1977).

Page 168: **researchers at a Chicago hospital:** Roberta Pollack Scid, *Never Too Thin* (New York: Prentice Hall, 1989), p. 291.

Page 171: **23 percent leaner than the average woman:** Naomi Wolf, *The Beauty Myth* (New York: Doubleday, 1991), p. 192.

Page 172: **Sales of diet books ... and are climbing:** *Healthy Weight Journal* quoted in NAAFA Newsletter, 23 (2): 3 (August/September 1994).

Page 179: **Over 80 percent of traditional societies:** Peter J. Brown and Melvin Konner, "An Anthropological Perspective on Obesity," *Annals of the New York Academy of Sciences* 499 (1987): 41.

Page 179: **Chinese associate ... fatness symbolizes beauty:** Mervat Nasser, "Culture and Weight Consciousness," *Journal of Psychosomatic Research* 32 (6): 573–77 (1988).

CHAPTER 9: BREASTS, THIGHS, HIPS, STOMACHS, LEGS, AND OTHER BODY PARTS

Page 197: **connection between physical attractiveness and romantic popularity:** Alan Feingold, "Gender Differences in Effects of Physical Attractiveness on Romantic Attraction: A Comparison Across Five Research Paradigms," *Journal of Personality and Social Psychology* 59 (5), 1990, p. 985.

Page 197: **Sue Browder:** Sue Browder, "Too Good to Be True," *New Woman,* November 1994, pp. 88, 133–35.

CHAPTER 10: POSITIVE AGING

Page 208: **television actresses:** Donald Davis, "Portrayals of Women in Prime Time Network Television: Some Demographic Characteristics," *Sex Roles* 23 (5/6): 325–32.

Page 208: **Academy Award:** Elizabeth Mehren; "Women in Films: Age of Anxiety," *Los Angeles Times,* June 18, 1991, p. F8.

Page 208: **hags, nags, witches:** Ibid., p. F1.

Page 208: **One study found:** Paula England, Alice Kuhn, and Teresa Gardner, "The Ages of Men and Women in Magazine Advertising," *Journalism Quarterly* 58 (1981): 468–71.

Page 209: **most old people rate their health as good:** Dr. John Rowe, "Healthy Aging," presentation at 92nd Street YMHA, New York City, January 26, 1995.

Page 210: **In another study:** Betty Friedan, *The Fountain of Age* (New York: Simon & Schuster, 1993), p. 151.

Page 210: **"become motivated to stretch. . . .":** Gail Sheehy, "Part 2: Ordinary Women Inventing Extraordinary Lives," *New Woman,* November 1993, p. 21.

Page 210: **Rosalind Barnett and Grace Baruch:** Betty Friedan, *Fountain of Age,* p. 139.

Page 210: **what makes for healthy and happy aging:** Rowe, "Healthy Aging."

Page 210: **It is also important to note . . . rote memory losses:** Friedan, *Fountain of Age,* pp. 22, 415–26.

Page 210: **Deborah Tannen:** Deborah Tannen, *You Just Don't Understand* (New York: Morrow, 1990), pp. 24–25.

CHAPTER 11: "SHE LOOKS SO GOOD, I JUST HATE HER": DEALING WITH OTHER WOMEN

Page 230: **Jean Baker Miller:** Jean Baker Miller, Toward a New *Psychology of Women* (Boston: Beacon, 1976), p. xx.

Page 231: **"uses their intellectual. . . .":** Ibid., p. xx.

Page 231: **"men as well as women. . . .":** Ibid., p. 83.

CHAPTER 12: LETTING THE GLINT IN YOUR EYES CAPTURE THE GLINT IN HIS (OR HERS): FINDING AND KEEPING A MATE

Page 240: **Fallon and Rozin:** April Fallon and Paul Rozin, "Sex Differences in Perceptions of Desirable Body Shape," *Journal of Abnormal Psychology* 94 (1): 102–5 (1985).

Page 241: **Rozin and Fallon:** Paul Rozin and April Fallon, "Body Image, Attitudes to Weight, and Misperceptions of Figure Preferences of the Opposite Sex: A Comparison of Men and Women in Two Generations," *Abnormal Psychology* 97 (3): 342–45 (1988).

Page 241: **David B. Herzog:** David B. Herzog et al., "Body Image Satisfaction in Homosexual and Heterosexual Women," *International Journal of Eating Disorders* 11 (4): 391–96 (1992).

Page 243: **Teachers told average . . . pupils:** Robert Rosenthal and Lenore Jacobson, *Pygmalion in the Classroom* (New York: Holt, Rinehart and Winston, 1968), pp. 174–82.

Yes, I am interested in receiving information on Carolynn Hillman's:

_____ Audiocassettes of exercises found in *LOVE YOUR LOOKS*

_____ Seminars and workshops

_____ Sponsoring one of Carolynn's workshops

Please print:

Name: _____

Address: _____

_____
City   State   Zip

Telephone: _____

email: _____

Please cut out and mail this page to:

        Carolynn Hillman
        P.O. Box 934
        Teaneck, NJ 07666